JOHNSON'S SHAKESPEARE

Johnson's Shakespeare

G. F. PARKER

CLARENDON PRESS · OXFORD
1989

Oxford University Press, Walton Street, Oxford OX2 6DP
Oxford New York Toronto
Delhi Bombay Calcutta Madras Karachi
Petaling Jaya Singapore Hong Kong Tokyo
Nairobi Dar es Salaam Cape Town
Melbourne Auckland
and associated companies in
Berlin Ibadan

Oxford is a trade mark of Oxford University Press

Published in the United States
by Oxford University Press USA

British Library Cataloguing in Publication Data
Parker, G. F.
Johnson's Shakespeare.
1. Drama in English. Shakespeare, William,
1564–1616–Critical studies
I. Title
822.3' 3
ISBN 0-19-812974-2

Library of Congress Cataloging in Publication Data
Parker, G. F. (Graham Frederick), 1956–
Johnson's Shakespeare/G. F. Parker.
p. cm.
1. Johnson, Samuel, 1709–1784. Preface to Shakespeare's plays,
1765. 2. Johnson, Samuel, 1709–1784 — Knowledge — Literature.
3. Shakespeare, William, 1564–1616 — Criticism and interpretation-
-History — 18th century. 4. Shakespeare, William, 1564–1616-
-Tragedies. I. Johnson, Samuel, 1709–1784. II. Title.
PR2975.J643P37 1989 822.3' 3 — dc19   88-25420
ISBN 0-19-812974-2

Phototypeset by Dobbie Typesetting Limited,

Printed in Great Britain
by Biddles Ltd.
Guildford & King's Lynn

For Jan

Acknowledgements

THIS study has benefited from the criticisms, suggestions, and encouragement offered me by a number of individuals: Sue Boyle, Greg Clingham, Richard Gooder, John Newton, Jan Parker, Roy Park, Christopher Ricks, Felicity Rosslyn, and Wilbur Sanders. I am grateful to each of them for giving so generously of their time, their interest, and their knowledge. Part of the book was written while I was a Research Fellow at Clare College, and I take this opportunity of thanking the Master and Fellows for their support and goodwill. Specific obligations to published work on Johnson are recorded in their proper place, but I would like here to mention particularly W. J. Bate, *The Achievement of Samuel Johnson* (New York, 1955); Paul Fussell, *Samuel Johnson and the Life of Writing* (1972); W. R. Keast, 'The Theoretical Foundations of Johnson's Criticism' (in R. S. Crane (ed.), *Critics and Criticism: Ancient and Modern* (1952)); and also two unpublished lectures on Johnson's criticism by Mr John Newton, on which I have drawn very freely. I have also learned a good deal, I hope, from the experience of discussing these ideas with students at Clare in recent years; I have tried to write with their salutary scepticism in mind. Finally, I must record a special debt to Mr H. A. Mason for stimulating my thinking about literature and about Nature in a variety of ways; it was while reading his *To Homer through Pope* (1972) that the possible interest of this subject first struck me, and the reader who knows the range of his critical work will recognize the pervasiveness of my debt.

G.F.P.

Contents

Acknowledgements   vii

From Johnson's Preface to Shakespeare   xi

Note on References   xxi

1. Taking Johnson Seriously   1

2. Just Representations of General Nature   15

    Sceptical Thinking   28

    The Pleasure of Generality   42

    Not Heroic but Human   51

3. The Mind against the World   63

    The Idealist Imagination—Wordsworth—
    Falstaff—Hamlet   63

    The Defiant Imagination—Lear—Audience
    Identification and Dramatic Illusion   91

    Individuals or Species?   106

    Supernatural Creation—Caliban and
    Prospero   111

    Organic Unity—Wordplay—*Romeo and
    Juliet*   126

    Conclusion: On the Necessity of Choosing   153

4. Johnson and Tragedy   156

Index   199

From Johnson's
Preface to Shakespeare

The most fitting preface to this discussion of Johnson's Shakespeare is Johnson's own; the extracts from the *Preface to Shakespeare* which follow present the reader with Johnson's leading propositions. Page numbers refer to Volume VII of the Yale edition of Johnson's Works: *Johnson on Shakespeare*, ed. Arthur Sherbo (New Haven and London, 1968).

NOTHING can please many, and please long, but just representations of general nature. Particular manners can be known to few, and therefore few only can judge how nearly they are copied. The irregular combinations of fanciful invention may delight a-while, by that novelty of which the common satiety of life sends us all in quest; but the pleasures of sudden wonder are soon exhausted, and the mind can only repose on the stability of truth.

Shakespeare is above all writers, at least above all modern writers, the poet of nature; the poet that holds up to his readers a faithful mirrour of manners and of life. His characters are not modified by the customs of particular places, unpractised by the rest of the world; by the peculiarities of studies or professions, which can operate but upon small numbers; or by the accidents of transient fashions or temporary opinions: they are the genuine progeny of common humanity, such as the world will always supply, and observation will always find. His persons act and speak by the influence of those general passions and principles by which all minds are agitated, and the whole system of life is continued in motion. In the writings of other poets a character is too often an individual; in those of Shakespeare it is commonly a species.

It is from this wide extension of design that so much instruction is derived. It is this which fills the plays of Shakespeare with practical axioms and domestick wisdom. It was said of Euripides, that every verse was a precept; and it may be said of Shakespeare, that from his works may be collected a system of civil and oeconomical prudence. Yet his real power is not shewn in the splendour of particular passages, but by the progress of his fable, and the tenour of his dialogue; and he that tries to recommend him by select quotations, will succeed like the pedant in Hierocles, who, when he offered his house to sale, carried a brick in his pocket as a specimen.

It will not easily be imagined how much Shakespeare excells in accommodating his sentiments to real life, but by comparing him with other authours. It was observed of the ancient schools of declamation, that the more diligently they were frequented, the more was the student disqualified for the world, because he found nothing there which he should ever meet in any other place. The same remark may be applied to every stage but that of Shakespeare. The theatre, when it is under any other direction, is peopled by such characters as were never seen, conversing in a language which was never heard, upon topicks which will never arise in the commerce of mankind. But the dialogue of this authour is often so evidently determined by the incident which produces it, and is pursued with so much ease and simplicity, that it seems scarcely to claim the merit of fiction, but to have been gleaned by diligent selection out of common conversation, and common occurrences.

Upon every other stage the universal agent is love, by whose power all good and evil is distributed, and every action quickened or retarded. To bring a lover, a lady and a rival into the fable; to entangle them in contradictory obligations, perplex them with oppositions of interest, and harrass them with violence of desires inconsistent with each other; to make them meet in rapture and part in agony; to fill their mouths with hyperbolical joy and outrageous sorrow; to distress them as nothing human ever was distressed; to deliver them as nothing human ever was delivered, is the business of a modern dramatist. For this, probability is violated, life is misrepresented, and language is depraved. But love is only one of many passions, and as it has no great influence upon the sum of life, it has little operation in the dramas of a poet, who caught his ideas from the living world, and exhibited only what he saw before him. He knew, that any other passion, as it was regular or exorbitant, was a cause of happiness or calamity.

Characters thus ample and general were not easily discriminated and preserved, yet perhaps no poet ever kept his personages more distinct from each other. I will not say with Pope, that every speech may be assigned to the proper speaker, because many speeches there are which have nothing characteristical; but perhaps, though some may be equally adapted to every person, it will be difficult to find any that can be properly transferred from the present possessor to another claimant. The choice is right, when there is reason for choice.

Other dramatists can only gain attention by hyperbolical or aggravated characters, by fabulous and unexampled excellence or depravity, as the writers of barbarous romances invigorated the reader by a giant and a dwarf; and he that should form his expectations of human affairs from the play, or from the tale, would be equally deceived. Shakespeare has no heroes; his scenes are occupied only by men, who act and speak as the reader thinks that he should himself have spoken or acted on the same occasion: Even where the agency is supernatural the dialogue is level with life. Other writers disguise the most natural passions and most frequent incidents; so that he who contemplates them in the book will not know them in the world: Shakespeare approximates the remote, and familiarizes the wonderful; the event which he represents will not happen, but if it were possible, its effects would probably be such as he has assigned; and it may be said, that he has not only shewn human nature as it acts in real exigences, but as it would be found in trials, to which it cannot be exposed.

This therefore is the praise of Shakespeare, that his drama is the mirrour of life; that he who has mazed his imagination, in following the phantoms which other writers raise up before him, may here be cured of his delirious extasies, by reading human sentiments in human language; by scenes from which a hermit may estimate the transactions of the world, and a confessor predict the progress of the passions.

His adherence to general nature has exposed him to the censure of criticks, who form their judgments upon narrower principles. Dennis and Rhymer think his Romans not sufficiently Roman; and Voltaire censures his kings as not completely royal. Dennis is offended, that Menenius, a senator of Rome, should play the buffoon; and Voltaire perhaps thinks decency violated when the Danish usurper is represented as a drunkard. But Shakespeare always makes nature predominate over accident; and if he preserves the essential character, is not very careful of distinctions superinduced and adventitious. His story requires Romans or kings, but he thinks only on men. He knew that Rome, like every other city, had men of all dispositions; and wanting a buffoon, he went into the senate-house for that which the senate-house would certainly have afforded him. He was inclined to shew an usurper and a murderer not only odious but despicable; he therefore added drunkenness to his other qualities, knowing that kings love wine like other men, and that wine exerts its natural power upon kings. These are the petty cavils of petty minds; a poet overlooks the casual distinction of country and condition, as a painter, satisfied with the figure, neglects the drapery.

The censure which he has incurred by mixing comick and tragick scenes, as it extends to all his works, deserves more consideration. Let the fact be first stated, and then examined.

Shakespeare's plays are not in the rigorous and critical sense either tragedies or comedies, but compositions of a distinct kind; exhibiting the real state of sublunary nature, which partakes of good and evil, joy and sorrow, mingled with endless variety of proportion and innumerable modes of combination; and expressing the course of the world, in which the loss of one is the gain of another; in which, at the same time, the reveller is hasting to his wine, and the mourner burying his friend; in which the malignity of one is sometimes defeated by the frolick of another; and many mischiefs and many benefits are done and hindered without design.

Out of this chaos of mingled purposes and casualties the ancient poets, according to the laws which custom had prescribed, selected some the crimes of men, and some their absurdities; some the momentous vicissitudes of life, and some the lighter occurrences; some the terrours of distress, and some the gayeties of prosperity. Thus rose the two modes of imitation, known by the names of tragedy and comedy, compositions intended to promote different ends by contrary means, and considered as so little allied, that I do not recollect among the Greeks or Romans a single writer who attempted both.

Shakespeare has united the powers of exciting laughter and sorrow not only in one mind but in one composition. Almost all his plays are divided between serious and ludicrous characters, and, in the successive evolutions of the design, sometimes produce seriousness and sorrow, and sometimes levity and laughter.

That this is a practice contrary to the rules of criticism will be readily allowed; but there is always an appeal open from criticism to nature. The end of writing is to instruct; the end of poetry is to instruct by pleasing. That the mingled drama may convey all the instruction of tragedy or comedy cannot be denied, because it includes both in its alternations of exhibition, and approaches nearer than either to the appearance of life, by shewing how great machinations and slender designs may promote or obviate one another, and the high and the low co-operate in the general system by unavoidable concatenation. [pp. 61-7]

. . . Shakespeare engaged in dramatick poetry with the world open before him; the rules of the ancients were yet known to few; the publick judgment was unformed; he had no example of such fame as might force him upon imitation, nor criticks of such authority as might restrain his extravagance: He therefore indulged his natural disposition, and his disposition, as Rhymer has remarked, led him to comedy. In tragedy he often writes with great appearance of toil and study, what is written at last with little felicity; but in his comick scenes, he seems to produce without labour, what no labour can improve. In tragedy he is always struggling after some occasion to be comick, but in comedy he seems to repose, or to luxuriate, as in a mode of thinking congenial to his nature. In his tragick scenes there is always something wanting, but his comedy often surpasses expectation or desire. His comedy pleases by the thoughts and the language, and his tragedy for the greater part by incident and action. His tragedy seems to be skill, his comedy to be instinct.

The force of his comick scenes has suffered little diminution from the changes made by a century and a half, in manners or in words. As his personages act upon principles arising from genuine passion, very little modified by particular forms, their pleasures and vexations are communicable to all times and to all places; they are natural, and therefore durable; the adventitious peculiarities of personal habits, are only superficial dies, bright and pleasing for a little while, yet soon fading to a dim tinct, without any remains of former lustre; but the discriminations of true passion are the colours of nature; they pervade the whole mass, and can only perish with the body that exhibits them. The accidental compositions of heterogeneous modes are dissolved by the chance which combined them; but the uniform simplicity of primitive qualities neither admits increase, nor suffers decay. The sand heaped by one flood is scattered by another, but the rock always continues in its place. The stream of time, which is continually washing the dissoluble fabricks of other poets, passes without injury by the adamant of Shakespeare.

If there be, what I believe there is, in every nation, a stile which never becomes obsolete, a certain mode of phraseology so consonant and congenial to the analogy and principles of its respective language as to remain settled and unaltered; this stile is probably to be sought in the common intercourse of life, among those who speak only to be understood, without ambition of elegance. The polite are always catching modish innovations, and the learned depart from established forms of speech, in hope of finding or making better; those who wish for distinction forsake the vulgar, when the vulgar is right; but there is a conversation above grossness and below refinement, where propriety resides, and where this poet seems to have gathered his comick dialogue. He is therefore more agreeable to the ears of the present age than any other authour equally remote, and among his other excellencies deserves to be studied as one of the original masters of our language.

These observations are to be considered not as unexceptionably constant, but as containing general and predominant truth. Shakespeare's familiar dialogue is affirmed to be smooth and clear, yet not wholly without ruggedness or difficulty; as a country may be eminently fruitful, though it has spots unfit for cultivation: His characters are praised as natural, though their sentiments are sometimes forced, and their actions improbable; as the earth upon the whole is spherical, though its surface is varied with protuberances and cavities.

Shakespeare with his excellencies has likewise faults, and faults sufficient to obscure and overwhelm any other merit. I shall shew them in the proportion in which they appear to me, without envious malignity or superstitious veneration. No question can be more innocently discussed than a dead poet's pretensions to renown; and little regard is due to that bigotry which sets candour higher than truth.

His first defect is that to which may be imputed most of the evil in books or in men. He sacrifices virtue to convenience, and is so much more careful to please than to instruct, that he seems to write without any moral purpose. From his writings indeed a system of social duty may be selected, for he that thinks reasonably must think morally; but his precepts and axioms drop casually from him; he makes no just distribution of good or evil, nor is always careful to shew in the virtuous a disapprobation of the wicked; he carries his persons indifferently through right and wrong, and at the close dismisses them without further care, and leaves their examples to operate by chance. This fault the barbarity of his age cannot extenuate; for it is always a writer's duty to make the world better, and justice is a virtue independant on time or place.

The plots are often so loosely formed, that a very slight consideration may improve them, and so carelessly pursued, that he seems not always fully to comprehend his own design. He omits opportunities of instructing or delighting which the train of his story seems to force upon him, and apparently rejects those exhibitions which would be more affecting, for the sake of those which are more easy.

It may be observed, that in many of his plays the latter part is evidently neglected. When he found himself near the end of his work, and in view of his reward, he shortened the labour, to snatch the profit. He therefore remits his efforts where he should most vigorously exert them, and his catastrophe is improbably produced or imperfectly represented.

He had no regard to distinction of time or place, but gives to one age or nation, without scruple, the customs, institutions, and opinions of another, at the expence not only of likelihood, but of possibility. These faults Pope has endeavoured, with more zeal than judgment, to transfer to his imagined interpolators. We need not wonder to find Hector quoting Aristotle, when we see the loves of Theseus and Hippolyta combined with the Gothick mythology of fairies. Shakespeare, indeed, was not the only violator of chronology, for in the same age Sidney, who wanted not the advantages of learning, has, in his *Arcadia*, confounded the pastoral with the feudal times, the days of innocence, quiet and security, with those of turbulence, violence and adventure.

In his comick scenes he is seldom very successful, when he engages his characters in reciprocations of smartness and contests of sarcasm; their jests are commonly gross, and their pleasantry licentious; neither his gentlemen nor his ladies have much delicacy, nor are sufficiently distinguished from his clowns by any appearance of refined manners. Whether he represented the real conversation of his time is not easy to determine; the reign of Elizabeth is commonly supposed to have been a time of stateliness, formality and reserve, yet perhaps the relaxations of that severity were not very elegant. There must, however, have been always some modes of gayety preferable to others, and a writer ought to chuse the best.

In tragedy his performance seems constantly to be worse, as his labour is more. The effusions of passion which exigence forces out are for the most part striking and energetick; but whenever he solicits his invention, or strains his faculties, the offspring of his throes is tumour, meanness, tediousness, and obscurity.

In narration he affects a disproportionate pomp of diction and a wearisome train of circumlocution, and tells the incident imperfectly in many words, which might have been more plainly delivered in few. Narration in dramatick poetry is naturally tedious, as it is unanimated and inactive, and obstructs the progress of the action; it should therefore always be rapid, and enlivened by frequent interruption. Shakespeare found it an encumbrance, and instead of lightening it by brevity, endeavoured to recommend it by dignity and splendour.

His declamations or set speeches are commonly cold and weak, for his power was the power of nature; when he endeavoured, like other tragick writers, to catch opportunities of amplification, and instead of inquiring what the occasion demanded, to show how much his stores of knowledge could supply, he seldom escapes without the pity or resentment of his reader.

It is incident to him to be now and then entangled with an unwieldy sentiment, which he cannot well express, and will not reject; he struggles with it a while, and if it continues stubborn, comprises it in words such as occur, and leaves it to be disentangled and evolved by those who have more leisure to bestow upon it.

Not that always where the language is intricate the thought is subtle, or the image always great where the line is bulky; the equality of words to things is very often neglected, and trivial sentiments and vulgar ideas disappoint the attention, to which they are recommended by sonorous epithets and swelling figures.

But the admirers of this great poet have most reason to complain when he approaches nearest to his highest excellence, and seems fully resolved to sink them in dejection, and mollify them with tender emotions by the fall of greatness, the danger of innocence, or the crosses of love. What he does best, he soon ceases to do. He is not long soft and pathetick without some idle conceit, or contemptible equivocation. He no sooner begins to move, than he counteracts himself; and terrour and pity, as they are rising in the mind, are checked and blasted by sudden frigidity.

A quibble is to Shakespeare, what luminous vapours are to the traveller; he follows it at all adventures, it is sure to lead him out of his way, and sure to engulf him in the mire. It has some malignant power over his mind, and its fascinations are irresistible. Whatever be the dignity or profundity of his disquisition, whether he be enlarging knowledge or exalting affection, whether he be amusing attention with incidents, or enchaining it in suspense, let but a quibble spring up before him, and he leaves his work unfinished. A quibble is the golden apple for which he will always turn aside from his career, or stoop from his elevation. A quibble, poor and barren as it is, gave him such delight, that he was content to purchase it, by the sacrifice of reason, propriety and truth. A quibble was to him the fatal Cleopatra for which he lost the world, and was content to lose it. [pp. 69–74]

. . . The necessity of observing the unities of time and place arises from the supposed necessity of making the drama credible. The criticks hold it impossible, that an action of months or years can be possibly believed to pass in three hours; or that the spectator can suppose himself to sit in the theatre, while ambassadors go and return between distant kings, while armies are levied and towns besieged, while an exile wanders and returns, or till he whom they saw courting his mistress, shall lament the untimely fall of his son. The mind revolts from evident falsehood, and fiction loses its force when it departs from the resemblance of reality.

From the narrow limitation of time necessarily arises the contraction of place. The spectator, who knows that he saw the first act at Alexandria, cannot suppose that he sees the next at Rome, at a distance to which not the dragons of Medea could, in so short a time, have transported him; he knows with certainty that he has not changed his place; and he knows that place cannot change itself; that what was a house cannot become a plain; that what was Thebes can never be Persepolis.

Such is the triumphant language with which a critick exults over the misery of an irregular poet, and exults commonly without resistance or reply. It is time therefore to tell him, by the authority of Shakespeare, that he assumes, as an unquestionable principle, a position, which, while his breath is forming it into words, his understanding pronounces to be false. It is false, that any representation is mistaken for reality; that any dramatick fable in its materiality was ever credible, or, for a single moment, was ever credited.

The objection arising from the impossibility of passing the first hour at Alexandria, and the next at Rome, supposes, that when the play opens the spectator really imagines himself at Alexandria, and believes that his walk to the theatre has been a voyage to Egypt, and that he lives in the days of Antony and Cleopatra. Surely he that imagines this may imagine more. He that can take the stage at one time for the palace of the Ptolemies, may take it in half an hour for the promontory of Actium. Delusion, if delusion be admitted, has no certain limitation; if the spectator can be once persuaded, that his old acquaintance are Alexander and Caesar, that a room illuminated with candles is the plain of Pharsalia, or the bank of Granicus, he is in a state of elevation above the reach of reason, or of truth, and from the heights of empyrean poetry, may despise the circumscriptions of terrestrial nature. There is no reason why a mind thus wandering in extasy should count the clock, or why an hour should not be a century in that calenture of the brains that can make the stage a field.

The truth is, that the spectators are always in their senses, and know, from the first act to the last, that the stage is only a stage, and that the players are only players. They come to hear a certain number of lines recited with just gesture and elegant modulation. The lines relate to some action, and an action must be in some place; but the different actions that compleat a story may be in places very remote from each other; and where is the absurdity of allowing that space to represent first Athens, and then Sicily, which was always known to be neither Sicily nor Athens, but a modern theatre.

By supposition, as place is introduced, time may be extended; the time required by the fable elapses for the most part between the acts; for, of so much of the action as is represented, the real and poetical duration is the same. If, in the first act, preparations for war against Mithridates are represented to be made in Rome, the event of the war may, without absurdity, be represented, in the catastrophe, as happening in Pontus; we know that there is neither war, nor preparation for war; we know that we are neither in Rome nor Pontus; that neither Mithridates nor Lucullus are before us. The drama exhibits successive imitations of successive actions, and why may not the second imitation represent an action that happened years after the first; if it be so connected with it, that nothing but time can be supposed to intervene. Time is, of all modes of existence, most obsequious to the imagination; a lapse of years is as easily conceived as a passage of hours. In contemplation we easily contract the time of real actions, and therefore willingly permit it to be contracted when we only see their imitation.

It will be asked, how the drama moves, if it is not credited. It is credited with all the credit due to a drama. It is credited, whenever it moves, as a just picture of a real original; as representing to the auditor what he would himself feel, if he were to do or suffer what is there feigned to be suffered or to be done. The reflection that strikes the heart is not, that the evils before us are real evils, but that they are evils to which we ourselves may be exposed. If there be any fallacy, it is not that we fancy the players, but that we fancy ourselves unhappy for a moment; but we rather lament the possibility than suppose the presence of misery, as a mother weeps over her babe, when she remembers that death may take it from her. The delight of tragedy proceeds from our consciousness of fiction; if we thought murders and treasons real, they would please no more.

Imitations produce pain or pleasure, not because they are mistaken for realities, but because they bring realities to mind. [pp. 76–8]

. . . Voltaire expresses his wonder, that our authour's extravagances are endured by a nation, which has seen the tragedy of *Cato*. Let him be answered, that Addison speaks the language of poets, and Shakespeare, of men. We find in *Cato* innumerable beauties which enamour us of its authour, but we see nothing that acquaints us with human sentiments or human actions; we place it with the fairest and the noblest progeny which judgment propagates by conjunction with learning, but *Othello* is the vigorous and vivacious offspring of observation impregnated by genius. *Cato* affords a splendid exhibition of artificial and fictitious manners, and delivers just and noble sentiments, in diction easy, elevated and harmonious, but its hopes and fears communicate no vibration to the heart; the composition refers us only to the writer; we pronounce the name of *Cato*, but we think on Addison.

The work of a correct and regular writer is a garden accurately formed and diligently planted, varied with shades, and scented with flowers; the composition of Shakespeare is a forest, in which oaks extend their branches, and pines tower in the air, interspersed sometimes with weeds and brambles, and sometimes giving shelter to myrtles and to roses; filling the eye with awful pomp, and gratifying the mind with endless diversity. Other poets display cabinets of precious rarities, minutely finished, wrought into shape, and polished unto brightness. Shakespeare opens a mine which contains gold and diamonds in unexhaustible plenty, though clouded by incrustations, debased by impurities, and mingled with a mass of meaner minerals. [p. 84]

. . . There is a vigilance of observation and accuracy of distinction which books and precepts cannot confer; from this almost all original and native excellence proceeds. Shakespeare must have looked upon mankind with perspicacity, in the highest degree curious and attentive. Other writers borrow their characters from preceding writers, and diversify them only by the accidental appendages of present manners; the dress is a little varied, but the body is the same. . . . Shakespeare, whether life or nature be his subject, shews plainly, that he has seen with his own eyes; he gives the image which he receives, not weakened or distorted by the intervention of any other mind; the ignorant feel his representations to be just, and the learned see that they are compleat. [pp. 88–90]

Note on References

In the references 'Yale' signifies *The Yale Edition of the Works of Samuel Johnson*, ed. Allen T. Hazen *et al.* (1958–); 'Hazlitt', *The Complete Works of William Hazlitt*, ed. P. P. Howe (21 vols.; 1930–4); and 'Schlegel', A. W. Schlegel, *Kritische Schriften und Briefe*, ed. Edgar Lohner (7 vols.; Stuttgart, 1962–74). Unless otherwise stated, in all references the place of publication is London, and all quotations from Shakespeare are taken from the text of Johnson's edition of 1765. Translations from German writers are my own, and references are therefore to the German texts.

1

TAKING JOHNSON SERIOUSLY

The great preoccupation of pedagogues, when they are faced with authors of some boldness who yet are classics, is to render them inoffensive; and I often wonder that the work of years should so naturally contribute to this. After a little it seems as though the edge of new thoughts gets worn away and also, from growing in some sort accustomed to them, we are able to handle them without fear of injury.

(ANDRÉ GIDE)

Shakespeare is above all writers, at least above all modern writers, the poet of nature.[1]

JOHNSON'S experience of Shakespeare as the poet of nature animates the whole of his account in the *Preface to Shakespeare*; on that central perception he rests his claim for Shakespeare's abiding greatness, and from it all his other observations flow. The present study inquires what it is to read Shakespeare in that way; it endeavours to grasp Johnson's meaning sympathetically enough to begin to see Shakespeare through Johnson's eyes, and to reflect on the implications of his appreciation for our own ways of reading. 'Nature' no longer has wide currency in the language of criticism, and for a modern reader it is not easy to see how Johnson's proposition could be going to the heart of the matter. Up to a point—the point of platitude—one recognizes, of course, broadly what is meant: the plays give us thoroughly convincing characters by whose feelings and actions we find ourselves to be powerfully moved; but if Johnson had no more to say to us than this we should hardly wish to lend him our attention. It would be no service to Johnson's Shakespeare to dwell upon its self-evidently sound and unexception-able aspects: better, even at the risk of some distortion, to insist upon its unfamiliarity, its 'questionable shape', in the hope of an encounter like that of T. S. Eliot with his 'dead master' in *Little Gidding*, 'Too strange to each other for misunderstanding'. What needs to be emphasized about the *Preface to Shakespeare* is not its good sense

[1] *Yale*, vii. 62.

(though it has some), nor yet its historical importance, but rather the way in which it continues to offer us radical criticism of Shakespeare: radical in that it reaches to fundamental thoughts about why the plays are worth reading, and radical also in both challenging and being challenged by other, more immediately congenial, approaches to the plays.

To remind oneself that Johnson's Shakespeare has not been comfortably assimilated by subsequent criticism, one need only recall certain other propositions from the *Preface*:

In the writings of other poets a character is too often an individual; in those of Shakespeare it is commonly a species.[2]

His disposition, as Rhymer has remarked, led him to comedy. In tragedy he often writes with great appearance of toil and study, what is written at last with little felicity.[3]

. . . he seems to write without any moral purpose.[4]

The plots are often so loosely formed, that a very slight consideration may improve them, and so carelessly pursued, that he seems not always fully to comprehend his own design.[5]

Whenever he solicits his invention, or strains his faculties, the offspring of his throes is tumour, meanness, tediousness, and obscurity.[6]

The equality of words to things is very often neglected, and trivial sentiments and vulgar ideas disappoint the attention, to which they are recommended by sonorous epithets and swelling figures.[7]

He is not long soft and pathetick without some idle conceit, or contemptible equivocation.[8]

. . . the spectators are always in their senses, and know, from the first act to the last, that the stage is only a stage, and that the players are only players.[9]

Such propositions as these are plainly radical enough, and provide a test for any claim to understand why Johnson thought Shakespeare a classic; only when his more remarkable findings become intelligible as part of a coherent response to the plays can we be at all confident that we know what it is that Johnson is praising in Shakespeare's 'just representations of general nature'.[10]

Taking Johnson seriously, then, implies the endeavour to bring the praise and the censure together as related parts of his total

---

[2] *Yale*, vii. 62   [3] Ibid. 69.   [4] Ibid. 71.   [5] Ibid.   [6] Ibid. 73.
[7] Ibid. 73 f.   [8] Ibid. 74.   [9] Ibid. 77.   [10] Ibid. 61.

response; and it implies the working assumption that what Johnson says about Shakespeare indeed expresses his response to *Shakespeare*, and that we shall therefore need to go to the plays in order to understand what Johnson is saying. This last point may seem elementary: but in both the existing full-length studies of Johnson's Shakespeare the grounds for what Johnson says are sought and found not in Shakespeare's plays but in the critical formulae of Johnson's contemporaries and predecessors. Arthur Sherbo has divided up the critical portion of the *Preface* into some sixty-odd separate elements, for each of which he produces parallel passages from earlier criticism; from this he infers that 'Johnson is the spokesman for his age', whose 'superior command of language enabled him to say more strikingly and more memorably what his predecessors had said before him'.[11] (He does not suppose that this superior power with language makes any difference to what is being communicated.) R. D. Stock has also demonstrated how the *Preface* can be seen as a representative document in the history of eighteenth-century critical thought; with rather more subtlety than Sherbo he has shown how it reflects the tension between the competing critical trends of 'rationalism' and 'sentimentalism', Johnson being generally inclined to the older view but sensitive to the arguments raised against it.[12] But about *Shakespeare*'s influence on the *Preface to Shakespeare* there is, in both these formidably well-documented studies, scarcely a word. They set up their terms of inquiry in such a way as wholly to assimilate the *Preface* to the history of literary-critical ideas, explaining Johnson's judgements in historical terms which never intersect with the question of their relation to the plays themselves; and in so far as they offer what are in effect studies of the history of Johnson's critical vocabulary as tolerably complete accounts of the whole matter they resemble the good Dr Busby of Pope's *Dunciad*: 'Words are Man's province, Words we teach alone.'[13] There must inevitably be something reductive about any discussion of Johnson's 'general nature' that refers to the theories of Rapin, Dryden, Gildon,

---

[11] Arthur Sherbo, *Samuel Johnson, Editor of Shakespeare* (Urbana, Ill., 1956), 60; see also pp. 125–8.

[12] See R. D. Stock, *Samuel Johnson and Neoclassical Dramatic Theory: The Intellectual Context of the Preface to Shakespeare* (Lincoln, Nebr., 1973), p. xxi, for a summary of his argument.

[13] *Twickenham Edition of the Poems of Alexander Pope*, ed. John Butt *et al.* (11 vols.; 1961–9), v. 356 (*Dunciad*, iv, l. 150).

Theobald, and Hurd without also bringing in Macbeth, or Othello, or Falstaff. To suppose otherwise would be to put Johnson on a level with Dick Minim, the pert young critic described in numbers 60 and 61 of the *Idler*, who

> was able to tell, in very proper phrases, that the chief business of art is to copy nature . . . Of the great authors he now began to display the characters, laying down as an universal position that all had beauties and defects. His opinion was, that Shakespear, committing himself wholly to the impulse of nature, wanted that correctness which learning would have given him . . .[14]

Minim has stolen some of Johnson's vocabulary, but he does not possess the experience which he is talking about; his opinions exist in a vacuum, and may be abstracted without injury from the literature to which they nominally refer, and wholly explained in terms of what others had said before him and were saying around him. He is the ideal subject for a certain kind of history of literary criticism.

With Johnson it is otherwise. And the attempt to relieve him of the responsibility for his own perceptions by suggesting that these are merely the product of his age is not only reductive, but also misleading. For it is interesting to note that a number of Johnson's original reviewers found some of Johnson's propositions very dubious indeed. Writing in the *St James's Chronicle*, George Colman could not accept Johnson's endorsement of Rymer's judgement that Shakespeare's disposition is for comedy:

> This opinion in which Mr. J. concurs with the Arch Zoilus of our Author, is however very disputable; and we cannot help thinking that what is said in this place, as well as what is afterwards thrown out on this head, in speaking of his faults, is infinitely too strong. A good comment on parts of Othello, Hamlet, Lear, Macbeth, and other tragick scenes of Shakespeare, or perhaps a mere perusal of them, would be the best method of confuting these assertions.[15]

William Kenrick's article in the *Monthly Review* dismissed Johnson's objection to Shakespeare's lack of moral purpose; Shakespeare, Kenrick argued, does not

---

[14] *Yale*, ii. 186. See Paul Fussell, *Samuel Johnson and the Life of Writing* (1972), 173 f.: 'Johnson's "thought" is not a great fixed structure . . . Johnson's criticism operates only within living contexts of actions, reactions, and generic purposes. If you remove the contexts, you misrepresent the criticism.'

[15] George Colman, *Prose on Several Occasions* (3 vols.; 1787), ii. 65.

conceive himself bound, as a *poet*, to write like a *philosopher*. He carries his persons, therefore, indifferently through right and wrong for the same reason as he makes them laugh and cry in the same piece, and is justifiable on the same principles . . . He did not presume to limit the designs of providence to the narrow bounds of poetical justice; but hath displayed the sun shining, as it really does, both on the just and the unjust.[16]

Kenrick also found Johnson's account of Shakespeare's faults in tragedy to be hugely and indefensibly exaggerated, and he regarded Johnson's discussion of dramatic illusion as a wilful departure from common sense:

The dramatic unities, if necessary, are necessary to support the *apparent probability*, not the *actual credibility* of the drama . . . We do not pretend to say that the spectators are not always in their senses; or that they do not know (if the question were put to them) that the stage is only a stage, and the players only players. But we will venture to say that they are often so intent on the scene as to be absent with regard to every thing else. A spectator properly affected by a dramatic representation makes no reflections about the fiction or the reality of it.[17]

In the *Critical Review*, William Guthrie took issue with Johnson's emphasis on generality, his assertion that Shakespeare's characters are not individuals but species:

Shakespeare has succeeded better in representing the oddities of nature than her general properties, which characterise a Menander, a Terence, or an Addison. . . . Can a Falstaff, a Malvolio, a Benedick, a Caliban; in short can any of Shakespeare's successful characters in comedy be termed a species? or rather, do they not please by being oddities, or, if Mr. Johnson pleases, individuals?[18]

Guthrie also joined in the chorus of indignation at the reservations about Shakespeare's tragic writing, believing that Johnson must have 'read himself out of a true taste for nature, and . . . studied himself into a disregard for the passions'; like Sir John Hawkins later,[19] he found something wilfully exaggerated in the account of Shakespeare's faults, and could only suppose that Johnson had 'thrown the blemishes of his author in too odious a light' in order

---

[16] Brian Vickers (ed.), *Shakespeare: The Critical Heritage* (6 vols.; 1973–81), v. 186.

[17] Ibid. 190.   [18] Ibid. 214.

[19] See John Hawkins, *The Life of Dr Samuel Johnson* (*The Works of Samuel Johnson*, i; 1787), 536.

'to preserve the character of impartiality'.[20] We also hear from
Hawkins that 'for thus detracting from the merit of his favourite,
Mr. Garrick was to the highest degree exasperated with Johnson',[21]
and from Boswell that the *Preface* 'excited much clamour against him
at first'.[22] Garrick, admittedly, had his own reasons for irritation,
but criticisms as substantial as these plainly challenge the idea
that Johnson was simply the spokesman for his age and that the
problematic remarks in the *Preface* have a straightforward historical
explanation.

Instead, they allow this possibility: that Guthrie and Garrick were
right to sense something wilful in the manner of Johnson's strictures,
and that in such problematic passages Johnson is more or less
deliberately opposing himself to other ways of reading Shakespeare
which he believes prejudicial to a true appreciation of Shakespeare's
classic status. 'The truth is', Johnson writes, emphatically, 'that the
spectators are always in their senses'; against that kind of engagement
with the plays which tends to take Shakespeare's power over the
imagination as its own authentication—an enthusiasm of a kind to
be kindled, perhaps, by the acting of Garrick—Johnson rudely insists
on the operation of a sceptical critical intelligence that remains firmly
in its senses, not flying on the viewless wings of Poesy but enforcing
a principled attention to all that the dull brain can offer which
perplexes and retards. This notion of a semi-deliberate resistance best
explains the fact that it is when Johnson is being most controversial,
most startling to the enthusiast for Shakespeare, that he sounds most
massively assertive, as though what he were proposing did not admit
of question at all. 'In tragedy he is always struggling after some
occasion to be comick'; 'the offspring of his throes is tumour,
meanness, tediousness, and obscurity'; '. . . he seldom escapes
without the pity or resentment of his reader'.[23] The overbearingly
positive manner in which Johnson advances such highly questionable
propositions has made many readers give him up as a critic of
Shakespeare; instead of thinking about such remarks in relation to
the plays, they turn instead, understandably enough, to diagnosing
the deficiencies of a critic so seemingly obtuse to the possibility of

---

[20] Vickers, *Shakespeare: The Critical Heritage*, v. 218 f.

[21] Hawkins, *Life of Johnson*, p. 442.

[22] *Boswell's Life of Johnson: Together with Boswell's Journal of a Tour to the
Hebrides and Johnson's Diary of a Journey into North Wales*, ed. G. B. Hill, rev.
edn. L. F. Powell (6 vols.; 1934–50), i. 449.

any more imaginative and appreciative response. Yet this is to miss the way in which such obtuseness is consciously polemical, 'not dogmatically but deliberatively written';[24] the intolerantly emphatic note itself represents a kind of intelligence about, or at least sensitivity to, the attraction of the way of reading which is opposed. To take a somewhat parallel case, when Johnson 'refutes' the idealism of Berkeley by kicking a stone,[25] or when he opposes the scepticism of Hume with the remark that he would not trust one of Hume's followers 'with young ladies, for *there* there is always temptation',[26] this, as philosophical criticism, is obtuse, but as a counter to his inter-locutor's brand of enthusiasm for the ideas of Berkeley or of Hume it may well have its point. Its tactical obtuseness as philosophical argument serves to indicate the true direction of the attack: not philosophy, but the uses and attractions of philosophy. Johnson never talks more overbearingly than when his opponent has a strongly attractive case to make; and although his loudness of voice can in itself demonstrate nothing but the strength of his opposition, this is not to say that his grounds for opposition are not worth taking seriously.

Consider, for example, one of the most alienating footnotes in the entire Shakespeare edition:

Juliet plays most of her pranks under the appearance of religion; perhaps Shakespeare meant to punish her hypocrisy.[27]

Three different tones of voice are to be heard in such an overtly insensitive remark as this. One is that of the magisterial dogmatist, distorting Shakespeare's sympathetic presentation of Juliet beneath the weight of his fixed preconceptions. A second tone of voice, also present, is more uneasy; it makes itself heard in the very trenchancy with which Johnson overrides aspects of *Romeo and Juliet* which he finds unacceptable or positively disturbing—the celebration of passionate love, and the absence of any obvious moral framework within which such love might be contained. Both these voices are generally recognized in discussions of Johnson; both (where present) tend to disqualify him as a critic. What has not always been so clearly recognized, however, is the presence of a third, more genial, challengingly deliberate tone:

[23] *Yale*, vii. 69, 73.   [24] Ibid. 80.
[25] Boswell, *Life of Johnson*, i. 471.
[26] Ibid. i. 444.   [27] *Yale*, viii. 953.

Yes, I know very well that to speak of Juliet's strategems here as 'pranks' and 'hypocrisy' is likely to outrage your feelings; but my purpose in being thus outrageous—thus woodenly unimaginative, if you will—is to suggest something rather too easy in the unqualified sympathy with Juliet which one readily feels at this point, but which depends on certain truths of the situation being kept out of sight. The intrusiveness of my remark simply reflects the exclusiveness of a certain kind of likely imaginative engagement with the play.

Johnson's full account of *Romeo and Juliet* will be discussed in more detail later; for the moment it is enough to say that the presence of this tone of genial challenge shows how Johnson could be taken seriously even in such an unpromising note as this. We may disagree with his assertions, but we should be foolish to discount them as obtuse on the ground of their tone; and in disagreeing with him we shall have to acknowledge the possibility that he equally disagrees with us.

I am not suggesting that Johnson strikes *only* the genial note. All three tones—the dogmatic and the uneasy-aggressive, as well as the genially challenging—can be heard in the remark on Juliet, and are present in varying proportions in all of his more rebarbative comments on Shakespeare, so that we may imagine these being spoken with a half-smiling look of challenge *and* in a growl of assertion. The tones of precisely modulated irony that he was to command in the *Lives of the Poets* are missing or muffled here; Johnson is engaged both in giving life to a great commonplace about Shakespeare with which all of his readers will agree, and in insisting upon certain related propositions which many of those readers will find distinctly unwelcome, and on those latter points he seems never quite to have decided whether to challenge his reader's disagreement or to brush it aside. The possibility of a dissenting reader is neither addressed nor ignored; what is provocative in Johnson's phrasing seems to have been written for such a reader to hear, but Johnson will not engage with him directly.[28] If the idea of a permanently valuable Shakespeare criticism implies the greatest openness to the diversity of possible readings that is compatible with the decisive choice of one, then Johnson's positiveness of manner in the Shakespeare edition

---

[28] One recalls Wordsworth's apprehensiveness in the Preface to *Lyrical Ballads* that he might appear 'like a man fighting a battle without enemies'; see *The Poetical Works of William Wordsworth*, ed. E. de Selincourt and Helen Darbishire (5 vols.; 1940–9), ii. 393.

is both a strength and a weakness: for if in its trenchancy it shows itself to be alive to the attraction of what it resists, it also betrays an impatience to be rid of that attraction which has weakened his case with his readers from his day to our own. Yet while deploring this, we may also allow it to suggest a moral: that we should not ourselves be impatient to dismiss Johnson's more startling propositions without considering what is meant by them—that is, in what qualities of Shakespeare's writing they originate.

To establish this with any precision, however, is not a straight-forward matter. If Johnson had left us a book of essays on the plays, or an edition with detailed critical comment on each page, there would have been no need for a book like this. But Johnson's specifically critical notes are not only few, they are also rarely descriptive; and where they are descriptive, they are frequently too brief to be thoroughly illuminating. This may have been partly because of Johnson's unwillingness to recognize that Shakespeare could be intelligently read in different ways, partly because of his belief that 'the reader . . . is seldom pleased to find his opinion anticipated; it is natural to delight more in what we find or make, than in what we receive',[29] and partly because he doubted that Shakespeare's 'real power' would in any case give itself up to close analysis, being a power 'not shewn in the splendour of particular passages, but by the progress of his fable, and the tenour of his dialogue'.[30] The depression of spirit which we know that he suffered during the years he was working on the edition may also have been a factor.[31] But, whatever the reasons for it, the paucity of descriptive notes which show how Johnson read specific passages or scenes makes it difficult for us to give to the generalizations of the *Preface* the kind of sharp application that would fill them out with meaning. My argument is that it is only through Shakespeare that we can hope to understand what Johnson means by 'the poet of nature': but this, it might reasonably be complained, is to seek to define one highly fluid, disputable, and various idea by another. There are many Shakespeares in existence: how shall we say with any precision *which* readings of Falstaff, of *King Lear*, of Shakespeare's comedy are grounded in general nature as Johnson understood the idea?

---

[29] *Yale*, vii. 104. [30] Ibid. 62.
[31] See W. J. Bate, *Samuel Johnson* (1978), 371–89, and Charles E. Pierce, *The Religious Life of Samuel Johnson* (1983), 130–41.

I overstate the difficulty, to be sure; some controls are to be had from the notes, from Johnson's thinking in other contexts, and from the evocative force of some of the writing in the *Preface*; but there is still a danger that one may be not so much recovering Johnson's Shakespeare as substituting a Shakespeare of one's own.

In this situation, it is helpful to hold on to Johnson's more questionable and challenging propositions, even at the risk of over-emphasizing what is polemical in his account. By concentrating on those areas where we can readily see points of conflict with other critical attitudes, we can replace the problematic question, 'What does "nature" mean in the *Preface to Shakespeare*?' by the more constructive inquiry, 'What is *not* meant by "nature"? What readings of Shakespeare does Johnson's emphasis on nature exclude?'—somewhat in the spirit of Karl Popper's definition of the informative content of a theory as 'the set of statements which are incompatible with the theory'.[32] By drawing the boundaries of Johnson's Shakespeare, we shall better be able to see its shape; the cutting edge of his account will become apparent in the context of a strong claim to refute or 'falsify' it.

Just such a claim is to be found in the romantic appreciation of Shakespeare—'romantic' being a word used throughout this study as a convenient shorthand for elements common to the Shakespeare criticism of August Wilhelm Schlegel, Samuel Taylor Coleridge, and William Hazlitt. Although these three critics do not always speak with one voice, their making common cause against Johnson, and the degree of sympathy that exists between their accounts, make it reasonable to find in their work a single approach to Shakespeare. Coleridge's debt to Schlegel, or at any rate his concurrence with Schlegel, is well known; Schlegel's *Lectures* were enthusiastically reviewed by Hazlitt,[33] who, after going on to write his *Characters of Shakespear's Plays*, believed that he had done more to vindicate Shakespeare against his detractors 'than any one except Schlegel';[34] and Schlegel returned the compliment in his opinion that Hazlitt had surpassed him as an 'ultra-Shakspearian'.[35] Despite their differences, what these critics had in common was an approach to Shakespeare that has been enduringly influential in challenging and displacing Johnson's way of reading the plays. The prestige and influence

---

[32] Karl Popper, *Unended Quest: An Intellectual Autobiography* (1976), 26.
[33] See Hazlitt, xvi. 57–99 ('Schlegel on the Drama').   [34] Ibid. xii. 122.
[35] *The Journal of Thomas Moore, 1818–1841*, ed. Peter Quennell (1964), 58.

of Schlegel's *Lectures on Dramatic Art and Literature*, both in England and throughout Europe, was immense;[36] a recent study of Coleridge's Shakespeare criticism has argued cogently that Coleridge's approach 'has become part and parcel of most of the subsequent criticism of Shakespeare' and that the positions which Coleridge sought to establish now 'often form tacit assumptions in our minds';[37] and René Wellek similarly finds that Schlegel (together with his brother) 'best formulated a view of literature and criticism which was transmitted by Coleridge to the English-speaking world and is, on many essential points, accepted by recent English and American criticism'.[38] If Johnson's Shakespeare is strange to us now, this may be in part because Schlegel, Coleridge, and Hazlitt have done their job well. Certainly, it is true of all of them that, where Shakespeare is concerned, Johnson is the enemy. Hazlitt devotes the preface of his *Characters of Shakespear's Plays* to the shortcomings of Johnson's account of Shakespeare, quoting Schlegel approvingly by way of contrast, and seeking to explain Johnson's otherwise unintelligible judgements by his lack of imagination. His sense of the fundamental incompatibility of Johnson's approach to Shakespeare with his own gives rise to the admirably unequivocal conclusion: 'If Dr. Johnson's opinion was right, the following observations on Shakespear's Plays must be greatly exaggerated, if not ridiculous.'[39] Coleridge, we learn from Crabb Robinson, devoted at least two of his 1811–12 course of Shakespeare lectures to an attack on what he elsewhere described as Johnson's 'strangely over-rated contradictory & most illogical Preface'.[40] He seems to have regarded an attack on Johnson as a proper part of a course on Shakespeare, since the advertisement for his 1813–14 lectures in Bristol speaks of two lectures on Shakespeare and four on Milton, these to include 'an examination of Dr. Johnson's Preface to Shakespeare'.[41] Unfortunately, we have no record of these lectures on the *Preface*, but their general tenor may be inferred from Crabb Robinson's diary notes:

[36] See Josef Körner, *Die Botschaft der deutschen Romantik an Europa* (Augsburg, 1929), 69–74 and *passim*.

[37] M. M. Badawi, *Coleridge: Critic of Shakespeare* (1973), 194 f.

[38] René Wellek, *A History of Modern Criticism: 1750–1950* (7 vols.; 1955–), ii. 73.　　　　　　　　　　　　　　　　　　　　[39] Hazlitt, iv. 178.

[40] *Collected Letters of Samuel Taylor Coleridge*, ed. E. L. Griggs (6 vols.; 1956–71), iv. 642 (no. 1010: to Daniel Stuart, 13 May 1816).

[41] Samuel Taylor Coleridge, *Shakespearean Criticism*, ed. T. M. Raysor, 2nd edn. (2 vols.; 1960), ii. 208.

Evening, Coleridge's lecture on Johnson's Preface. C. succeeded admirably in the exposure of Johnson, and tho' he was sometimes obscure, the many palpable and intelligible *hits* must have given general satisfaction.[42]

Schlegel too is emphatic that his approach to Shakespeare represents a clean break with the eighteenth-century English commentators:

. . . there I must separate myself from them entirely. What they say is hardly ever true, and certainly never profound . . . The recent editors go further still, both in their prefaces, which are just meant as rhetorical exercises on the theme of praising the poet, and in their notes on particular passages. Not only do they concede that his plays offend against the rules, which is to examine them by wholly inappropriate criteria, but they also accuse him of bombast, of a confused, ungrammatical, conceited way of writing, and of the most improper buffoonery.[43]

It soon becomes clear in the *Lectures* that it is Johnson whom he regards as his principal antagonist. He declares Johnson's criticism to stem from a mechanical view of art which disables him from appreciating Shakespeare,[44] attacks Johnson's statement that Shakespeare's characters are not individuals but species,[45] takes issue with Johnson over Shakespeare's effects of pathos,[46] finds Johnson's reservations about the tragic in Shakespeare to be hardly worthy of formal refutation,[47] defends Shakespeare's fondness for word-play,[48] and argues that Johnson's defence of Shakespeare's 'mingled drama' is both theoretically unsound and grossly inadequate to the facts of our experience.[49] Schlegel's earlier essays on *Hamlet* and *Romeo and Juliet* also make reference to Johnson and are, to a large extent, attempts to meet Johnson's dissatisfaction with those plays.[50]

In opposing Johnson's account to the romantic reading of Shakespeare, and in seeking to give him the strongest possible reply to those who claimed to supersede him, it is not my intention to argue that

---

[42] Ibid. 173.   [43] Schlegel, vi. 115 f.   [44] Ibid. 128.
[45] Ibid. 131.   [46] Ibid. 132.   [47] Ibid. 133.
[48] Ibid. 133 f.   [49] Ibid. 137 f.
[50] See ibid. i. 88–140. It seems to have been Schlegel's own decision to take Johnson, rather than, for example, Voltaire, as the malignant authority that had to be overthrown; earlier German admirers of Shakespeare hardly mention him, and, although he would have been known through his edition, the *Preface* was not translated and was far less well-known in Germany than that of Pope. See L. M. Price, *English Literature in Germany* (University of California Publications in Modern Philology; Berkeley, Calif. 1953), 217; and Hans Wolffheim (ed.), *Die Entdeckung Shakespeares: Deutsche Zeugnisse des 18. Jahrhunderts* (Hamburg, 1959), 39.

Johnson was simply right about Shakespeare where the romantics were wrong. The criticism of literature is not a wholly objective discipline any more than it is a wholly subjective one; every critical account of Shakespeare must involve an element of choice from amongst competing possibilities as well as an element of attention to what is there in the text. What I wish to establish is that the choices informing Johnson's finding of 'general nature' in Shakespeare are just as tenable and as unquestionably responsive to a real potentiality in the plays as those preferred by its great romantic antagonist, and that each set of choices acquires a larger and more precise significance in the context of the other. In relation to Johnson, that is, the romantic view is most usefully seen as neither a development nor a refutation but a powerful alternative. That Schlegel comes after Johnson is in itself no reason to suppose him an *advance*; one notes that Goethe, who had heard Schlegel's arguments and who will not easily be convicted of a prosaic cast of mind, chose nevertheless to reaffirm Johnson's conviction that Shakespeare is the poet of nature:

It is the interest of what lies within this world that quickens Shakespeare's great spirit into life. For although prophecy and madness, dreams, intimations, portents, fairies and gnomes, ghosts, magicians and unearthly beings do create an element of magic which, at the right moments, makes itself felt in his plays, still these figures of illusion are in no way central to his works, which rest instead on the fundamental truth and health of his feeling for life; and this is why everything that comes from him in that spirit strikes us as so genuine, sound, and substantial. He has accordingly been recognized to belong not so much to the modern, 'romantic' poets but rather to the 'naive' kind, for the value of his work rests on the reality of the present; barely at its most sensitive, most extreme point does it touch the emotion of desire for something other than this world affords.[51]

Goethe, there, was deliberately opposing the view of Shakespeare put forward by Schlegel and his brother Friedrich. What Johnson offered in 1765 as a great commonplace—albeit half conscious that it carried certain polemical implications—had in 1815 to be advanced by Goethe as a fighting proposition, and it is only as a fighting proposition that it is likely to quicken our understanding now. And the fight in question is something more interesting and more crucial

---

[51] Johann Wolfgang Goethe, *Werke*, ed. Erich Trunz (14 vols.; Hamburg, 1949–60), xii. 290 f. ('Shakespeare und kein Ende'). 'The emotion of desire for something other than this world affords' translates the German *Sehnsucht*.

than a matter of simple critical disagreement; it corresponds in large part to choices and tensions both exhibited by and dramatized within Shakespeare's plays themselves.

This, however, is to anticipate. The romantic reading of Shakespeare will be discussed in Chapter 3. In preparation for that discussion I shall need first to describe certain leading characteristics of Johnson's feeling for 'general nature', and in particular to defend it against the common charge that it is both untenable in theory and self-contradictory in practice.

2

JUST REPRESENTATIONS
OF GENERAL NATURE

. . . the purpose of playing; whose end, both at the first and now, was
and is, to hold as 'twere the mirror up to nature

(HAMLET)

imitari, is nothing: so doth the hound his master, the ape his keeper,
the tired horse his rider

(HOLOFERNES, a Schoolmaster)

In a course of lectures on aesthetics which he gave in 1801,
A. W. Schlegel applied a withering common sense to the notion that
the imitation of nature could properly be said to be the aim of art:

As Nature is already present and available, it's a little hard to understand
why one should go to the trouble of bringing a second precisely similar
version of it into being as art . . .

There have been some, however, who, realising how vague and broad
this principle is, have . . . declared that art ought to imitate *la belle nature*
. . . But this gets us nowhere: either one imitates nature as one finds it,
in which case it may well turn out not to be beautiful, or one re-creates
nature as beautiful, in which case there can no longer be any question of
imitation.[1]

This straightforward argument appears to have considerable force.
The charge that Johnson treats art as life, or, in mitigated form, that
he reads Shakespeare's plays as though they were naturalistic novels,
commonly features in unfavourable accounts of the *Preface*. The
modern Shakespearean finds it easier to believe that in his more
startling propositions Johnson is entangled by some flaw in his
fundamental approach, than that he is responding to certain qualities
that are really in the plays. The apologist for Johnson's Shakespeare
must, therefore, show that Schlegel's is not the knock-down argument
which it appears to be: that is, he must establish, firstly, that what

[1] Schlegel, ii. 84 f.

Johnson seeks and finds in Shakespeare is not a mere duplication of our daily experience of the world, and, secondly, that there is, notwithstanding, nothing contradictory about his emphasis on 'nature', 'truth', and 'realities'.

In order to understand what is so special about Shakespeare's truth to nature, inquiry must turn to Johnson's feeling for *generality*: the plays, we recall, are 'just representations of general nature'. But, before doing so, a common misconception about Johnson's Shakespeare needs to be examined. The 'nature' which Johnson finds in the plays is not only 'general', it also carries with it 'instruction'—'it is from this wide extension of design that so much instruction is derived'[2]—and it is sometimes thought that the 'nature' Johnson wanted from Shakespeare was nature moralized. Leavis, for example, believed that Johnson wished the dramatist 'to manipulate his puppets so as to demonstrate and enforce . . . a conscious and abstractly formulated moral'.[3] This is untrue. The moral usefulness of Shakespeare, in the narrow sense which Leavis has in mind, is for Johnson quite clearly incidental to the main thing, the power of nature:

It was said of Euripides, that every verse was a precept; and it may be said of Shakespeare, that from his works may be collected a system of civil and oeconomical prudence. Yet his real power is not shewn in the splendour of particular passages, but by the progress of his fable, and the tenour of his dialogue.[4]

Addison's impeccably edifying tragedy *Cato* 'affords a splendid exhibition of artificial and fictitious manners, and delivers just and noble sentiments, in diction easy, elevated and harmonious', but Johnson nevertheless adduces it as the merest foil to Shakespeare's drama, for 'its hopes and fears communicate no vibration to the heart'.[5] 'Of the agents we have no care: we consider not what they are doing, or what they are suffering; we wish only to know what they have to say.'[6]

Admittedly, Johnson observes it as a fault in Shakespeare that 'his precepts and axioms drop casually from him', and that 'he carries his persons indifferently through right and wrong'. 'He sacrifices

---

[2] *Yale*, vii. 62.   [3] F. R. Leavis, *The Common Pursuit* (1952), 111.
[4] *Yale*, vii. 62.   [5] Ibid. 84.
[6] Samuel Johnson, *Lives of the English Poets*, ed. G. B. Hill (3 vols.; 1905), ii. 132.

virtue to convenience, and is so much more careful to please than to instruct, that he seems to write without any moral purpose.'[7] Here it might indeed seem that the prescriptive moralist is making his presence felt. There is a degree of truth in this; Johnson recognizes that there are 'laws of higher authority than those of criticism'.[8] But he did not in practice invoke those laws with any great emphasis or frequency: to look through his edition for notes which illustrate his moral strictures in the *Preface* is to find that in reading Shakespeare he was very far from preoccupied by specifically moral questions, and very little disturbed by the absence of manifest moral purpose. The one crucial exception to this is Johnson's response to the tragedies: certain notes on *Hamlet*, *Othello*, *King Lear*, and *Macbeth* express feelings of shock and dismay altogether different from the tone of good-humoured reproof employed by Johnson elsewhere. (His response to what is tragic in Shakespeare's tragedies raises separate questions, and will be reserved for discussion in the last chapter of this study.) But in looking through the thirty-two plays which remain, I have counted only thirteen notes which carry the general objection voiced in the *Preface*. Of these, no fewer than six are concerned with *All's Well* and *Measure for Measure*.[9] Johnson questions both the morality and the dramatic effectiveness of the bids for sympathetic forgiveness for Bertram and Angelo which the plays make at their respective conclusions; the implication is that the kind of sympathy elicited by Isabella's uncertainly motivated intercession, or by Shakespeare's invoking in *All's Well* the conventions of romance, cannot comprehend the moral reality so forcefully presented in Angelo and Bertram. Clearly, there is nothing narrowly moralistic in that objection; both plays are generally agreed to be experimental and problematic works. A somewhat similar mistrust of any attempt to turn moral realities into the stuff of romance lies behind three other notes: Johnson remarks Belarius's unconcern in *Cymbeline* for 'the injury which he has done to the young princes, whom he has robbed of a kingdom only to rob their father of heirs',[10] regrets Shakespeare's omission of 'the dialogue between the usurper and the hermit' as blurring over Frederick's wonderful conversion from evil to good at the end of *As You Like It*,[11] and finds that the comic

[7] *Yale*, vii. 71.
[8] Ibid. 339.
[9] See ibid. 193, 213, 214, 400, 401, 404.
[10] Ibid. viii. 892.
[11] Ibid. vii. 265.

ending to *Twelfth Night* 'wants credibility and fails to produce the proper instruction required in the drama, as it exhibits no just picture of life'.[12] Whatever one may think of Johnson's attitude to romance comedy, these grumbles at the stylization of reality conventional to romance are not what one would expect from a critic who wanted his nature moralized: the 'instruction' which he desiderates is simply that which, in his view, flows from a 'just picture of life'. The four other notes observe relatively small matters: Johnson objects to the frequency of profanity in *Merry Wives*,[13] wonders at the loyalty of Oswald to Goneril in *King Lear*,[14] remarks (in passing) the dramatic impropriety of the 'horrid wish' for Cade's damnation 'with which Iden debases his character' in *2 Henry VI*,[15] and expresses indignation at the apparent neutrality with which Shakespeare represents the 'horrible violation of faith' with which Lancaster and Westmoreland engineer the defeat of the rebels in *2 Henry IV*.[16] (On that last point, a modern critic might claim that the irony intended is perfectly clear; but it has not always been found so.) For the insistent moralist that Johnson is sometimes supposed to be, this is no very substantial list of complaints.

The relative slightness of those notes lends support, then, to the suggestion that when Johnson asserts that Shakespeare seems to write without any moral purpose, it is with a strong implicit distinction between the moral purpose of the writer and the general moral effect of the work. As a moralist, Johnson deplored Shakespeare's willingness to sacrifice virtue to convenience, just as he applauded the 'purity and excellence'[17] of Addison's literary purposes; but as a critic of literature he found *Cato* to be frigid and Shakespeare's plays to give immense and enduring pleasure of the most valuable kind. There is no contradiction here; the two sets of judgements refer to different kinds of thing. It is even possible to glimpse in Johnson's *Preface* the suggestion that Shakespeare's general moral power is actually enhanced by the lack of any conscious didactic aim, if one puts the proposition that Shakespeare 'is so much more careful to please than to instruct' next to the assertion that 'the end of poetry is to instruct by pleasing'.[18] Thus to interpret the Horatian *delectando pariterque monendo* is to make pleasure prior, and

[12] Ibid. 326.   [13] Ibid. 339.   [14] Ibid. viii. 694.
[15] Ibid. 595.   [16] Ibid. vii. 512.
[17] Johnson, *Lives of the Poets*, ii. 125.   [18] *Yale* vii. 71, 67.

instruction consequent: it is precisely *because* Shakespeare cares so much for pleasing—with that special pleasure which nature affords—that his works give so much instruction. *C'est avoir profité que de sçavoir s'y plaire*:[19] the words Boileau uses of Homer also express Johnson's attitude to Shakespeare.

This response to Shakespeare is the more significant in that Johnson felt quite differently about the contemporary novel. In a *Rambler* essay written in 1750, shortly after the publication of *Tom Jones*, he insisted on the need for clear moral purposiveness in the novel. In so far as the novelist shows us vice in association with attractive other qualities, he can hardly avoid glamorizing it; such a representation of life may well be not unrealistic, but will also be potentially corrupting in its effect:

> It is justly considered as the greatest excellency of art, to imitate nature; but it is necessary to distinguish those parts of nature, which are most proper for imitation: greater care is still required in representing life, which is so often discoloured by passion, or deformed by wickedness.[20]

'Nature' here is a much less comprehensive idea than it becomes in the context of Shakespeare, where Johnson makes no such overriding demand for selectivity and 'care' in the representation of nature, and where he can observe with unqualified pleasure and approval that 'the character which Shakespeare delighted to draw' was 'a fellow that had more wit than virtue'[21]—precisely the kind of character which the *Rambler* essay warns against. We need not infer that Johnson's position changed between 1750 and 1765; what this difference recognizes is the difference between 'just representations of general nature' and the kind of realism achieved by such novelists as Richardson, Smollett, and Fielding:

> They are engaged in portraits of which every one knows the original, and can detect any deviation from exactness of resemblance. Other writings are safe, except from the malice of learning, but these are in danger from every common reader; as the slipper ill executed was censured by a shoemaker who happened to stop in his way at the Venus of Apelles.[22]

---

[19] Nicolas Boileau-Despréaux, *Œuvres complètes*, ed. F. Escal (Paris, 1966), 176 (*L'Art poétique*, iii, l. 308).

[20] *Yale*, iii. 22 (*Rambler* no. 3).

[21] Ibid. vii. 399. Johnson is thinking in the first place of Parolles and Falstaff.

[22] Ibid. iii. 20 (*Rambler* no. 4).

There is a striking contrast between this and what Johnson says of the power of enlightenment possessed by Shakespeare's truth to nature:

He who has mazed his imagination, in following the phantoms which other writers raise up before him, may here be cured of his delirious extasies, by reading human sentiments in human language; by scenes from which a hermit may estimate the transactions of the world, and a confessor predict the progress of the passions.[23]

The experience of Shakespearean nature has the power to rectify false opinion and bring new understanding, to give the hermit and the confessor knowledge of modes of life with which they have no first-hand familiarity. The kind of recognition possible for the shoemaker, on the other hand, can be only of what he already knows, and knows that he knows; such realism as he can verify gives us what we can normally also get from our quotidian experience of the world—which is why Johnson supposes that this new kind of fiction will matter chiefly to the inexperienced, 'the young, the ignorant, and the idle, to whom they serve as lectures of conduct, and introductions into life'.[24] And there is the further point that the shoemaker is a specialist as the reader of Shakespeare is not; 'particular manners can be known to few':[25] when presented with a Venus, not every man's attention will be riveted by her footwear; the sense in which an eighteenth-century Englishwoman of the middle classes would have special authority to judge of the truth of, say, Richardson's Clarissa is not at all the same as that in which she might perceive the truth of Desdemona, or Cleopatra, or Macbeth. It is as 'just copyers of human manners'[26] that Johnson describes the prac- titioners of the new art of the novel, 'manners' being a term which he regularly uses for modes of behaviour peculiar to a particular historical period or social grouping, and which he regularly distinguishes from the generality of nature. 'Dryden knew more of man in his general nature, and Pope in his local manners';[27] the comic characters in *Troilus and Cressida* 'are of the superficial kind, and exhibit more of manners than nature';[28] in *Julius Caesar* Shakespeare's 'adherence to the real story, and to Roman manners, seems to have impeded the natural vigour of his genius'.[29] An earlier editor, Warburton,

---

[23] Ibid. vii. 65.   [24] Ibid. iii. 21 (*Rambler* no. 4).   [25] Ibid. vii. 61.
[26] Ibid. iii. 20 (*Rambler* no. 4).   [27] Johnson, *Lives of the Poets*, iii. 222.
[28] *Yale*, viii. 938.   [29] Ibid. 836.

had seen in Polonius a 'weak, pedant, minister of state' whose
pedantry reflected the vices of Elizabethan practice; Johnson granted
that knowledge of the manners of the Elizabethan court was relevant
to Polonius's 'mode of oratory', but denied that such shoemaker-like
knowledge could in itself comprehend the more general representation of 'dotage encroaching upon wisdom' which he found in the
character: 'The commentator makes the character of Polonius, a
character only of manners, discriminated by properties superficial,
accidental, and acquired. The poet intended a nobler delineation of
a mixed character of manners and of nature.'[30] Particular manners
can be known to few: 'nothing can please many, and please long,
but just representations of general nature'.[31] The Shakespearean
truth to nature is something clearly distinct from the realism
characteristic of the novelist, and this difference makes finally
unnecessary the directive moral purpose upon which Johnson had
insisted in the case of the novel. Shakespeare's representations of
general nature, it would seem, penetrating as they do beneath
qualities 'superficial, accidental, and acquired', reach to a depth at
which fidelity to the truth of the world and fidelity to moral truth
become one.

This returns us to the question of what Johnson means by generality,
and by aligning generality with nature. Most of his commentators
here may be said to take one of two lines: the high road of ideality,
where 'general' is taken to imply some kind of ideal order, or
the low road of empiricism, where 'general' implies the power to
draw generalizations from the particularities of experience. Both
roads lead to contradiction. On the high road are to be found
W. K. Wimsatt, who relates Johnson's principle of generality to
'the neo-Platonic drive in literary theory', Jean Hagstrum ('nature
as some kind of general order'), R. D. Stock ('he apparently uses the
word in its general or ideal sense'), and Arieh Sachs ('a transcendence
of the limits of particularity and of temporal life').[32] But there is in
fact nothing that suggests the 'ideal' in any of Johnson's discussions

---

[30] Ibid. 973 f.   [31] Ibid. vii. 61.

[32] W. K. Wimsatt and Cleanth Brooks, *Literary Criticism: A Short History*
(New York, 1957), 331; Jean H. Hagstrum, *Samuel Johnson's Literary Criticism*
(Minneapolis, Minn., 1952), 56; R. D. Stock, *Samuel Johnson and Neoclassical
Dramatic Theory: The Intellectual Context of the Preface to Shakespeare* (Lincoln,
Nebr., 1973), 28; Arieh Sachs, *Passionate Intelligence: Imagination and Reason in
the Work of Samuel Johnson* (Baltimore, Maryland, 1967), 81.

of generality;[33] such an emphasis on ideality would run strangely counter to the strongly sceptical and empirical tendency of his thought, and seems hardly compatible with his warm praise of Shakespeare for exhibiting 'the real state of sublunary nature, which partakes of good and evil, joy and sorrow, mingled with endless variety of proportion and innumerable modes of combination', and in which 'many mischiefs and many benefits are done and hindered without design'.[34] It is 'this chaos of mingled purposes and casualties',[35] Johnson says, that Shakespeare truly represents; those commentators determined to find in general nature 'some kind of general order' are driven to conclude that in that passage Johnson 'has abandoned all notions of general or ideal nature' (Stock), that by 'nature' he means not one thing but two—'particular reality' and 'ordered reality' (Hagstrum), and that the *Preface* accordingly exhibits 'an unresolved tension between the neoclassic conscience and the liberating impulse' (Wimsatt).[36] However, Johnson fares no better with those commentators who take the alternative line and see the generality he desiderates as something akin to generalization—generalization based on the unideal world of sublunary nature. Leopold Damrosch, for example, holds that 'Johnson simply means that the general (and unchanging) principles of human experience must be deduced from the chaos of mingled purposes and casualties in which we normally meet them', a process which Damrosch describes as one of 'abstraction'.[37] F. R. Leavis takes an essentially similar view in connecting Johnson's terms for Shakespeare with the 'radically undramatic', statement-like generalities of Johnson's own verse.[38] Clearly, this is not a favourable interpretation. Shakespeare's art does not characteristically work through abstractions; if it were true that Johnson saw Shakespeare as 'deducing' and 'abstracting'

---

[33] For corroboration, see Howard D. Weinbrot, 'The Reader, the General, and the Particular: Johnson and Imlac in Chapter Ten of *Rasselas*', *Eighteenth-Century Studies*, 5 (1971–2), 80–96, esp. p. 90.

[34] *Yale*, vii. 66.   [35] Ibid.

[36] Stock, *Samuel Johnson and Neoclassical Dramatic Theory*, p. 69; Hagstrum, *Samuel Johnson's Literary Criticism*, p. 74; *Samuel Johnson on Shakespeare*, ed. W. K. Wimsatt (1960), p. xxi.

[37] Leopold Damrosch, Jun., *The Uses of Johnson's Criticism* (Charlottesville, Va., 1976), 24 f., 27. See also Emerson R. Marks, *The Poetics of Reason: English Neoclassical Criticism* (New York, 1968), 135.

[38] Leavis, *Common Pursuit*, p. 118, and see 'Johnson as Critic', *Scrutiny*, 12 (1944–5), 187–204.

generality from the real particulars of sublunary life, he would seem uncomfortably like the critic that the romantics found him to be—one, in Hazlitt's words, whose 'general powers of reasoning overlaid his critical susceptibility', and who

found the general species or *didactic* form in Shakespeare's characters, which was all he sought or cared for; he did not find the individual traits, or the *dramatic* distinctions which Shakespear has engrafted on this general nature, because he felt no interest in them.[39]

It would be easy enough to cite passages that contradict such a view. Johnson was obviously thinking of Shakespeare, for example, when he wrote that

Milton would not have excelled in dramatick writing; he knew human nature only in the gross. . . . His images and descriptions of the scenes or operations of Nature do not seem to be always copied from original form, nor to have the freshness, raciness, and energy of immediate obervation.[40]

Or, at the level of linguistic detail, one might note that in the scene of Ophelia's funeral, Johnson found the Folio 'virgin rites' inferior to the Quarto 'virgin crants' because it gave 'no certain or definite image'.[41] But a commentator such as Leavis would simply reply that these are merely instances of the way in which Johnson's perception intermittently 'transcends his training';[42] like other commentators, Leavis ends by depicting a critic divided against himself to the point of self-contradiction.

This commonly held view of Johnson's account of Shakespeare depends, then, on a line of thought which may be summarized as follows. The 'general nature' which Johnson seeks and finds in Shakespeare must be in some sense a step away from the lived reality of life—*must* be, partly because of preconceptions concerning Johnson's 'Augustanism' or 'neoclassicism', and partly because of a rather casual assumption that our immediate experience is always only of particulars, but more importantly in order to defend Johnson against the charge that he treats Shakespeare's art 'as a piece or slice of life'.[43] Yet Johnson also finds Shakespeare to exhibit the real

[39] Hazlitt, iv. 175 f; see also Schlegel, ii. 31.
[40] Johnson, *Lives of the Poets*, i. 189, 178.   [41] *Yale*, viii. 1003.
[42] Leavis, *Common Pursuit*, p. 109.
[43] René Wellek, *A History of Modern Criticism: 1750–1950* (7 vols.; 1955–), i. 79. For Johnson and 'neoclassicism', see the enlightening discussion by P. J. Smallwood,

state of sublunary nature with all the freshness, raciness, and energy of immediate observation. In this, therefore, he is in conflict with himself; as René Wellek sees it, 'the abstract neoclassicism clashes with the new realism'.[44]

This apparent contradiction is, I believe, very largely of the commentators' own making; by 'general nature' and 'sublunary nature' Johnson means, in fact, the same thing. The error in the line of argument summarized above lies in its assumption that our observation of the world is ordinarily 'immediate', that the real state of nature in which we live is normally or commonly the object of our experience. For Johnson it is axiomatic that this is not so. 'The mind of man is never satisfied with the objects immediately before it.'[45] 'Perhaps, if we speak with rigorous exactness, no human mind is in its right state.'[46] The vanity of human wishes is but one manifestation of the general truth that the mind and the world are not well matched, so that the one does not map easily, accurately, or securely on to the other. As the hermit is unfamiliar with the world and the confessor with the passions, so are we unfamiliar with the experience of nature: our ordinary experience of life is such as to produce that dissatisfied restlessness of the mind, ceaselessly oscillating between satiety and the hunger of imagination for something striking and new, which is the theme of all Johnson's

'Samuel Johnson and the Myth of Neoclassicism: A Re-examination of Johnson's Criticism', Ph.D. thesis (London, 1980). Howard Weinbrot's exposition in 'The Reader, The General, and the Particular' is exceptional in deriving Johnson's generality from real, non-ideal experience without implying that such generality ends in abstraction. He expounds Imlac's doctrine thus: 'Several particular tulips are unified in the poet's mind and poem, make a "general" tulip which, in turn, evokes or, in Johnson's term recalls, an original and particular tulip in the reader's mind' (pp. 90 f.). On this view, the function of generality is in its power to evoke the particular, to mediate between the poet's experience of particulars and the reader's. This interpretation might seem to find room for all sides of Johnson's approach; however, it does not fit either Shakespeare's poetic practice (all Weinbrot's examples of such generality come from eighteenth-century writing) or what Johnson says in the *Preface*, where generality is spoken of not as a means of representation and communication but as itself the matter to be represented and communicated: Johnson finds in Shakespeare not general representations of nature but representations of general nature.

[44] Wellek, *History of Modern Criticism*, i. 85; see also M. J. C. Hodgart, *Samuel Johnson and his Times* (1962), 107, and M. M. Badawi, *Coleridge: Critic of Shakespeare* (1973), 55.

[45] *Yale*, iii. 9 (*Rambler* no. 2).

[46] *The Works of Samuel Johnson, LLD* (11 vols.; Oxford, 1825), i, 292 f. (*Rasselas*, ch. xliv).

moral writing.[47] In the context of this scepticism, his central proposition about Shakespeare is revealed to be a thought of great power:

Nothing can please many, and please long, but just representations of general nature. Particular manners can be known to few, and therefore few only can judge how nearly they are copied. The irregular combinations of fanciful invention may delight a-while, by that novelty of which the common satiety of life sends us all in quest; but the pleasures of sudden wonder are soon exhausted, and the mind can only repose on the stability of truth.[48]

Instead of reflecting 'a state, in which much is to be endured, and little to be enjoyed',[49] representations of general nature are found to 'please many, and please long'—and pleasure, according to Johnson's first illustrative quotation in the *Dictionary*, implies that the mind and the world find themselves (for once) well matched: '*Pleasure*, in general, is the consequent apprehension of a suitable object, suitably applied to a rightly disposed faculty.'[50] Or, as 'Boileau justly remarks', books which please many and please long are 'adequate to our faculties, and agreeable to nature'.[51] The felicity of the term 'nature' as Johnson handles it is that it suggests both our innermost, 'natural' feelings and what is 'out there', the way the world really is, and so, where both these connotations are simultaneously present, it can imply a correspondence or rapport between the two. The way things really are is, extraordinarily, shown to be such as to feel 'natural' to us; what is suggested is a transformation in the relations normally obtaining between the reader's self and his experience of the world.

'But if nature is not what we commonly experience, how is it that we recognize it *as natural*?' To answer this we need to observe that Johnson, in an unsystematic and *ad hoc* way, regularly distinguishes between what may crudely be called two levels of the self, the mind and the heart. Beneath the conscious ego which produces all

[47] For the importance of this idea in Johnson's thinking, see W. J. Bate, *The Achievement of Samuel Johnson* (New York, 1955), 63–91 (ch. 2).

[48] *Yale*, vii. 61 f.

[49] Imlac's description of human life; see Johnson, *Works* (1825), i. 226 (*Rasselas*, ch. xi).

[50] The quotation comes from Robert South's sermon on the text, 'Her Ways are Ways of Pleasantness', in *Sermons Preached upon Several Occasions*, 5th edn. (3 vols.; 1722), i. 2.

[51] *Yale*, iv. 122 (*Rambler* no. 92); for the allusion, see Boileau, *Œuvres*, pp. 523–7 (Réflexion vii).

those ideas and expectations of the world against which Johnson's scepticism is steadily directed, and with which we normally identify ourselves, lies a deeper seat of self. Consider this not untypical passage from the *Rambler*; the subject is the decay of close friendship:

Exchange of endearments and intercourse of civility may continue, indeed, as boughs may for a while be verdant, when the root is wounded; but the poison of discord is infused, and though the countenance may preserve its smile, the heart is hardening and contracting.[52]

The rhythm and logical structure of that sentence are echoed by the sentence in the *Preface*, just quoted, which starts 'The irregular combinations of fanciful invention' and ends with 'the stability of truth'; in both sentences we begin with the specious testimony of an experience which is then displaced by the inexorable rising into consciousness of a more substantial truth. By the figure of speech which allows 'the countenance' and 'the heart' each to be the subject of its own active verb, Johnson allows to each a certain independent life and so holds open the question of where the experiencing self is to be located; the smile of the countenance is no simply deliberate hypocrisy, and yet any clear-cut division between conscious and unconscious would be inappropriate, given that the movements of the heart, although not, in general, objects of consciousness, are nevertheless felt from within: '. . . the heart feels innumerable throbs, which never break into complaint. Perhaps, likewise, our pleasures are for the most part equally secret, and most are borne up by some private satisfaction, some internal consciousness, some latent hope.'[53] 'Secret', 'private', 'internal', 'latent'—such words are regularly used by Johnson to evoke a distinction between what is known and clearly acknowledged by the mind and what is frequently secret to our consciousness of ourselves, the knowledge of the heart.

The distinction between these two different levels of our experience is central to Johnson's understanding of how literature works on us. The poet's first and indispensable task is to 'fix attention', to interest and engage the mind, to offer something striking and new which can shake the mind free from its habits of stock response and its jadedness with familiarity—'the common satiety of life'. 'Works of imagination excel by their allurement and delight; by their power

---

[52] *Yale*, iii. 343 (*Rambler* no. 64).   [53] Ibid. 359 (*Rambler* no. 68).

of attracting and detaining the attention.'[54] No critic places more importance than Johnson on the power of original invention— 'the highest praise of genius'[55]—or is more willing to dismiss accomplished writing simply on the grounds that it is tedious. Prior's *Solomon* possesses 'many excellences', but 'wanted that without which all others are of small avail, the power of engaging attention and alluring curiosity'.[56] Addison, in his verse, 'thinks justly; but he thinks faintly'.[57] But in the form of that judgement on Addison lies the problem which confronts every poet: for, if Johnson's first demand is that poetry should seize his attention, he is also aware that what most readily stimulates attention is the eccentric, the bizarre, the merely ingenious. The 'false magnificence' of Dryden's heroic drama is a case in point:

It was necessary to fix attention; and the mind can be captivated only by recollection or by curiosity; by reviving natural sentiments or impressing new appearances of things: sentences were readier at his call than images; he could more easily fill the ear with some splendid novelty than awaken those ideas that slumber in the heart.[58]

To engage the mind at all, most writers have to tickle the palate with novelty, 'impressing new appearances of things', producing 'the irregular combinations of fanciful invention'; such are Dryden's magniloquent protagonists, the conceits of the metaphysicals, the fantastic happenings of romance. Johnson is very far from despising these things, but they do not give him that more satisfying pleasure which Shakespeare provides. For, when nature touches the heart the effect on the mind is not that of activity and stimulation but rather one which Johnson thinks of as 'repose', a stilling of intellectual activity which permits the mind, exceptionally, to attend to what lies beyond its own aegis. Ideas which strike no deeper than the mind— which fail, in Johnson's words, to find 'the passes of the mind'[59] —may fix attention for a time, but there will still be something wanting:

In the perusal of the *Davideis*, as of all Cowley's works, we find wit and learning unprofitably squandered. Attention has no relief; the affections are

---

[54] Johnson, *Lives of the Poets*, i. 454.

[55] Ibid. 194. In the *Preface* Johnson states, 'Perhaps it would not be easy to find any authour, except Homer, who invented so much as Shakespeare' (*Yale*, vii. 90).

[56] Johnson, *Lives of the Poets*, ii. 206.

[57] Ibid. 127.   [58] Ibid. i. 458 f.   [59] Ibid. iii. 227.

never moved; we are sometimes surprised, but never delighted, and find much to admire, but little to approve.[60]

Where the appeal is to the mind and not through the mind, so to speak, nature cannot make itself felt; when Shakespeare, by contrast, 'awakens those ideas that slumber in the heart', the experience is one which Johnson can describe as a form of 'recollection', a 'reviving' of sentiments which are to the reader 'at once natural and new'.[61] Nature is thought of as a medium in which we all move but of which few of us are ordinarily much aware; to recollect our participation in it means that the hunger of the mind, which has otherwise to feed on ideal creations of its own, can find satisfaction in the world as it is.

Sceptical Thinking

Johnson's distinction between two levels of our experience—'the mind' and 'the heart', or sometimes 'the ear' and 'the mind'—is one which he shares with Boileau:

> Rien n'est beau, je reviens, que par la verité.
> C'est par elle qu'on plaist, et qu'on peut long-temps plaire.
> L'esprit lasse aisément, si le coeur n'est sincere.[1]

If his own writings possess this power of truth, Boileau claims, it is because in them *le coeur* is to be found 'toûjours conduisant mon esprit'.[2] The classic truth possessed by a Greek poet such as Hesiod lay in the power of penetration which his precepts could attain:

> Et par tout des esprits ses preceptes vainqueurs,
> Introduits par l'oreille entrerent dans les coeurs.[3]

Such precepts are *vainqueurs des esprits*: to convince the mind is to overcome the mind, or—in Johnson's words—to find the passes of the mind. We know from Mrs Thrale that Johnson 'delighted exceedingly in Boileau's works', and from Arthur Murphy that he was 'a professed admirer of Boileau', whom he 'seldom found mistaken'.[4] To recognize Johnson's affinity with Boileau—and also with another French critic contemporary with Boileau, Dominique Bouhours,

---

[60] Ibid. i. 55.   [61] Ibid. 20.
[1] Boileau, *Œuvres*, p. 135 (Epître ix).   [2] Ibid. 134 (Epître ix).
[3] Ibid. 184 (*L'Art poétique*, iv, ll. 161 f.).
[4] *Johnsonian Miscellanies*, ed. G. B. Hill (2 vols.; 1897), i. 334; ibid. 416; Johnson, *Lives of the Poets*, i. 385.

whom Johnson also warmly commended—is both to relate Johnson's general scepticism to the way of thinking worked out in the particular context of literary criticism by the French critics, and to place Johnson in a 'classical' tradition of critical thought that is clearly distinguishable from the doctrinaire neoclassicism of a d'Aubignac or a Le Bossu. It was Bouhours and Boileau whom Addison cited in the *Spectator* as the most illuminating exponents of the principle that 'it is impossible for any Thought to be beautiful which is not just, and has not its Foundation in the Nature of things';[5] where they differed from their neoclassicizing contemporaries was, as Borgerhoff has argued in *The Freedom of French Classicism*, in their 'belief in the validity of affective rather than intellectual awareness'.[6] Both men were centrally concerned with the recognition in literature of 'the extraordinary, the mysterious, the inexplicable',[7] and this corresponded to their awareness that, in life, *la vérité* is not commonly present to the mind. The nature of life in such a highly polished, highly mannered society as that of the *grand siècle* was, for Boileau in particular, a striking expression of a permanent and fundamental truth:

> Cessons de nous flatter. Il n'est Esprit si droit
> Qui ne soit imposteur et faux par quelque endroit.
> Sans cesse on prend le masque, et quittant la Nature,
> On craint de se montrer sous sa propre figure.[8]

L'Esprit de l'Homme est naturellement plein d'un nombre infini d'idées confuses du Vrai, que souvent il n'entrevoit qu'à demi; et rien ne lui est plus agreable que lors qu'on luy offre quelqu'une de ces idées bien éclaircie, et mise dans un beau jour.[9]

Literature can release us from this semi-blindness and allow us to see clearly; a great artist like Molière causes nature to rise to the

---

[5] The *Spectator*, ed. Donald F. Bond (5 vols.; Oxford, 1965), i. 268 (no. 62).

[6] E. B. O. Borgerhoff, *The Freedom of French Classicism* (Princeton, NJ, 1950), 238; see also pp. 186–211. For complementary accounts of Boileau, see Jules Brody, *Boileau and Longinus* (Geneva, 1958), esp. pp. 36–53 ('Un Savoir Secret . . .'); and H. A. Mason, 'Hommage à M. Despréaux: Some Reflections on the Possibility of Literary Study', *Cambridge Quarterly*, 3, 51–71, and 'The Miraculous Birth: or The Founding of Modern European Literary Criticism', *Cambridge Quarterly*, 11, 281–97, esp. pp. 287–91. For the influence of Boileau and Bouhours on the idea of 'nature' in English criticism, see A. F. B. Clark, *Boileau and the French Classical Critics in England 1660–1830* (Paris, 1925), p. 385 and *passim*.

[7] Borgerhoff, *Freedom of French Classicism*, p. 209.

[8] Boileau, *Œuvres*, p. 134 (Epître ix).   [9] Ibid. 1 (Préface de 1701).

surface, so to speak, of the world of manners and appearances within which we might have thought ourselves to be confined:

> Un geste la découvre, un rien la fait paroistre:
> Mais tout esprit n'a pas des yeux pour la connoistre.[10]

Both Boileau and Bouhours are explicit that such experience escapes the conceptual categories that might seem to define it; an experience which strikes deeper than the mind is not to be comprehended by the mind alone. Here is Boileau, for example, refusing to chop logic with one Pierre-Daniel Huet who had disputed whether the opening passages of Genesis could properly be called '*sublime*':

A cela je pourrois vous respondre en general, sans entrer dans une plus grande discussion, que le Sublime n'est pas proprement une chose qui se prouve et qui se demonstre; mais que c'est un Merveilleux qui saisit, qui frappe, et qui se fait sentir.[11]

The 'certain agrément' which causes a work of literature to please many and please long, Boileau remarks elsewhere, is 'un je ne scay quoy qu'on peut beaucoup mieux sentir, que dire'.[12] Bouhours devotes an entire dialogue to this subject of the *je ne sais quoi* which enables language to go to the heart:

'Cét agrément, ce charme, cét air ressemble à la lumiere qui embellit toute la nature, et qui se fait voir à tout le monde, sans que nous sçachions ce que c'est; de sorte qu'on n'en peut mieux parler à mon gré, qu'en disant qu'on ne peut ni l'expliquer, ni le concevoir. En effet c'est quelque chose de si delicat, et de si imperceptible, qu'il échappe à l'intelligence la plus penetrante, et la plus subtile: l'esprit humain qui connoist ce qu'il y a de plus spirituel dans les Anges, et de plus divin en Dieu, pour parler ainsi, ne connoist pas ce qu'il y a de charmant dans un objet sensible qui touche le coeur.'

'Si cela est,' dit Eugene, 'il faut démentir les Philosophes qui ont soûtenu de tout temps que la connoissance precede l'amour; que la volonté n'aime rien qui ne soit connu de l'entendement.'[13]

---

[10] Ibid. 178 (*L'Art poétique*, iii, ll. 371 f.).
[11] Ibid. 546 (Réflexion x).
[12] Ibid. 1 (Préface de 1701).
[13] Dominique Bouhours, *Les Entretiens d'Ariste et d'Eugène*, ed. F. Brunot (Paris, 1962), 142.

But more important than their explicit statements of this principle is the way in which it informs both critics' manner of discussion. Their criticism regularly gives the impression of meaning more than it says; each general proposition is finely qualified by the sense that it comes out of an agile play of mind—a species of wit—that eludes formulation. The irony which Boileau deploys so tellingly as a satirist modulates into the more delicate and pervasive irony proper to the mind's endeavour to communicate an experience which it cannot define. 'So *vast* is Art, so *narrow* Human Wit.'[14] At crucial points in the argument images are substituted for definitions, or definitions are used with a conscious circularity, sounding the 'note of tentativeness' which for Jules Brody, in *Boileau and Longinus*, 'seems to betoken, as well as an inability to explain, an undissimulated willingness to welcome and live with the inexplicable'.[15] Criteria conventionally opposed are paired together—*bon sens* and *bel esprit*, *délicatesse* and *force*, *sublimité* and *simplicité*—suggesting, like Johnson's 'at once natural and new', the shift to a level of experience at which those conceptual oppositions no longer obtain and the mind can be released from its oscillation between the poles of 'fanciful invention' and the 'satiety of life':

Le vray bel esprit . . . est inseparable du bon sens; et c'est se méprendre, que de le confondre avec je ne sçay quelle vivacité qui n'a rien de solide . . . Il a du solide et du brillant dans un égal degré: c'est à le bien definir, le bon sens qui brille. Car il y a une espece de bon sens sombre et morne, qui n'est gueres moins opposé à la beauté de l'esprit, que le faux brillant. Le bon sens dont je parle, est d'une espece toute differente: il est gay, vif, plein de feu, comme celuy qui paroist dans les Essais de Montaigne.[16]

Not surprisingly, the attempt to press such writing for definitive doctrine yields only a set of vague and insipid criteria that virtually cancel one another out, the body of thought 'généralement banale et médiocre' that Audra finds in both Boileau's *Art poétique* and Pope's *Essay on Criticism* (which was both based on and permeated by the spirit of Boileau's work): 'Ce n'est pas tellement l'affirmation d'une doctrine que l'expression de son goût personnel que commandait

[14] *Twickenham Edition of the Poems of Alexander Pope*, ed. John Butt *et al.* (11 vols.; 1961–9), i. 246 (*Essay on Criticism*, l. 61).
[15] Brody, *Boileau and Longinus*, p. 55.
[16] Bouhours, *Entretiens*, p. 115.

une intelligence honnête et claire, mais superficielle.'[17] But to make the point in that way, divorcing hard doctrinal content from what is seen as the merely personal and incidental manner of its expression, is to fail to recognize that Boileau is not trying to propose a doctrine but to render an experience; his implicit conviction that theoretical terms only have meaning in so far as they communicate the experience to which they refer becomes explicit in his admiration for Longinus:

Longin ne s'est pas contenté . . . de nous donner des preceptes tous secs et dépoüillés d'ornemens. Il n'a pas voulu tomber dans le defaut qu'il reproche à Cecilius, qui avoit, dit-il, écrit du Sublime en stile bas. En traitant des beautez de l'Elocution, il a employé toutes les finesses de l'Elocution. Souvent il fait la figure qu'il enseigne; et en parlant du Sublime, il est lui-mesme tres-sublime.[18]

That remark was echoed by Bouhours[19] and by Pope,[20] and also calls to mind Johnson's comment that in his criticism Dryden 'proves his right of judgement by his power of performance',[21] but Gibbon's is perhaps the best commentary:

Till now, I was acquainted only with two ways of criticizing a beautifull passage; The one, to shew, by an exact anatomy of it, the distinct beauties of it, and from whence they sprung; the other, an idle exclamation, or a general encomium, which leaves nothing behind it. Longinus has shewn me that there is a third. He tells me his own feelings upon reading it; and tells them with such energy, that he communicates them.[22]

In Gibbon's terms, the critical approach of Boileau and Bouhours, and of Pope in the *Essay on Criticism*, is one of 'communication' rather than 'exact anatomy', which is why commentary which seeks to anatomize their writings and to abstract from them a body of coherent theory yields such disappointing results. The Twickenham

---

[17] E. Audra, *L'Influence française dans l'œuvre de Pope* (Paris, 1931), 230, 223.

[18] Boileau, *Œuvres*, p. 333 (*Traité du Sublime*, Préface); see also p. 562 (Réflexion xii).

[19] See Dominique Bouhours, *La Manière de bien penser dans les ouvrages d'esprit* (Paris, 1715: facsimile repr., Brighton, 1971), 158.

[20] See *Poems of Alexander Pope*, i. 316 (*Essay on Criticism*, ll. 675-80).

[21] Johnson, *Lives of the Poets*, i. 412.

[22] *Gibbon's Journal: To January 28th, 1763: My Journal, i, ii, & iii and Ephemerides*, ed. D. M. Low (1929), 155. Gibbon was reading Longinus in the Tollius edition of 1694, which printed Boileau's translation and notes together with the Greek text.

editors, for example, find themselves obliged to go outside the poem
to expound what Pope means by 'Nature' in the *Essay on Criticism*:

> Throughout the *Essay* Pope is working with a set of assumptions which,
> if they are not entirely clear from the poem alone, are easily recoverable
> from other contemporary writings. These assumptions suggest, moreover,
> a body of thought which conforms closely to Dennis's own thinking about
> Nature as it is revealed in that critic's work.
>
> Fundamental to 'neo-classical' thought about Nature is the conception
> of a cosmos which, in its order and regularity and harmony, reflects the
> order and harmony in the Divine Mind of its Creator.[23]

But if the idea of an ordered cosmos is so fundamental, it is hard
to understand why Pope found Nature supremely in the Homer
whose 'wild Paradise' he contrasted to the 'regularity' and 'order'd
Garden' of inferior art,[24] hard to explain how such an idea could
have helped Boileau to single out Molière and Racine from amongst
their rivals, and hard too to see why Johnson, who was so scathing
about Soame Jenyns's offer to demonstrate the harmony of the
cosmos, and so emphatically unimpressed by the thought in the *Essay
on Man*, should nevertheless have considered that the *Essay on
Criticism* placed Pope 'among the first critics and the first poets'.[25]
Dennis was, in fact, according to his lights, quite right to complain
of Pope's failure to say 'what he means by Nature, and what it is
to write or judge according to Nature',[26] just as Barbier d'Aucour
was entirely accurate in attacking Bouhours for failing to put forward
any coherent aesthetic in the *Entretiens d'Ariste et d'Eugène*: 'Son
plaisir lui tient lieu de raison; il ne cite que cela, et il ne parle pas
même de l'Approbation publique qu'ont eu les livres qui lui plaisent.
Quelle façon de juger . . . toute absolue et indépendante de toute
raison!'[27] This, as we have seen, is a charge to which Bouhours was
delighted to plead guilty; the categories which he uses are deployed
with a delicate consciousness of their ultimate inadequacy, so as
to point beyond themselves to a quality of response which is not
susceptible of more direct exposition. The endeavour at definition
and rationalization illuminates, rightly handled, the experience of

---

[23] *Poems of Alexander Pope*, i. 219.   [24] Ibid. vii. 3 (Preface to the *Iliad*).
[25] Johnson, *Lives of the Poets*, iii. 228.
[26] John Dennis, *The Critical Works*, ed. E. N. Hooker (2 vols.; Baltimore, Md.,
1939–43), i. 403.
[27] Barbier d'Aucour, *Sentimens de Cleante sur les entretiens d'Ariste et d'Eugène*,
4th edn. (Paris, 1738), 51.

which it falls short; when Johnson wrote in the *Preface* 'there is always an appeal open from criticism to nature', he was not rising up against the tradition of critical thought represented by Bouhours and Boileau but, on the contrary, showing how well he had assimilated it.

(This assimilation was a developing process; it is suggestive to set Johnson's remark between two others, one made earlier and one later:

It is, however, the task of criticism to establish principles; to improve opinion into knowledge; and to distinguish those means of pleasing which depend upon known causes and rational deduction, from the nameless and inexplicable elegances which appeal wholly to the fancy, from which we feel delight, but know not how they produce it, and which may well be termed the enchantresses of the soul.

That this is a practice contrary to the rules of criticism will be readily allowed; but there is always an appeal open from criticism to nature.

I suspect this objection to be the cant of those who judge by principles rather than perception.[28]

These passages were written in 1751, 1765, and 1780; there is a good deal of continuity between them (the third quotation does not contradict the first: to 'judge by principles' is not the same as to 'establish principles'), but also a perceptible shift in emphasis. Although it would be unwise to draw any very precise inference concerning an evolution in Johnson's thought, as the manner in which he expresses himself varies according to its context quite as much as it evolves over time, it would be broadly true to say that while Johnson's scepticism remains pretty much the same throughout his years as a writer, he exhibits a growing confidence in the constructive potential of that scepticism, and communicates an increasing pleasure through its operation. Arguably, he views the vanity of human wishes in *Rasselas* (1759) with an awareness of comic possibility that is not present in the poem of 1749; and in *Rambler* no. 156 (1751) he defends Shakespeare's mingling of tragic and comic on exactly the same grounds as those adduced in the 1765 *Preface*, but with very much less assurance. The work on Shakespeare reflects this changing emphasis and was also, one may suppose, in some measure its stimulus and provocation.)

---

[28] *Yale*, iv. 122 (*Rambler* no. 92); ibid. vii. 67 (*Preface to Shakespeare*); *Lives of the Poets*, iii. 248.

In conversation, Johnson cited Bouhours, 'who shews all beauty to depend on truth', as 'an example of true criticism'.[29] The work of Bouhours which most directly sets out to show that beauty depends on truth is the first of the four dialogues in *La Manière de bien penser dans les ouvrages d'esprit*, a work that exemplifies the flexibility of mind that is able to pass from the inadequacy of even the truest general principle to 'survey the *Whole*'.[30] The two speakers who take part in this dialogue are so described as to suggest the polarity of the *solide* and the *brillant*:

> Eudoxe a le gout trés-bon, et rien ne luy plaist dans les ouvrages ingénieux qui ne soit raisonnable et naturel. . . . Pour Philinthe, tout ce qui est fleuri, tout ce qui brille, le charme. Les Grecs et les Romains ne valent pas à son gré les Espagnols et les Italiens.[31]

Philinthe suspects that what is '*raisonnable*' may be incompatible with the '*brillant*' and is keen to champion the rights of imagination against what he fears may be a heavy and limited common sense; the task of Eudoxe is to lead his friend to see that what is required is a union of both qualities. He begins by asserting that, in order to be satisfying, a thought, description, or figure of speech must be true, must '*représente les choses fidellement*'.[32] Philinthe immediately makes the plausible objection that many of the universally acknowledged beauties of literature are, strictly speaking, fictions. Eudoxe replies with a distinction analogous to that between the *vrai* and the *vraisemblable* worked out by earlier commentators on Aristotle:

> Ne confondons rien, s'il vous plait, reprît Eudoxe; et souffrez que je m'explique pour me faire entendre. Tout ce qui paroist faux ne l'est pas, et il y a bien de la difference entre la fiction et la fausseté: l'une imite et perfectionne en quelque façon la nature; l'autre la gâte, et la détruit entierement.[33]

The reader narrows his eyes at this and, properly enough, wonders whether Bouhours is making a real or a merely verbal distinction. This very uncertainty and provisionality, however, proves functional:

---

[29] *Boswell's Life of Johnson. Together with Boswell's Journal of a Tour to the Hebrides and Johnson's Diary of a Journey into North Wales*, ed. G. B. Hill, rev. edn. L. F. Powell (6 vols.; 1934–50), ii. 90.

[30] *Poems of Alexander Pope*, i. 266 (*Essay on Criticism*, l. 235).

[31] Bouhours, *Manière de bien penser*, p. 2.   [32] Ibid. 12.

[33] Ibid. 12 f. Cf. Boileau: 'De toute fiction l'adroite fausseté | Ne tend qu'à faire aux yeux briller la Verité' (*Œuvres*, p. 134: Epître ix).

in what follows, the same essential movement is repeated again and again, so that our attention gradually slips away from the question of definition to grow sensitive to the spirit informing the movement and structure of the dialogue. One complication after another is raised—the fabulous, the *'merveilleux'*, metaphor, mixed wit, the *'équivoque'*, hyperbole, comic distortion, factual falsehood—and in each case Eudoxe agrees that some of these 'falsehoods' in fact give us the truth, while insisting that other examples within the same category *are* false and unsatisfactory and that no plea of poetic licence can excuse them. We become aware of a tightrope being walked, and that awareness grows increasingly sharp as the dialogue goes on: there is a continuous movement of statement, challenge, and qualification, the mind immediately taking up and modifying whatever theoretical position is offered as a final resting-place. On the one hand there is a sharpening of focus, thanks to the abundance of specific poetic examples discussed; on the other hand, and at the same time, there is a dissolving away of any available fixed formulation as Eudoxe repeatedly qualifies and restates his criterion in the new context provided by each new example. This criterion is eternally not quite what the straightforward Philinthe believes that he now understands it to be: 'Hills peep o'er Hills, and *Alps* on *Alps* arise!'[34] Bouhours's criterion of 'truth' is modified again and again, twisting and turning with great suppleness, almost but never quite collapsing into a purely subjective 'taste', saving itself from this by an ever finer verbal poise and precision, so that we, along with Philinthe, are brought safely across the tightrope to the understanding of this criterion as indeed a real and communicable principle, but one which is too fine to be caught in the net of logic. The dialogue form is marvellously right for the expression of such a poise: Eudoxe can say all that can be said, he can formulate the ideal doctrine and even the ideal flexibility as well as can be done, and yet the dialogue form (like Boileau's 'voix legere', passing 'du grave au doux, du plaisant au severe')[35] is always teasing us into an awareness of a stance larger, subtler, and more intelligent than any conceptual formulation. The dialogue movement makes for a repeated refinement of

---

[34] *Poems of Alexander Pope*, i. 265 (*Essay on Criticism*, l. 232).
[35] Boileau, *Œuvres*, pp. 158 f. (*L'Art poétique*, i, ll. 75 f.). See Peter France, *Rhetoric and Truth in France: Descartes to Diderot* (1972), 162 f. for fuller description of this suppleness of voice in Boileau and its relation to the idea of truth.

approximation as we come only gradually to understand what Bouhours's *bon sens* is; the sense in which the dialogue offers something more alive and more supple than doctrine is given by the way that we *need* Philinthe in order to get to the heart of the matter, in order to provide the situation in which the gently swinging pendulum of thought is able to describe the full figure.

This sceptical sense of the relationship of idea to reality is basic to all Johnson's thinking, not only his thinking about literature. '*Definitions are hazardous*', he wrote in the *Rambler*, thinking no doubt of the work for the *Dictionary* on which he was then engaged:

Definition is, indeed, not the province of man; every thing is set above or below our faculties. The works and operations of nature are too great in their extent, or too much diffused in their relations, and the performances of art too inconstant and uncertain, to be reduced to any determinate idea. It is impossible to impress upon our minds an adequate and just representation of an object so great that we can never take it into our view, or so mutable that it is always changing under our eye, and has already lost its form while we are labouring to conceive it.

Definitions have been no less difficult or uncertain in criticism than in law. Imagination, a licentious and vagrant faculty, unsusceptible of limitations, and impatient of restraint, has always endeavoured to baffle the logician, to perplex the confines of distinction, and burst the inclosures of regularity.[36]

The movement of Bouhours's dialogue is here repeated in a more urgent and energetic form. Locke had stressed the vigilance required if our words are to stand for clear and distinct ideas, but for Johnson the difficulty of getting our words to correspond to our ideas is only one aspect of the greater difficulty of getting our ideas to correspond to the way things are—a difficulty at once epistemological, psychological, and moral. In the context of cognition, the more clear and distinct the ideas which one manages to form of any complex reality, the less truth there is likely to be in them; in the context of volition, the reach of man's mind regularly exceeds his grasp: no man is 'satisfied with himself, because he has done much, but because he can conceive little'.[37] In this situation the mind's tendency is to free-wheel away from engagement with actualities, to live 'only in

---

[36] *Yale*, iv. 300 (*Rambler* no. 125).
[37] Johnson, *Works* (1825), v. 42 (Preface to the *Dictionary*).

idea';[38] the optimism of Soame Jenyns,[39] the literary criticism of Dick Minim,[40] the stoicism of the philosopher in *Rasselas* who nonetheless breaks down on the death of his daughter,[41] the celebration by Cowley of the pleasures of solitude and retirement,[42] are all examples of the universal human tendency to take the ideas of the mind for realities, to indulge in, or fall victim to, that habit of thinking which, at the level of language, expresses itself as 'cant'— the knowingness and wordiness that come with talking about experience one does not oneself possess. We are all, so to speak, given to 'false wit' and 'unnatural flights' in our living as well as in our taste in poetry; our *bel esprit* is not characteristically reconciled to *bon sens*.

Johnson's response is not, in general, that we should moderate our imaginings, prudently cutting our ideas down to conform to our actual experience. Such a response is one that he believed neither possible nor desirable, as can be seen from his dislike of stoicism, or from such a typical remark as this:

Irresolution and mutability are often the faults of men, whose views are wide, and whose imagination is vigorous and excursive, because they cannot confine their thoughts within their own boundaries of action . . . for want of that calm and immoveable acquiescence in their condition, by which men of slower understandings are fixed for ever to a certain point.[43]

Although the disparity between idea and actuality produces many evils, it is not itself felt as an evil but as a vital tension, an element in what makes us human that cannot be gainsaid. To communicate and indeed to heighten that vital tension is one of the functions of the peculiar Johnsonian style, as most deliberately articulated in the *Rambler* essays. Take, for example, this sentence from the passage already quoted on the difficulty of definition: 'Imagination, a licentious and vagrant faculty, unsusceptible of limitations, and impatient of restraint, has always endeavoured to baffle the logician,

---

[38] *Yale*, iii. 10 (*Rambler* no. 2).

[39] See Johnson's 'Review of a Free Enquiry into the Nature and Origin of Evil', in *Works* (1825), vi. 47–76.

[40] See *Yale*, ii. 184–93 (*Idler* nos. 60 f.).

[41] See Johnson, *Works* (1825), i. 239–41 (*Rasselas*, ch. xviii).

[42] See *Yale*, iii. 32–5 (*Rambler* no. 6), and Johnson, *Lives of the Poets*, i. 15–17.

[43] *Yale*, iii. 337 (*Rambler* no. 63); see also *Yale*, iii. 221–5 (*Rambler* no. 41) and ix. 148 (*Journey to the Western Islands*: on Iona). For Johnson's dislike of stoicism, see e.g. *Yale*, iii. 174–6, 255–7, 349 f. (*Rambler* nos. 32, 47, 66).

to perplex the confines of distinction, and burst the inclosures of regularity.' The most immediately striking feature of that style is the way that elements of syntax are set in parallel with one another, as when imagination is stated to be 'unsusceptible of limitations, and impatient of restraint'. This is not quite saying the same thing twice—imagination being viewed from outside, as it were, in the first phrase and from within in the second—but this difference is a fine one, so that the mind has to pause and reflect and work in order to make it, acknowledging the existence of at least two distinct perspectives in which the unruly imagination may be viewed, and realizing in the process that both phrases are really a kind of range-finding for a quality which the words cannot altogether contain, a quality which—the phrasing obliges us to see—exists independently of the attempt to catch it in the net of language and ideas. The effect is of something 'not dogmatically but deliberatively written',[44] and the less dogmatically as the more deliberatively, for the deliberation that is given a kind of bodily, almost muscular, presence by the reach of the Johnsonian diction and the damming and releasing of energy effected by the syntax carries the knowledge that the categories of language are not those of reality; Johnson's style is, amongst other things, a technique for allowing full and vigorous play to the mind while not talking cant, while keeping the object of thought from being taken over and swallowed up by the activity of thinking. The strong rhythmic and intellectual impulse towards a satisfying comprehensiveness seems inevitably to require an additional qualifying term, another comparative phrase, a further complicating encounter of the large general proposition with the awkward particular case; each phrase, each sentence, presses towards an authoritative finality, but turns out to be only a provisional resting-place in a more fluid, more truly comprehensive process.

This movement of mind informs not only the handling of language but also the logical structure of argument; in the *Rambler* essays in particular one learns to expect that any strikingly convincing paragraph setting out Johnson's thinking on some subject is sure to lead to a 'but' or 'however' and a second paragraph that sets out with equal cogency an opposite (though not contradictory) set of considerations.[45] (Johnson's experience of parliamentary debate and

<hr>

[44] *Yale*, vii. 80.
[45] This is well described in Paul Fussell, *Samuel Johnson and the Life of Writing*

interest in legal advocacy are to the point.) Assertion of the dangers of living in our imaginings of the future is followed by the argument that the exercise of such imagination is vitally necessary to our humanity.[46] A sharp satirical portrait is followed by a challenging of our right to criticize.[47] Shakespeare has 'faults sufficient to obscure and overwhelm any other merit'.[48] One can see why Sir John Hawkins felt that 'in all Johnson's disquisitions, whether argumentative or critical, there is a certain even-handed justice that leaves the mind in a strange perplexity',[49] and why Hazlitt too objected that in his essays Johnson never finally gets anywhere:

One clause answers to another in measure and quantity, like the tagging of syllables at the end of a verse; the close of the period follows as mechanically as the oscillation of a pendulum, the sense is balanced with the sound . . . Dr. Johnson is also a complete balance-master in the topics of morality. He never encourages hope, but he counteracts it by fear; he never elicits a truth, but he suggests some objection in answer to it. . . . 'He runs the great circle, and is still at home.'[50]

Allowing for Hazlitt's antagonism, this is no bad description of Johnson's manner in the *Rambler*, yet it need not lead to the diagnosis of 'timidity' and 'morbid apprehension' which Hazlitt gives; the positive function of thinking that arrives only at a 'conclusion, in which nothing is concluded'[51] may be suggested by Rasselas's remark to Nekayah in the debate on marriage: 'Thus it happens, when wrong opinions are entertained, that they mutually destroy each other, and leave the mind open to truth.' Such opinions are not, however, 'wrong' in the sense that better ones could be put in their place; the passage continues:

'I did not expect,' answered the princess, 'to hear that imputed to falsehood, which is the consequence only of frailty. To the mind, as to the eye, it is difficult to compare, with exactness, objects, vast in their extent, and various in their parts. . . . Of two systems, of which neither can be surveyed, by any human being, in its full compass of magnitude, and multiplicity of

---

(1972), 157–71; see also Robert Voitle, *Samuel Johnson the Moralist* (Cambridge, Mass., 1961), 45.

[46] See *Yale*, iii. 9 f. (*Rambler* no. 2).

[47] See ibid. v. 277–81 (*Rambler* no. 200).   [48] Ibid. vii. 71.

[49] John Hawkins, *The Life of Dr Samuel Johnson* (*The Works of Samuel Johnson*, i; 1787), 482.

[50] Hazlitt, vi. 102.   [51] The title of the final chapter of *Rasselas*.

complication, where is the wonder, that, judging of the whole by parts, I am alternately affected by one and the other, as either presses on my memory or fancy? We differ from ourselves, just as we differ from each other, when we see only part of the question.'[52]

Truth lies in the whole, but the human intellect is limited and, except for the merest statements of facts or propositions in mathematics whose truth is logically demonstrable, our opinions can be only of the parts. This is one of Johnson's favourite thoughts.[53] And it follows from this that the apprehension of truth cannot rest in any single opinion or proposition but will be something struck out of the collision of differing opinions, or out of the sudden encounter of opinion with experience: 'Human experience, which is constantly contradicting theory, is the great test of truth.'[54] Experience, Johnson believes, is always best seen as contradicting, rather than corroborating, theory; intelligence operates through an essentially sceptical movement. It is relevant here to recall how in conversation Johnson was prepared to take either side of virtually any question (unless religion were the subject), and also how in both his conversation and his writing he is often happiest when he can reply to a proposition already advanced rather than having to develop one of his own. He was expressing a principle fundamental to his thinking when he wrote to Langton: 'I know not any thing more pleasant or more instructive than to compare experience with expectation, or to register from time to time the difference between Idea and Reality.'[55] Human life, to quote Montaigne, is 'a wonderfull, vaine, divers and wavering subject: it is very hard to ground any directly-constant and uniforme judgement' upon it. To be penetrated by this understanding is to give up 'living only in idea' and, since we cannot think at all except through ideas, to handle them more lightly, to allow one's mind to travel more freely round a subject in the understanding that there is no single, privileged point of view available to the intellect which is the right one. More of the truth is to be had this way. As Imlac says in *Rasselas*, 'Inconsistencies cannot both be right, but, imputed to man, they may

---

[52] Johnson, *Works* (1825), i. 259 (*Rasselas*, ch. xxviii).
[53] See e.g. *Yale*, ii. 440–5 (*Adventurer* no. 107) and iii. 336–8 (*Rambler* no. 63), and Boswell, *Life of Johnson*, i. 444 and ii. 361.
[54] Boswell, *Life of Johnson*, i. 454.
[55] *Letters of Samuel Johnson*, ed. R. W. Chapman (3 vols.; 1952), i. 110 (no. 110: to Bennet Langton, 27 June 1758).

both be true'[56]—a distinction which, in the little jolt of pleasure that comes with the unexpected shift from the perspective of logic to that of experience, itself exhibits the kind of ironic poise or wit that can accommodate the disparity of idea and reality. That pleasure comes from seeing beyond the one-sidedness of mental categories and the restlessness and frustration these bring with them; it is the pleasure that comes when, in the moment before thinking crystallizes back into thought, the mind feels itself in correspondence with things as they are.

The Pleasure of Generality

This emphasis on pleasure may seem misplaced, given Johnson's famous description of human life as a state 'in which much is to be endured, and little to be enjoyed'. Not everyone will agree that the author of *Rasselas* is an inspiriting writer; recent commentators have spoken of Johnson's bleakly 'absurdist view', his 'Christian pessimism', and his 'tragic sense of life'.[1] Certainly, materials for all three of these (distinct) attitudes can be found in Johnson; certainly, his thinking about human life and human nature is regularly disillusioned and disillusioning. But, although the process of disillusionment is generally a painful one, that which drives the illusions out is not in itself felt as an evil. Rather, it might be called an extraordinarily strong sense of fact, of the experiential reality of life as something constantly qualifying and contradicting the ideas of the mind; the primary and tonic emphasis is not concerned with whether the facts in question are benign or hostile, but is simply that they exist, that they are there. The first thing one feels about Johnson's prose is its weightiness, its solidity of substance:

Let us endeavour to see things as they are, and then enquire whether we ought to complain. Whether to see life as it is will give us much consolation I know not, but the consolation which is drawn from truth, if any there

---

[56] Johnson, *Works* (1825), i. 216 (*Rasselas*, ch. viii).

[1] Charles E. Pierce, 'The Conflict of Faith and Fear in Johnson's Moral Writing', *Eighteenth-Century Studies*, 15 (1981–2), 334; Sachs, *Passionate Intelligence*, pp. 78, 95 and see also pp. 3–65 *passim*; Leopold Damrosch, Jun., *Samuel Johnson and the Tragic Sense* (Princeton, NJ, 1972), *passim*. For persuasive readings of *Rasselas* as an affirmative work, see M. M. Lascelles, '*Rasselas*: A Rejoinder', *Review of English Studies*, 21 (1970), 49–56, and Ian White, 'On *Rasselas*', *Cambridge Quarterly*, 6 (1972), 6–31.

be, is solid and durable, that which may be derived from errour must be like its original fallacious and fugitive.[2]

If the disillusioning reality on which Johnson insists is often a painful one, this is because the mind generally cherishes optimistic and comforting ideas. 'Very little of the pain, or pleasure, which does not begin and end in our senses, is otherwise than relative.'[3] It is because of the mind's confidence in its powers of discernment that things as they are present us with an incalculable web of contingencies and contradictions that mock human rationality; it is because of the mind's tendency to think well of human nature (especially its own) that the realities of egotism, vice, and injustice are such disillusioning ones. Where the occasion requires it, Johnson is equally ready to take up the opposite point of view: if he is generally hard on mankind's dreams of happiness, he is equally so on Boswell's dreams of melancholy; if his common theme is the inadequacy of the intellect, he can speak equally strongly of man's dignity as a thinking being; if he believes that the majority of men are wicked,[4] he also finds it wonderful that 'the worst man . . . does more good than evil'.[5] The characteristic tendency of his thinking is given, the more clearly because somewhat too deliberately, in this passage from the *Rambler*:

If the general disposition of things be estimated by the representation which every one makes of his own state, the world must be considered as the abode of sorrow and misery. . . . If we judge by the account which may be obtained of every man's fortune from others, it may be concluded, that we are all placed in an elysian region . . .[6]

To see things as they are is to feel how life always escapes our ideas by being composed of what appear to the mind as contrary qualities. Johnson's primary concern in his moral writing is to resist the impulse of the mind to limit the largeness and variousness of life by making some particular intellectual or emotional sense of it. And to do this releases a degree of pleasure, felt in the quotation above in the way that the tone hints at a potential, at least, for humour.

In reviewing *Middlemarch*, Henry James spoke of 'that supreme sense of the vastness and variety of human life . . . which it belongs only to the greatest novels to produce'.[7] In Johnson's

---

[2] *Letters of Samuel Johnson*, i. 111 (no. 116: to Bennet Langton, 21 Sept. 1758).
[3] *Yale*, iii. 282 (*Rambler* no. 52).   [4] See *Yale*, v. 159 f. (*Rambler* no. 175).
[5] Boswell, *Life of Johnson*, iii. 236 f.   [6] *Yale*, iv. 317 (*Rambler* no. 128).
[7] David Carroll (ed.), *George Eliot: The Critical Heritage* (1971), 357.

mostly discursive prose this sense is evoked only indirectly, through the opposing of experience to speculation, the stylistic deliberateness that suggests its own arbitrariness, the wit that plays between two or more perspectives on experience and makes us feel how neither can be final. What Johnson values so highly in Shakespeare, we can now say, is his power directly to communicate this largeness of life. This is his description of Shakespeare's 'mingled drama', in defending which he was doing what no critic of Shakespeare had done before him:[8]

Shakespeare's plays are not in the rigorous and critical sense either tragedies or comedies, but compositions of a distinct kind; exhibiting the real state of sublunary nature, which partakes of good and evil, joy and sorrow, mingled with endless variety of proportion and innumerable modes of combination; and expressing the course of the world, in which the loss of one is the gain of another; in which, at the same time, the reveller is hasting to his wine, and the mourner burying his friend; in which the malignity of one is sometimes defeated by the frolick of another; and many mischiefs and many benefits are done and hindered without design.[9]

What is striking about that passage is that no pattern or order or meaning is found in 'this chaos of mingled purposes and casualties',[10] yet the overall impression is powerfully affirmative, strongly conveying Johnson's sense of pleasure in the rightness of such a state. The pendulum movement of the prose resists any impulse of interpretation or simple emotional response, yet implies something positive in that very resistance, allows us to feel 'the real state of sublunary nature' not as a terrain across which man wanders but as his proper home. We register the achievement when we notice that in this paragraph Johnson is merely *describing* Shakespeare's mingled drama, with the formal defence yet to come: I take it that every reader feels that the essential justification—and celebration—is already there in the description.

If the power to feel and to represent life in this way is what Johnson means by just representations of general nature, I cannot see that 'general' need imply any element of either the ideal or the abstract.

---

[8] For Johnson's originality here, see Arthur Sherbo, *Samuel Johnson, Editor of Shakespeare* (Urbana, Ill., 1956), 59 f., and R. D. Stock, *Samuel Johnson and Neoclassical Dramatic Theory*, pp. 57–64.

[9] *Yale*, vii. 66.   [10] Ibid.

The point of the experience is precisely that it is as little of a mental construction as may be; 'the stability of truth' is knowledge of a directly experiential, not conceptual, kind. We know the mourner and the reveller and their coexistence, which is quite different from knowing (as Dick Minim may know) that mourning and revelry coexist. What the word 'general' suggests is, perhaps, akin to what Dryden meant by finding in both Chaucer and Shakespeare a 'comprehensive' power:[11] not simply that Shakespeare, like Chaucer, gives us an extraordinarily large and varied world, although that is certainly to the point, but that this largeness of possibility is present to us at any one moment, is felt to play around specific actualities of experience so that we apprehend them with an unusual wholeness. We know that Johnson greatly admired Dryden's encomium of Shakespeare;[12] in the *Dictionary* he quotes Dryden on Chaucer's 'wonderful comprehensive nature' and defines 'comprehensive', 'Having the power to comprehend or understand many things at once', which recalls the importance of simultaneity in his own description of 'the real state of sublunary nature': we are made aware of the mourner and the reveller 'at the same time'. Generality of this kind means the truth felt at those moments when one is released from the limitations of the individual viewpoint and becomes aware of one's participation in the common nature of humanity, penetrating the relatively superficial distinctions of character and situation to the level at which 'a man loves and hates, desires and avoids, exactly like his neighbour':[13]

His persons act and speak by the influence of those general passions and principles by which all minds are agitated, and the whole system of life is continued in motion. In the writings of other poets a character is too often an individual; in those of Shakespeare it is commonly a species.[14]

A species implies differentiation within a common *genus*; an individual, sheer differentiation. What Johnson finds in Shakespeare, as the context makes clear, is not so much the power to classify and typify individual particulars in a general form (as one might say that Falstaff is the type of all ageing debauchees) but rather the power to perceive and preserve the general in the particular, to make us

<hr/>

[11] See *Essays of John Dryden*, ed. W. P. Ker (2 vols.; 1900), i. 79 (on Shakespeare) and ii. 262 (on Chaucer).

[12] See *Yale*, vii. 111 f.; and Johnson, *Lives of the Poets*, i. 412.

[13] *Yale*, ii. 427 (*Adventurer* no. 95).   [14] Ibid. vii. 62.

feel how Falstaff, in all his personal specificity, participates in the same human nature which we all share.

What is it like to become aware of nature, to feel oneself to be a species rather than an individual? Part of the answer is that the boundaries of the self seem less absolute: the sense of self is relaxed, the opposition between all that one is and all that one is not becomes less imperious: one finds oneself less a spectator of and more a participant in a life larger than one's own. Johnson found Dryden to write a supremely natural prose, and gathers up his praise of it in these terms: 'He who writes much will not easily escape a manner, such a recurrence of particular modes as may be easily noted. Dryden is always "another and the same".'[15] Another and the same: Johnson salutes in Dryden's prose the quality which, with rather less sureness of touch, he desiderated in the *Rambler*:

There are animals that borrow their colour from the neighbouring body, and, consequently, vary their hue as they happen to change their place. In like manner it ought to be the endeavour of every man to derive his reflections from the objects about him; for it is to no purpose that he alters his position, if his attention continues fixed to the same point. The mind should be kept open to the access of every new idea, and so far disengaged from the predominance of particular thoughts, as easily to accommodate itself to occasional entertainment.[16]

'Another and the same' is the phrase in which Dryden describes Ovid's reborn phoenix in 'Of the Pythagorean Philosophy',[17] one of a number of passages in the *Fables* in which sublunary nature is seen as a never-ending, ever-changing flux in which all the forms of life are constantly interpenetrating and succeeding one another. This thought is most fully explicit in the great argument by which Theseus, in Dryden's version of *The Knight's Tale*, seeks to show that mourning need not exclude revelry:

---

[15] Johnson, *Lives of the Poets*, i. 418.

[16] *Yale*, iii. 28 (*Rambler* no. 5). Note also the motto to the *Rambler*, 'Nullius addictus jurare in verba magistri, | Quo me cunque rapit tempestas, deferor hospes' (Horace, *Epistles*, I. i. 14 f.), thus rendered by Pope: 'Sworn to no Master, of no Sect am I: | As drives the storm, at any door I knock, | And house with Montagne now, or now with Lock.' (*The First Epistle of the First Book of Horace Imitated*, ll. 24–6: *Poems of Alexander Pope*, iv. 281.)

[17] *The Poems of John Dryden*, ed. James Kinsley (4 vols.; 1958), iv. 1732; 'Of the Pythagorean Philosophy', ll. 578–81: 'All these receive their Birth from other Things | But from himself the *Phoenix* only springs: | Self-born, begotten by the Parent Flame | In which he burn'd, another and the same.'

This Law th'Omniscient Pow'r was pleas'd to give,
That ev'ry Kind should by Succession live;
That Individuals die, his Will ordains:
The propagated Species still remains.[18]

The individual lives on 'by succession' in his children and in his
fellow human beings, rather as Ovid and Chaucer live on in Dryden's
verse, where they too are 'another and the same'. By applying that
phrase to the naturalness of Dryden's prose, Johnson is pointing to
something delightfully light and mobile and provisional in the sense
of self which Dryden's prefaces communicate, something which calls
out an answering generosity and good humour in the reader: 'He
may be thought to mention himself too frequently; but while he forces
himself upon our esteem, we cannot refuse him to stand high in his
own. Every thing is excused by the play of images and the spriteliness
of expression.'[19]

Johnson sees good humour of this kind as marking our moments
of release from the strain of the perpetual competitiveness of our
relationships, as individuals, with other individuals. In no. 72 of the
Rambler he calls it 'a habit of being pleased', or 'the act or emanation
of a mind at leisure to regard the gratification of another';[20] it can
commonly be called into being only by those who have no great claim
on our admiration or respect and so, confessing or betraying their
frail and foolish humanity from the outset, make it possible for us
to loosen somewhat the tightness of our grip on our own claims as
individuals:

It is by some unfortunate mistake that almost all those who have any claim
to esteem or love, press their pretensions with too little consideration of
others. . . . We are most inclined to love when we have nothing to fear,
and he that encourages us to please ourselves, will not be long without
preference in our affection.[21]

The supreme exemplar of this quality, Johnson says in the same
essay, is Falstaff:

It is remarked by Prince Henry, when he sees Falstaff lying on the ground,
that 'he could have better spared a better man.' He was well acquainted
with the vices and follies of him whom he lamented, but while his conviction

---

[18] Ibid. 1527 ('Palamon and Arcite', iii, ll. 1054-7).
[19] Johnson, Lives of the Poets, i. 418.
[20] Yale, iv. 13.   [21] Ibid. 16, 15.

compelled him to do justice to superior qualities, his tenderness still broke out at the remembrance of Falstaff, of the chearful companion, the loud buffoon, with whom he had passed his time in all the luxury of idleness, who had gladded him with unenvied merriment, and whom he could at once enjoy and despise.[22]

The word 'despise' prevents us from finding anything sentimentalizing in Johnson's feeling for the tenderness which Falstaff inspires; it is only because he is despised that his merriment can be 'unenvied' and tenderness can flow: we are most inclined to love when we have nothing to fear. But this fact about human nature, however unpalatable it may be to the sentimentalist, takes nothing away from the feelings of love and tenderness which ensue, feelings which reach out beyond the fearful enclosure of the individual ego. His note on Falstaff in the Shakespeare edition makes it clear that for Johnson Hal's tenderness at that moment reflected the generosity of our own response:

But Falstaff unimitated, unimitable Falstaff, how shall I describe thee? Thou compound of sense and vice; of sense which may be admired but not esteemed, of vice which may be despised, but hardly detested. Falstaff is a character loaded with faults, and with those faults which naturally produce contempt. He is a thief, and a glutton, a coward, and a boaster, always ready to cheat the weak, and prey upon the poor; to terrify the timorous and insult the defenceless. At once obsequious and malignant, he satirises in their absence those whom he lives by flattering. He is familiar with the Prince only as an agent of vice, but of this familiarity he is so proud as not only to be supercilious and haughty with common men, but to think his interest of importance to the Duke of Lancaster. Yet the man thus corrupt, thus despicable, makes himself necessary to the prince that despises him, by the most pleasing of all qualities, perpetual gaiety, by an unfailing power of exciting laughter, which is the more freely indulged, as his wit is not of the splendid or ambitious kind, but consists in easy escapes and sallies of levity, which make sport but raise no envy. . . .

    The moral to be drawn from this representation is, that no man is more dangerous than he that with a will to corrupt, hath the power to please; and that neither wit nor honesty ought to think themselves safe with such a companion when they see Henry seduced by Falstaff.[23]

The generosity of this lies in the way that our knowledge of Falstaff is felt also to be a kind of self-discovery: if it is our contempt for

---

[22] Ibid. 15.   [23] Ibid. vii. 523 f.

Falstaff that allows us to enjoy him in the first place, that enjoyment tells us something about ourselves which overturns our sense of superiority even as we come to feel it—hence the fine discriminations of 'admired but not esteemed . . . despised, but hardly detested'. Those discriminations are what distinguish Johnson's response from the run-of-the-mill contemporary enthusiasm for Falstaff expressed, for example, by Corbyn Morris, who found that 'the good *Sense* which he possesses comes also to his Aid, and saves him from being *despicable*, by forcing your Esteem for his real Abilities'.[24] Johnson vigorously admires Falstaff's real abilities, but he does not esteem them, and although he agrees with Morris that 'it is impossible to *hate* honest *Jack Falstaff*',[25] this does not prevent him, any more than it prevents Hal, from finding the fat knight despicable. Such a combination of attitudes could not have been predicted: one would normally think of 'admire' and 'esteem', and 'despise' and 'detest', as near synonyms, and one might also have supposed that a character whom one found despicable could hardly possess such irresistible and admirable power to please. This unexpectedness in Johnson's discriminations, together with the tone of delighted wonder with which he measures the solidity of Shakespeare's achievement against its theoretical improbability, express his recognition of what Leo Salingar has described as Falstaff's 'inexhaustible resilience, his predictable unpredictability. . . . Falstaff's personality seems always in movement, going against the stream of opinion.'[26] Salingar suggests that our pleasure in this arises from 'the mental jolt of expecting to see a logical or moral rule at work but finding instead that the mechanism of the rule had been overcome',[27] and this recalls Johnson's general statement in the *Preface*: 'His comedy often surpasses expectation or desire.'[28] Knowledge of Johnson's moral writing reveals this as extraordinary praise. The condition of mankind is one in which desire regularly exceeds enjoyment, and expectation is regularly disappointed by the reality. But just as 'there is always an appeal open from criticism to nature', so there is also

---

[24] Corbyn Morris, *An Essay Towards Fixing the True Standards of Wit, Humour, Raillery, Satire, and Ridicule. To Which is Added, an Analysis of the Characters of an Humourist, Sir John Falstaff, Sir Roger De Coverly, and Don Quixote* (1744), 27.

[25] Ibid. 29.

[26] Leo Salingar, *Dramatic Form in Shakespeare and the Jacobeans* (1986), 34, 37 ('Falstaff and the Life of Shadows').

[27] Ibid. 33 f.

[28] *Yale*, vii. 69.

an appeal from ⸱the mode of experience that is conditioned by mental categories to a more comprehensive, more adequate, sense of the multiplicity of things. Falstaff himself is a 'compound', rather as Shakespeare's plays are not 'either tragedies or comedies, but *compositions* [my italics] of a distinct kind', exhibiting a state 'in which, at the same time, the reveller is hasting to his wine, and the mourner burying his friend': Johnson found in Hal's speech over the 'dead' Falstaff 'a very natural mixture of the serious and ludicrous'.[29] The vitality supremely embodied in Falstaff, and in Hal's relationship with Falstaff, is for Johnson a power characteristically and pervasively Shakespearean:

Parolles has many of the lineaments of Falstaff, and seems to be the character which Shakespeare delighted to draw, a fellow that had more wit than virtue. Though justice required that he should be detected and exposed, yet his 'vices sit so fit in him' that he is not at last suffered to starve.[30]

That power to combine clarity of moral judgement with the *caritas* that flows from recognition of our common humanity may remind one of George Eliot, but where Johnson, with Shakespeare, goes beyond George Eliot is in his power to feel *delight* in such a situation. The whole of the note on Falstaff is devoted to Falstaff's irresistible 'power to please' and hence to his extreme dangerousness and our extreme susceptibility—'neither wit nor honesty ought to think themselves safe with such a companion when they see Henry seduced by Falstaff'—but the tone in which Johnson contemplates this state of affairs is not anxious but exhilarated. It was, perhaps, because he possessed a good deal of this comic power himself that he was able to respond so strongly to its presence in Shakespeare; Fanny Burney tells the following splendid anecdote:

. . . 'And yet,' continued the doctor, with the most comical look, 'I have known all the wits, from Mrs. Montagu down to Bet Flint!'

'Bet Flint!' cried Mrs Thrale; 'pray who is she?'

'Oh, a fine character, madam! She was habitually a slut and a drunkard, and occasionally a thief and a harlot.'

'And, for Heaven's sake, how came you to know her?'

'Why, madam, she figured in the literary world, too! Bet Flint wrote her own life, and called herself Cassandra, and it was in verse;—it began:

---

[29] Ibid. 489.   [30] Ibid. 399.

When Nature first ordained my birth,
A diminutive I was born on earth:
And then I came from a dark abode,
Into a gay and gaudy world.

'So Bet brought me her verses to correct; but I gave her half-a-crown, and she liked it as well. Bet had a fine spirit;—she advertised for a husband, but she had no success, for she told me no man aspired to her! Then she hired very handsome lodgings and a footboy; and she got a harpsichord, but Bet could not play; however, she put herself in fine attitudes, and drummed.'

Then he gave an account of another of these geniuses, who called herself by some fine name, I have forgotten what.

'She had not quite the same stock of virtue,' continued he, 'nor the same stock of honesty as Bet Flint; but I suppose she envied her accomplishments, for she was so little moved by the power of harmony, that while Bet Flint thought she was drumming very divinely, the other jade had her indicted for a nuisance!'

'And pray what became of her, sir?'

'Why, madam, she stole a quilt from the man of the house, and he had her taken up: but Bet Flint had a spirit not to be subdued; so when she found herself obliged to go to jail, she ordered a sedan chair, and bid her footboy walk before her. However, the boy proved refractory, for he was ashamed, though his mistress was not.'

'And did she ever get out of jail again, sir?'

'Yes, madam; when she came to her trial the judge acquitted her. "So now," she said to me, "the quilt is my own, and now I'll make a petticoat of it." Oh, I loved Bet Flint!'[31]

Not Heroic but Human

'No man can taste the fruits of autumn, while he is delighting his scent with the flowers of the spring', Nekayah reflects in *Rasselas*: 'nature sets her gifts on the right hand and on the left'.[1] The disposition of mind that can find so much in Falstaff and in good humour, that is so happy to promote the species over the individual and can embrace so readily the Erasmian praise of folly, will not find it easy to enter into a different area of imaginative possibility:

[31] *Diary and Letters of Madame D'Arblay*, ed. Charlotte Barrett (6 vols.; 1904–5), i. 82 f. Boswell's version adds the detail that the judge was a womanizer who 'loved a wench' and therefore 'summed up favourably' (*Life of Johnson*, iv. 103).

[1] Johnson, *Works* (1825), i. 263 (*Rasselas*, ch. xxix).

the idea of individual greatness, the idea of the heroic. This is certainly true of Johnson, whose biographical writing is pointedly free of what he sees as the common biographer's endeavour 'to hide the man that he may produce a hero':[2] no matter how great their qualities of mind, their achievements, or their sufferings, the subjects of Johnson's biographies are shown as foolish mortal creatures, seen by an intelligence not satirical only because possessed of a strong sense of human solidarity with them in their imperfections, absurdities, and failures.[3] And this, Johnson believes, is equally true of Shakespeare:

Other dramatists can only gain attention by hyperbolical or aggravated characters . . . Shakespeare has no heroes; his scenes are occupied only by men, who act and speak as the reader thinks that he should himself have spoken or acted on the same occasion.[4]

The immediate contrast with the heroics of Restoration tragedy merges into the larger thought that to become aware of what it is to be a human being is necessarily to understand how profoundly man has *not* been formed to be a hero. The first quotation for 'Man' in the *Dictionary* is this, from the night scene in *Henry V*:

The king is but a *man* as I am; the violet smells to him as it doth to me; the element shews to him as it doth to me, all his senses have but human conditions.

The passage continues: 'his ceremonies laid by, in his nakedness he appears but a man; and tho' his affections are higher mounted than ours, yet when they stoop, they stoop with the like wing.' This, for Johnson, is the Shakespearean ground-note, a note which he finds immensely congenial. Of Hal in *Henry IV* he remarks:

The Prince, who is the hero both of the comick and tragick part, is a young man of great abilities and violent passions, whose sentiments are right, though his actions are wrong; whose virtues are obscured by negligence, and whose understanding is dissipated by levity. In his idle hours he is rather loose than wicked, and when the occasion forces out his latent qualities, he is great without effort, and brave without tumult. The trifler is roused

---

[2] *Yale*, ii. 262 (*Idler* no. 84).
[3] See W. J. Bate, 'Johnson and Satire Manqué', in *Eighteenth-Century Studies in Honor of Donald F. Hyde*, ed. W. H. Bond (New York, 1970), 145–60; and Robert Folkenflik, *Samuel Johnson: Biographer* (1978), 29–55.   [4] *Yale*, vii. 64.

into a hero, and the hero again reposes in the trifler. This character is great, original, and just.[5]

Johnson evinces the greatest pleasure in the truth of such a 'mingled' hero, given to negligence and levity, whose heroism rings true ('without effort . . . without tumult') precisely because it is occasional and set off by the trifling of his idle hours. The phrasing of 'the trifler is roused into a hero, and the hero again reposes in the trifler' disallows any great significance to Hal's reformation at the end of Part 2 (which Johnson thought might just as well have come at the beginning of *Henry V*),[6] and the word 'reposes' makes the second proposition the more fundamental truth about Hal; the mind can only repose on the stability of truth: the hero is always potentially the trifler. It is just such a hero that Johnson likes; anything more uniformly impressive than this would be elevated above the common feelings of the heart: the reader or spectator, instead of finding himself in the protagonist, another and the same, would be pressed back within himself by his admiration of the protagonist's extraordinary individuality, so that the feelings of nature could no longer flow. 'We are most inclined to love when we have nothing to fear.'

It is noteworthy that what Johnson says about Hal echoes what he says in the *Preface* about Shakespeare's situation in the history of the drama. Shakespeare was able to indulge his disposition for comedy, Johnson suggests, because he too had nothing to fear, no body of critical expectation 'of such authority as might restrain his extravagance', no heroic predecessor against whom he would have been obliged to measure his strength; the world of the drama was still 'open before him'.[7] And the result of thus indulging his disposition is that Hal-like mixture of greatness and trifling, that operation of 'great abilities . . . obscured by negligence, and . . . dissipated by levity', which overflows into other characters apart from Hal—'The character of the Bastard [in *King John*] contains that mixture of greatness and levity which this authour delighted to exhibit'[8]—and which calls out Johnson's pleasure and affection even while it provokes his censure. The tone in which he speaks of Shakespeare as having 'faults sufficient to obscure and overwhelm any other merit' hovers between the judicial and the comic: it has affinities with the way in which he marvels that a character so 'loaded

[5] Ibid. 523.   [6] See ibid. 522.   [7] Ibid. 69.   [8] Ibid. 428.

with faults' as Falstaff should notwithstanding possess such 'power to please'. Undeniably comic is the situation envisaged in 'his performance seems constantly to be worse, as his labour is more', as is also the splendid paragraph on Shakespeare's fascination with the quibble, 'the fatal Cleopatra for which he lost the world, and was content to lose it'.[9] To draw attention to Johnson's comic tone here is not to mitigate the force of his strictures, any more than the pleasure that Johnson takes in Falstaff softens his condemnation of his vices. But, when many commentators represent Johnson as divided between admiration for Shakespeare and a conflicting adherence to the criteria by which Shakespeare is found wanting, to acknowledge the element of humour in his adverse criticisms is to recognize that these went hand in hand with the warmest positive appreciation. Falstaff's contemptible qualities are greatly comic only because we see at the same time and as part of the same perception how much there is in him to be admired; Shakespeare's faults can only be felt as comic when there is a simultaneous apprehension of his greatness. And the manifestations of that greatness—which 'exigence forces out' in Shakespeare's case, and 'occasion forces out' in Hal's—are the more impressive for seeming to arise 'without effort' (Hal) and 'without labour' (Shakespeare).[10] In its negligence and levity, even a mind of such extraordinary powers as Shakespeare's does not transcend the common condition of humanity. It is a fact which Johnson is more inclined to celebrate than to deplore.

There is support for that suggestion in the ambivalence of the praise that Johnson gives to Milton and to Pope, two writers whose work *does* bear the true heroic stamp. In Milton's case, the grandeur of *Paradise Lost*—the grandeur both of the imagination which produced it, and the action represented in it—is something Johnson cannot but salute, but which deprives him of a pleasure he is loath to miss. Such grandeur is the expression of a mind not content to repose on the stability of truth and nature:

The appearances of nature and the occurrences of life did not satiate his appetite of greatness . . . The poet whatever be done is always great. . . . Reality was a scene too narrow for his mind . . . The reader feels himself in captivity to a higher and a nobler mind, and criticism sinks in admiration . . . Like other heroes he is to be admired rather than imitated. He that

[9] Ibid. 72 f., 74.
[10] Ibid. 73, 69 (for the phrases used of Shakespeare).

thinks himself capable of astonishing may write blank verse, but those that hope only to please must condescend to rhyme.[11]

For such a writer, the application of the Shakespearean formula 'not heroic but human' yields only negative results:

The want of human interest is always felt. *Paradise Lost* is one of the books which the reader admires and lays down, and forgets to take up again. None ever wished it longer than it is. Its perusal is a duty rather than a pleasure. We read Milton for instruction, retire harassed and overburdened, and look elsewhere for recreation; we desert our master, and seek for companions.[12]

Admiration is opposed to pleasure, human greatness to human interest; the 'higher and nobler mind' which makes itself felt in *Paradise Lost* intensifies rather than relaxes the reader's constricting sense of self, leaving him harassed and overburdened and in want of companions. Such individual prowess compels our admiration, and such imaginative grandeur elevates the mind; but Johnson does not enjoy being lifted so high.

It may be that Johnson's pleasure in Milton is also restricted by his subject-matter: in discussing Cowley's *Davideis* he remarks that

the whole system of life, while the Theocracy was yet visible, has an appearance so different from all other scenes of human action . . . that it is difficult even for imagination to place us in the state of them whose story is related, and by consequence their joys and griefs are not easily adopted.[13]

But in Johnson's account of Pope there are no such complicating factors. Johnson sees Pope's sense of self as inimical to the attitude of good humour described in the *Rambler* essay on Falstaff and Hal. That essay was followed a week later by a companion piece on the opposite disposition, 'ill humour' or 'peevishness', much of which reads like a commentary on Johnson's future portrait of Pope in the *Life*. Here are three of the more strikingly applicable passages:

A painful and tedious course of sickness frequently produces such an alarming apprehension of the least increase of uneasiness, as keeps the soul perpetually on the watch, such a restless and incessant solicitude, as no care or tenderness can appease.

He that gives himself up to his own fancy, and converses with none but such as he hires to lull him on the down of absolute authority, to sooth

---

[11] Johnson, *Lives of the Poets*, i. 177, 180, 178, 190, 194.
[12] Ibid. 183 f.   [13] Ibid. 51.

him with obsequiousness, and regale him with flattery, soon grows too slothful for the labour of contest, too tender for the asperity of contradiction, and too delicate for the coarseness of truth; a little opposition offends, a little restraint enrages, and a little difficulty perplexes him; having been accustomed to see every thing give way to his humour, he soon forgets his own littleness, and expects to find the world rolling at his beck, and all mankind employed to accommodate and delight him.

It sometimes happens that too close an attention to minute exactness, or a too rigorous habit of examining every thing by the standard of perfection, vitiates the temper, rather than improves the understanding, and teaches the mind to discern faults with unhappy penetration. It is incident likewise to men of vigorous imagination to please themselves too much with futurities, and to fret because those expectations are disappointed, which should never have been formed. Knowledge and genius are often enemies to quiet, by suggesting ideas of excellence, which men and the performances of men cannot attain.[14]

Johnson's critical, though not finally unsympathetic, account of Pope in the *Life* is of just such an ill-humoured man, confined within himself by the effects of chronic illness and by the consciousness of his own great powers, nervous of his dignity, 'flattered till he thought himself one of the moving powers in the system of life',[15] and therefore acutely sensitive to criticism, obstruction, or attack:

The indulgence and accommodation which his sickness required had taught him all the unpleasing and unsocial qualities of a valetudinary man. He expected that every thing should give way to his ease or humour, as a child whose parents will not hear her cry, has an unresisted dominion in the nursery.

> C'est que l'enfant toujours est homme,
> C'est que l'homme est toujours enfant.[16]

Given the connection he makes between good humour and the power of comedy, Johnson's observation may be noted that Pope 'sometimes condescended to be jocular with servants or inferiors; but by no merriment, either of others or his own, was he ever seen excited to laughter.'[17] And in the letters of both Swift and Pope Johnson reports 'such narrowness of mind as makes them insensible of any excellence that has not some affinity with their own.'[18] This is the opposite of the power to be 'always another and the same'.

---

[14] *Yale*, iv. 24, 25, 27 (*Rambler* no. 74).
[15] Johnson, *Lives of the Poets*, iii. 154.
[16] Ibid. 198.   [17] Ibid. 202.   [18] Ibid. 212.

However, the above are all biographical remarks: where the same thoughts about Pope are active in Johnson's account of his qualities as a poet they produce an altogether more complex and more appreciative judgement, one that suggests how the human failing, the restless, embattled sense of self, may have been the poet's strength:

> Pope was not content to satisfy; he desired to excel, and therefore always endeavoured to do his best: he did not court the candour, but dared the judgement of his reader, and, expecting no indulgence from others, he shewed none to himself. He examined lines and words with minute and punctilious observation, and retouched every part with indefatigable diligence, till he had left nothing to be forgiven.[19]

> Pope had likewise genius; a mind active, ambitious, and adventurous, always investigating, always aspiring; in its widest searches still longing to go forward, in its highest flights still wishing to be higher; always imagining something greater than it knows, always endeavouring more than it can do.[20]

This is praise of a kind that could not go to a writer whose excellence is his good humour, or to one whose mind characteristically reposes on the stability of truth; the mind with which one makes contact in Pope's poetry reposes neither on the sense of human fellowship nor on any pleasure which nature can afford. It is not so much that Johnson has reservations in his praise as that for Pope's particular achievement in poetry, as for any human achievement, there was a price to be paid, and the price in Pope's case was a substantial one. This becomes clear when his 'indefatigable diligence' is contrasted with Dryden's vigorous negligence in a way that works finally to the disadvantage of Pope, who 'left nothing to be forgiven'. Dryden left much to be forgiven: 'when he pleased others, he contented himself'[21]—a characteristic in which he exactly resembles Shakespeare: 'I am indeed far from thinking, that his works were wrought to his own ideas of perfection; when they were such as would satisfy the audience, they satisfied the writer.'[22] Pope, however, 'was not content to satisfy'; he expected no indulgence from others, and, as a poet if not as a man, requires none, whereas in Dryden 'every thing is excused':[23] Dryden's great need for critical forgiveness helps to make possible a more relaxed, 'easy' relationship between himself and his readers, giving pleasure even though it may forfeit esteem.

[19] Ibid. 221.   [20] Ibid. 217.   [21] Ibid. 220.
[22] Yale, vii. 91.   [23] Johnson, Lives of the Poets, i. 418.

'We are most inclined to love when we have nothing to fear, and he that encourages us to please ourselves will not be long without preference in our affection': Johnson's preference for Dryden over Pope indeed involves, as he acknowledges, 'some partial fondness for the memory of Dryden'.[24]

At the same time, it would be wrong to imply that Pope is *only* the foil to Dryden in Johnson's account. The description of Pope's genius, 'always imagining something greater than it knows, always endeavouring more than it can do', amply acknowledges an energy that cannot be subordinated to any merely limiting judgement, but is a real and fundamental part of our human potential. As he also does with Milton, Johnson there acknowledges that the heroic impulse to go beyond the given cannot be simply identified with egotism, however it may manifest itself as egotism in his subject's life. But, as again with Milton, the form of Johnson's acknowledgement shows how uncongenial it is to the natural tendency of his thought, a tendency which he found so happily met by Shakespeare.

The difference between Johnson's preferred apprehension of the heroic and Pope's can be illustrated from Johnson's note on lines spoken by Coriolanus as, banished, he prepares to leave Rome; he reminds his weeping mother of her own precepts concerning a noble fortitude in adversity:

> Fortune's blows,
> When most struck home, being gentle wounded, craves
> A noble cunning.

The sense is, When fortune strikes her hardest blows, to be wounded, and yet continue calm, requires a generous policy. He calls this calmness 'cunning', because it is the effect of reflection and philosophy. Perhaps the first emotions of nature are nearly uniform, and one man differs from another in the power of endurance, as he is better regulated by precept and instruction.

> They bore as heroes, but they felt as man.[25]

That final quotation is from the last book of Pope's *Iliad* (line 646), where Priam kneels to Achilles and moves him to compassion by urging him to think of his own father: the appositeness to *Coriolanus*, and to the next occasion on which Coriolanus will meet with his mother, is clear. However, the implication of the line as Johnson quotes and glosses it is significantly different from its force in Pope's

---

[24] Ibid. iii. 223.   [25] *Yale*, viii. 813.

translation. The opposition of 'heroes' to 'man' belongs to Pope not Homer, who makes no reference in this passage to heroes or the heroic:

τὼ δὲ μνησαμένω, ὁ μὲν Ἕκτορος ἀνδροφόνοιο
κλαῖ' ἀδινὰ προπάροιθε ποδῶν Ἀχιλῆος ἐλυσθείς,
αὐτὰρ Ἀχιλλεὺς κλαῖεν ἑὸν πατέρ', ἄλλοτε δ' αὖτε
Πάτροκλον· τῶν δὲ στοναχὴ κατὰ δώματ' ὀρώρει.

[Memories came upon them both; the one, sprawling at Achilles' feet, wept bitterly for man-killing Hector, but Achilles wept for his own father and for Patroclus by turns; and their cries of grief went up through the house.][26]

Pope's reason for introducing the heroic explicitly here (as also two lines before) is to emphasize that there is true greatness in Achilles' thus yielding to the feelings of general nature; his note on Achilles' immediately ensuing speech makes this clear:

There is not a more beautiful Passage in the whole *Ilias* than this before us: *Homer* to shew that *Achilles* was not a mere Soldier, here draws him as a Person of excellent Sense and sound reason . . . And it was a piece of great Judgment thus to describe him; for the Reader would have retain'd but a very indifferent Opinion of the Hero of a Poem, that had no Qualification but mere Strength . . . By these means he fixes an Idea of his Greatness upon our Minds, and makes his Hero go off the Stage with Applause.[27]

Shakespeare makes *his* hero go off the stage very differently:

> O mother, mother!—
> [*Holds her by the hands, silent.*
> What have you done? behold the heav'ns do ope,
> The Gods look down, and this unnatural scene,
> They laugh at.

At the climax of Pope's *Iliad*, the heroic and the human reinforce one another; Achilles is in Pope's view never so much the hero as when he here shows himself to feel also as a man; the point of Pope's line is that in Priam and Achilles at this moment the heroic and the human are felt as one, and Pope accordingly underlines what he finds

[26] Homer, *Iliad*, ed. D. B. Monro and T. W. Allen, 3rd edn. (2 vols.; Oxford, 1920), xxiv, ll. 509–12.
[27] *Poems of Alexander Pope*, viii. 564.

to be the grandeur and dignity of their sympathy in grief, departing
from Homer's text by explicitly reminding us that these men are heroes
and introducing the idea of fortitude in endurance ('They *bore* as
heroes'). In the preceding line he describes their weeping as 'solemn',
and two lines below, following and amplifying Homer, he speaks
of 'divine Achilles' (δῖος Ἀχιλλεύς): 'From the high Throne divine
Achilles rose'. But in *Coriolanus* the yielding of the protagonist's
wrath to his humanity breaks the heroic against the human: the hero,
as hero, is offered up to the gods' derision. And Johnson's note
reflects and reinforces this difference, for he quotes Pope's line only
in a context and after a gloss that effectively reverses its implication:
Volumnia can draw no strength from her own precepts now, and
all Johnson's writing bears witness to his conviction that the qualities
by which men differ from one another, such as the power to be
'regulated by precept and instruction', are superficial and incidental
by comparison with 'the first emotions of nature' which all men have
in common. After Johnson's gloss, Pope's words come to suggest that
the heroic is merely the foil to the human, a power to endure in one's
outward behaviour which interests us principally as it is felt to resist
the deeper truth of human feeling within.

This 'anti-heroic' aspect of Johnson's thought about Shakespeare
needs no special exposition to be shown as tenable. Many readers of
Shakespeare would, on the whole, agree with these two propositions:
that an uninhibited, although not necessarily destructive, scepticism
is allowed to play on virtually every character in Shakespeare who
has claims to greatness of any kind; and that it is characteristic of
Shakespeare's power to trace the texture of our common humanity
in the alien, exalted, or otherwise outstanding individual—the king,
the malcontent, the lover, the machiavel, the Jew. These propositions
would become contentious perhaps only with regard to the tragedies.
Yet here too the position which states that Shakespeare has no heroes
is not only tenable but frequently held; Eliot's remarks on Othello's
bovarysme[28] are only one extreme position in a continuing debate
over whether, and in what sense, one can speak of the grandeur of
Hamlet, Othello, Lear, or Antony, when there is so much in their
respective plays that calls that grandeur in question. The arguments
on both sides of the case have great force: it is likely that the critical

[28] See T. S. Eliot, *Elizabethan Essays* (1934), 38–40 ('Shakespeare and the
Stoicism of Seneca').

debate corresponds to what is being dramatized in the plays themselves. The question of Coriolanus's greatness is a crucial and
consuming question for Coriolanus himself as well as for his critics.
And here one sees how the tone in which Johnson comes down so
decisively on one side of the question may be said, with regard to
these five or six plays, to fall short of their full interest, treating as
a binary opposition (not heroic but human) what would be better
felt as a polarity. For, even supposing that we take the line, with
Johnson, that not one of Shakespeare's protagonists possesses heroic
stature of the order that impresses us in Homer's Achilles, still we
must feel that the *possibility* of the heroic is forcefully present in the
tragedies, so that its unattainability is, to the protagonists, an agony.
They do not so much come to 'repose' on their non-heroic human
nature as are crucified upon it.

The relationship between Johnson's attitude to the heroic and his
response to the tragedies will be further discussed at the end of this
study. In the mean time, it should be reiterated that his disinclination
for the heroic is inseparably bound up with his powerful appreciation
of general nature in the plays; if it is a defect, it is the defect of his
virtues, and one which, moreover, Shakespeare may well be thought
in large measure to share with him. George Bernard Shaw's elevation
of Bunyan over Shakespeare is outrageously perverse, but it is the
perversion of a true perception:

Shakespear wrote for the theatre because, with extraordinary artistic powers,
he understood nothing and believed nothing. Thirty-six big plays in five blank
verse acts, and (as Mr Ruskin, I think, once pointed out) not a single hero!
Only one man in them all who believes in life, enjoys life, thinks life worth
living, and has a sincere, unrhetorical tear dropped over his death-bed; and
that man—Falstaff! What a crew they are—these Saturday to Monday
athletic stockbroker Orlandos, these villains, fools, clowns, drunkards,
cowards, intriguers, fighters, lovers, patriots, hypochondriacs who mistake
themselves (and are mistaken by the author) for philosophers, princes without
any sense of public duty, futile pessimists who imagine they are confronting
a barren and unmeaning world when they are only contemplating their own
worthlessness, self-seekers of all kinds, keenly observed and masterfully
drawn from the romantic-commercial point of view. . . .

All that you miss in Shakespear you find in Bunyan, to whom the true
heroic came quite obviously and naturally. The world was to him a more
terrible place than it was to Shakespear; but he saw through it a path at
the end of which a man might look not only forward to the Celestial City,
but back on his life and say:— 'Tho' with great difficulty I am got hither,

yet now I do not repent me of all the trouble I have been at to arrive where I am. My sword I give to him that shall succeed me in my pilgrimage, and my courage and skill to him that can get them.' The heart vibrates like a bell to such an utterance as this.[29]

Johnson approaches that perception from an opposite point of view. What he looks for in Shakespeare above all else is the power to deliver the mind from its restless desire to go beyond what life gives, the power to bring us home to our participation in that general human nature which unites us. From this position, the heroic can be spared; it is because Johnson values so highly the affirmation involved in the experience of nature, and feels it so strongly, that he reads Shakespeare always with these priorities, these fundamental pleasures, in mind.

But it is on those priorities that the romantic account of Shakespeare makes war; in place of nature, it brings to Shakespeare a radically opposed but hardly less fundamental set of needs.

[29] *Shaw on Shakespeare*, ed. Edwin Wilson (1962), 221 f.

3

THE MIND
AGAINST THE WORLD

He that has pictured a prospect upon his fancy, will receive little pleasure
from his eyes.

(JOHNSON)[1]

The Idealist Imagination—
Wordsworth—Falstaff—Hamlet

WHEN, in 1785, Mrs Thrale wrote up her anecdotes of Johnson,
it was already clear to her that Johnson's account of Shakespeare
tensed itself against one possible way of reading the plays in favour
of another. She spoke of Johnson's

extreme distance from those notions which the world has agreed, I know
not very well why, to call romantic. It is indeed observable in his preface
to Shakespeare, that while other critics expatiate on the creative powers and
vivid imagination of that matchless poet, Dr. Johnson commends him for
giving so just a representation of human manners, 'that from his scenes a
hermit might estimate the value of society, and a confessor predict the
progress of the passions.'[2]

What was dimly present in that tendency of other critics to exalt
Shakespeare's 'creative powers and vivid imagination' *as opposed to*
his powers of just representation became articulate some twenty-five
years later in the work of Schlegel and Coleridge, under the stimulus
of Kant's argument that the mind is not an organ of passive perception but itself gives laws and form to the world of phenomena.
Coleridge in particular waged unceasing war on the pernicious notion
of the mind as the passive register of a world of things, a view which
threatened to drain away all spiritual and ethical significance from
human life: 'The pith of my system is to make the senses out of the

---

[1] *Yale*, ii. 182 (*Idler* no. 58).
[2] *Johnsonian Miscellanies*, ed. G. B. Hill (2 vols.; 1897), i. 313.

mind—not the mind out of the senses'.[3] For Coleridge the mind was above all an active, creative power, and this creativity was supremely manifest in the creativity of poetry; hence his antagonism to any description of great art which, by laying the emphasis on *representation*, seemed utterly to subordinate the powers of the mind to realities already given in experience. 'In all, that truly merits the name of *Poetry* in its most comprehensive sense', he wrote in *The Friend*, 'there is a necessary predominance of the Ideas (i.e. of that which originates in the artist himself), and a comparative indifference of the materials.'[4]

This is the core of Coleridge's opposition to Johnson. For, although Johnson certainly does not regard the mind as passive, it is nevertheless the case that in his experience of Shakespeare the mind is felt as the receiver rather than the giver, in 'repose', filled with interest and pleasure in a world not of its own or Shakespeare's making. Johnson could pay Shakespeare no higher compliment than to say that he 'must have looked upon mankind with perspicacity, in the highest degree curious and attentive'.[5] Coleridge, by contrast, repeatedly distinguishes mere 'observation' of the given external world from the Shakespearean process of 'meditation', or

the observation of that mind which, having formed a theory and a system in its own nature, has remarked all things as examples of the truth . . . Mercutio was a man possessing all the elements of a Poet: high fancy; rapid thoughts; the whole world was, as it were, subject to his law of association: whenever he wished to impress anything, all things became his servants.[6]

Johnson would hardly have cared for the suggestion that in the encounter between idea and world the idea should carry all before it, modifying experience without itself being modified in its turn. What Coleridge is there describing, he might have said, is the insanity of the astronomer in *Rasselas* who, in believing that he controls the weather, has precisely this power of remarking all things as exemplifying the truth of a theory formed a priori. But Coleridge would have found in such an objection a fundamental misunderstanding of the way the poetic imagination works: the materials

---

[3] *Table Talk of Samuel Taylor Coleridge*, ed. Henry Morley (1884), 165 (25 July 1832).

[4] Samuel Taylor Coleridge, *The Friend*, ed. Barbara E. Rooke (2 vols.; 1969), i. 464.   [5] *Yale*, vii. 88.

[6] *Coleridge on Shakespeare: The Text of the Lectures of 1811–12*, ed. R. A. Foakes (1971), 78.

afforded by nature are neither represented nor, therefore, mis-represented by the process of art, but transmuted into something else: 'Shakespeare's characters from Othello or Macbeth down to Dogberry are ideal; they are not the things, but the abstracts of the things which a great mind may take into itself and naturalize to its own heaven.'[7]

At one level, this emphasis on the creativity of great art is not open to challenge. Shakespeare's plays are not (how could they be?) literal facsimiles of anything in nature, and while one may, with Johnson, hold the just representation of general nature to be the *end* of Shakespeare's art, it cannot rationally be maintained that the method by which Shakespeare achieves that end is in any straightforward sense mimetic. On the formal working of Shakespeare's imagination Coleridge is full of insight, while Johnson has little or nothing to say, so that even the most Johnsonian reader may go gratefully to Coleridge for stimulus and illumination. But Coleridge's concern with the method of Shakespeare's art comprehends his concern with its end and value, and it is here that the romantic insistence on the mind's creativity becomes the direct antagonist of Johnson's feeling for general nature. For if what *matters* is the process by which imagination 'turns | Bodies to spirit by sublimation strange',[8] then the value set on this process tends inevitably to devalue the 'mere' world of nature that stands in need of such transmutation; we are left with a dualism in which the claims of the mind are set over against the world.

Such a dualistic view is readily nourished by Kantian philosophy, as witness much of Kant's own discussion of art in the *Critique of Judgement*:

The imagination . . . is very powerful in creating what might be called a second nature out of the material given to it by actual nature. We entertain ourselves with it where experience proves too commonplace, and we even use it to re-model experience, always following laws of analogy, no doubt, but also in accordance with higher principles given by the reason. . . . By this means we gain a sense of our freedom from the law of association (which attaches to the empirical employment of that power [namely, imagination]), for although it is according to that law that we borrow material from nature,

---

[7] Ibid. 101.
[8] Samuel Taylor Coleridge, *Biographia Literaria*, ed. J. Shawcross (2 vols.; 1907), ii. 12. Coleridge is quoting from Sir John Davies's *Nosce Teipsum*.

we have the power to work that material into something quite other—namely, that which surpasses nature.[9]

Coleridge must have found that passage immensely congenial, with its firm distinction between an empirical employment of imagination bound by laws of association, and so dependent on the phenomenal qualities of things (called 'Fancy' in the *Biographia*), and a higher power whose operation, under Kant's analysis, figures forth the realm in which the mind rises free of the sensible world of causally determined phenomena; in poetry the mind is empowered 'to make use of nature on behalf of, and as a kind of schema for, the supersensible'.[10] It is just such a view of art that Coleridge finds confirmed in Shakespeare: 'The events themselves are immaterial, otherwise than as the clothing and manifestation of the spirit that is working within.'[11] Until transfigured by the indwelling spirit of imagination, the flesh of nature is of no account; nothing, therefore, could be more misguided than Johnson's stubborn reference of the value of Shakespeare's plays to the world of 'realities'. In a notebook entry, Coleridge argues that it is Johnson's perverse literal-mindedness, attending only to the 'facts' of the dramatic situation without regard to how those facts have been organized and transformed in the process of art, that leads him to such grossly inappropriate faultfinding; he speaks of the

vile Johnsonian Antithesis of Black & White/ One would suppose from Johnson's Preface that Sh. was a pie-bald Poet—& that he, the Critic, was standing by . . . pointing out as faults the conditio sine qua non of the acknowledged beauties!—The expecting of contradictions!—The Poet & his Subject, are they not as the Δημιουργος & ὕλή of Plato—if the ὕλη were not of itself reluctant & naked & ungratifying, what need of the Demiurge—and tho' he may hinder this, & alter it, & form, & educe perpetual good even out of the worst evil, can he annihilate the ὕλη without evanishment of the ιδεα?[12]

Later writers used the term ὕλή for that inchoate material from which Plato's craftsman-god, or Demiurge, fashions the universe—just as

---

[9] *Immanuel Kants Werke*, ed. Ernst Cassirer *et al.* (11 vols.; Berlin, 1912–22), v. 389 (*Kritik der Urteilskraft*, para. 49).

[10] Ibid. 402 (*Kritik der Urteilskraft*, para. 53).

[11] Coleridge, *Shakespearean Criticism*, ed. T. M. Raysor, 2nd edn. (2 vols.; 1960), i. 125. The immediate reference is to the history plays.

[12] *The Notebooks of Samuel Taylor Coleridge*, ed. Kathleen Coburn (1957–), iii. no. 3952.

Shakespeare, Coleridge suggests, fashions his plays out of the raw material of life. What Coleridge attacks in Johnson is the presumption that one may judge the created product by criteria drawn from that formless raw material; but what is revealing about Coleridge's attack is how life itself, prior to its 'sublimation strange' in poetry, is envisaged as 'reluctant & naked & ungratifying', the intrinsically unlovely ground on which imagination has to work.

Schlegel and Coleridge respond very differently to this dualistic tendency in their critical thought. Schlegel readily accepts and indeed embraces the devaluation of nature; this appears most clearly in the seminal distinction between classical and romantic art with which he begins the *Lectures on Dramatic Literature*. Greek culture he characterizes as 'a finished education in the school of Nature':

They accomplished all that man is capable of when imprisoned within the limits of the finite . . . But however great their achievement with regard to the beautiful and even the ethical, we cannot grant any higher character to their culture than that of a refined and ennobled sensuality . . . A higher wisdom teaches us that man has lost his way and through this great error has forfeited the place for which he was originally destined; the whole condition and end of his earthly existence is the striving to return to his lost position—although this is something he can never achieve by his own unaided efforts. The old religion of the senses sought nothing higher than blessings of an external, transient kind; immortality, insofar as it was believed in at all, was a dim and distant shadow, a dream faintly remembered in the sunny waking daytime of life. In the Christian perspective everything is reversed: the intuition of infinity has destroyed what is finite, and it is life which has become a world of shadow and darkness, while the eternal day of our real existence dawns only on a further shore. Such a religion necessarily brings into full consciousness the intimation sleeping in every sensitive heart, the intimation that we aspire to a happiness unattainable here, that no external object can ever entirely satisfy our souls, and that all enjoyment is a momentary, fleeting illusion . . . The poetry of the ancients was that of enjoyment, and ours is that of desire.[13]

This spiritually enlightened sense of alienation, Schlegel argues, is supremely realized in the art of Shakespeare.

Such a philosophy of two worlds—a lower realm of the world known to the senses and a higher, finally more substantial, world of the mind—was deeply attractive to Coleridge also. To a mind like

[13] Schlegel, v. 23, 25. Schlegel's distinction is echoed by Coleridge; see *Shakespearean Criticism*, i. 196.

his, teeming with the analogies suggested by every kind of experience, the sublimation of thing into thought, of the literal into the meta-phorical, was as natural as breathing; to the philosophical thinker who was to make such absolute distinctions between 'Nature and Spirit, the one being the *antithesis* to the other'[14] and also between the 'Understanding' which addresses the world of sense experience and the independently self-vindicating 'Reason' which transcends it,[15] this dualism of world and spirit held a strong appeal, as it did to the moralist for whom the idea of original sin and of the depravity of the will was of such central importance;[16] and it must have been congenial also to the Coleridge who was so ill at ease with his own body, the 'damaged archangel' who found himself so painfully cramped and disabled whenever it came to realizing his great powers, and great desires, in the world of fact and flesh. Yet there was another, no less essential, part of Coleridge that—during his years as poet and as critic, at least—emphatically rejected any such dichotomy. 'A Poet's *Heart* & *Intellect* should be *combined*, *intimately* combined and *unified*, with the great appearances in Nature', he had written in 1802:[17] this was the Coleridge of 'the one Life within us and abroad',[18] whose guiding principle of thought was always, in some form, the reconciling of opposites, and in whose best critical remarks immediacy of response and depth of reflection are manifestly and remarkably one. For *this* Coleridge, to call Shakespeare 'a profound Metaphysician' was no more than to say that he possessed an extraordinary, quasi-sensory '*Tact*':

for all sounds, & forms of human nature he must have the *ear* of a wild Arab listening in the silent Desert, the eye of a North American Indian tracing the footsteps of an Enemy upon the Leaves that strew the Forest—; the *Touch* of a Blind Man feeling the face of a darling Child—[19]

---

[14] Samuel Taylor Coleridge, *Aids to Reflection* (1901), 166.

[15] See ibid. 142–56.

[16] See ibid. 198–200; also A. O. Lovejoy, 'Coleridge and Kant's Two Worlds', *Essays in the History of Ideas* (Baltimore, Md., 1948), 254–76, and L. S. Lockridge, *Coleridge the Moralist* (1977), 53–77.

[17] *Collected Letters of Samuel Taylor Coleridge*, ed. E. L. Griggs (6 vols.; 1956–71), ii. 864 (no. 459: to William Sotheby, 10 Sept. 1802).

[18] *The Complete Poetical Works of Samuel Taylor Coleridge*, ed. E. H. Coleridge (2 vols.; 1912), i. 101 ('The Eolian Harp', l. 26).

[19] Coleridge, *Letters*, ii. 810 (no. 444: to William Sotheby, 13 July 1802).

and the 'imagination' was not a specialized faculty but 'simply life coming to consciousness', as L. C. Knights has described it, 'a function of the whole person, a dynamic integrating force'.[20] Coleridge's impulse toward integration was, during these years, not diminished by the fact that his own emphasis on the creativity of the mind was constantly bringing such integration into peril. Thus, despite his antagonism to Johnson, Coleridge is capable of describing Shakespeare's feeling for the wholeness of human life in entirely Johnsonian terms: 'In all his various characters, we still feel ourselves communing with the same human nature, which is everywhere present as the vegetable sap in the branches, sprays, leaves, buds, blossoms, and fruits.'[21] He differs from both Schlegel and Hazlitt in preserving the essential idea behind Johnson's assertion that Shakespeare's characters are not individuals but species: 'Shakspeare's characters are all *genera* intensely individualized'; 'Lady Macbeth, like all in Shakespeare, is a class individualized'.[22] And his marginal notes reveal how frequently he looked to the plays primarily for representations of men and women like ourselves, however awkwardly that approach may have sat to his more general theoretical emphasis. If Coleridge's first concern was to affirm the mind's creativity, he was clearly far from happy to relinquish general nature for the sake of that affirmation, despite the inconsistencies, or at least radically divergent emphases, which this created.

For the most part these two approaches simply lie alongside one another in the Shakespeare criticism; M. M. Badawi's full-length study identifies a 'dichotomy or polarity' between Coleridge's emphasis on imagination and his 'tendency towards naturalism'.[23] This may be vexing to the theory-hunter, but in itself it is not necessarily a weakness. Indeed, a strong case could be made that it represents Coleridge's distinction as a critic of Shakespeare, being fed by a corresponding dichotomy or creative tension at or near the centre of Shakespeare's art. To put the matter with painful simplicity, we can go to Shakespeare's men and women for some of the fullest representations of our common human nature that literature can supply, or we can regard what they say and do as the characters

---

[20] John Beer (ed.), *Coleridge's Variety: Bicentenary Studies* (1974), p. xxii.

[21] Coleridge, *The Friend*, i. 457.

[22] Coleridge, *Shakespearean Criticism*, i. 122, 64.

[23] See M. M. Badawi, *Coleridge: Critic of Shakespeare* (1973), esp. pp. 40–5, 64–6.

and symbols of a poetic language—a language used both to express
a particular vision of things, and to manifest the power and freedom
and scope of art itself. It is not obvious how, in the final analysis,
those approaches might be combined; yet Shakespeare would seem
to support, and indeed to demand, both. If, in this situation, the
essence of criticism is an act of choice that decisively promotes
some possibilities over others, we shall have to say that Coleridge
falls short of this; however, it is equally true that his inconsistencies
represent an openness to 'myriad-minded Shakespeare' that Johnson's
sometimes brutally decisive criticism does not afford. To appreciate
the value of that decisiveness we have first to supply Johnson with
an antagonistic point of view, but Coleridge, as often, is his own
best antagonist.

Nevertheless, Coleridge's criticism is open to challenge, not for
its inconsistency, but for its refusal to admit that any inconsistency
exists. Coleridge's inclination is to play down or gloss over the tension
between 'nature' and 'imagination'; by vigorously promoting the
claims of each, he comes to imply that the two emphases somehow
belong together and even reinforce one another, and in this he can
be a thoroughly misleading guide.

The account of Wordsworth in the *Biographia Literaria* is a telling
case in point, for much of Wordsworth's best poetry is concerned
to admit and explore just this tension between truth to nature and
the claims of imagination. Coleridge describes Wordsworth's aim
in *Lyrical Ballads* as that of

awakening the mind's attention from the lethargy of custom, and directing
it to the loveliness and the wonders of the world before us; an inexhaustible
treasure, but for which, in consequence of the film of familiarity and selfish
solicitude we have eyes, yet see not, ears that hear not, and hearts that neither
feel nor understand.[24]

Here the affirmation of 'the world before us' is primary, and from the
strength of Coleridge's phrasing it could seem that such affirmation
has his whole-hearted endorsement. Yet this is silently contradicted
when Coleridge goes on to identify the 'pre-eminent' characteristic
of Wordsworth's genius as 'IMAGINATION in the highest and strictest
sense of the word':

---

[24] Coleridge, *Biographia Literaria*, ii. 6.

To employ his own words, which are at once an instance and an illustration, he does indeed to all thoughts and to all objects

<blockquote>
add the gleam,
The light that never was, on sea or land.
The consecration, and the poet's dream.[25]
</blockquote>

Coleridge seems not to reflect that such an employment of the imagination implies a certain alienation from or dissatisfaction with the wonders of the world before us; specifically, he feels free to disregard the fact that the very poem from which he quotes those lines—'Elegiac Stanzas, Suggested by a Picture of Peele Castle, in a Storm'—is explicitly concerned with what is incompletely human about 'the poet's dream':

<blockquote>
So once it would have been,—'tis so no more;
I have submitted to a new control:
A power is gone, which nothing can restore;
A deep distress hath humanized my soul.

.   .   .   .

Farewell, farewell the heart that lives alone,
Housed in a dream, at distance from the Kind!
</blockquote>

The power of 'IMAGINATION' celebrated by Coleridge yields to experience; Wordsworth can no longer wish himself the freely creative artist, setting the castle 'amid a world how different from this', but must now endure, if not exactly submit to, the realities of grief and bereavement. In their context, the lines raise questions about the poetic imagination which Coleridge's quotation of them entirely fails to acknowledge.

No less revealing is Coleridge's discussion of the passage that he quotes from 'Resolution and Independence':

<blockquote>
My former thoughts returned; the fear that kills;
And hope that is unwilling to be fed;
Cold, pain, and labour, and all fleshly ills;
And mighty poets in their misery dead.
But now, perplex'd by what the old man had said,
My question eagerly did I renew,
'How is it that you live, and what is it you do?'
</blockquote>

---

[25] Ibid. 124.

He with a smile did then his words repeat;
And said, that gathering leeches far and wide
He travell'd; stirring thus about his feet
The waters of the ponds where they abide.
'Once I could meet with them on every side,
But they have dwindled long by slow decay;
Yet still I persevere, and find them where I may.'

While he was talking thus, the lonely place,
The old man's shape, and speech, all troubled me:
In my mind's eye I seemed to see him pace
About the weary moors continually,
Wandering about alone and silently.

Coleridge wishes the second of these stanzas away, finding it incongruously prosaic and flat by comparison with the power of imagination manifested in what comes before and after; he finds it a lapse of artistic judgement that Wordsworth should break the flow of his own troubled imaginings with the bare and unimpassioned renarration of the simple facts of the leech-gatherer's means of life.[26] But the 'bathos' of this is functional: it is precisely because the figure of the old man not only kindles but also resists the poet's imagination that the encounter is such a significant and healing one for Wordsworth. I continue the quotation from where Coleridge ends it:

While I these thoughts within myself pursued,
He, having made a pause, the same discourse renewed.

And soon with this he other matter blended,
Cheerfully uttered, with demeanour kind,
But stately in the main; and when he ended,
I could have laughed myself to scorn to find
In that decrepit Man so firm a mind.
'God,' said I, 'be my help and stay secure;
I'll think of the Leech-gatherer on the lonely moor!'

Wordsworth has got outside his melancholy, has gained access to a larger perspective: his restorative power to laugh himself to scorn is indebted to the smile with which the old man found himself obliged to repeat his story to the inattentive poet lost in his own imaginings.

[26] See ibid. 97–100.

Those imaginings are not, of course, merely decried, but have a genuinely creative force: by seeing the leech-gatherer as 'a Man from some far region sent | To give me human strength, and strong admonishment', Wordsworth's mind is made sensitive, one feels, for the reception of what is to follow. Yet what does follow is not any higher reach of the visionary imagination but rather a suspension of the mind's working, a still moment of unusual attentiveness to the nature of things, as embodied in the physical presence of the old man and the simple dignity and hardship of his life. 'He, having made a pause, the same discourse renewed': the 'pause' which the leech-gatherer makes in the imaginative movement of the poem itself, and which the flatness of the offending stanza enables us to feel, is in its effect not unlike the 'pauses of deep silence' described in the lines beginning 'There was a Boy'. The boy had the trick of blowing 'mimic hootings to the silent owls' across the lake, so that they would reply with

>   quivering peals,
> And long halloos, and screams, and echoes loud
> Redoubled and redoubled; concourse wild
> Of mirth and jocund din! And when it chanced
> That pauses of deep silence mock'd his skill,
> Then sometimes, in that silence, while he hung
> Listening, a gentle shock of mild surprise
> Has carried far into his heart the voice
> Of mountain torrents; or the visible scene
> Would enter unawares into his mind
> With all its solemn imagery, its rocks,
> Its woods, and that uncertain Heaven, receiv'd
> Into the bosom of the steady Lake.[27]

While the owls respond, it seems that all nature is subject to the boy's skill: but the moments that count are to this power a kind of anticlimax, the 'gentle shock' of encounter with a nature that comes to the self with something other than the echo of the self's own activity. It is an understanding of things deeply opposed to Coleridge's emphasis on the creative activity of the mind as expressed in, for example, his 'Dejection: An Ode':

---

[27] Wordsworth, *The Prelude: or Growth of a Poet's Mind: 1805*, ed. E. de Selincourt and rev. Helen Darbishire (1960), v, ll. 401–13.

O Lady! we receive but what we give,
And in our life alone does Nature live:
Ours is her wedding garment, ours her shroud!
And would we aught behold, of higher worth,
Than that inanimate cold world allowed
To the poor loveless ever-anxious crowd,
Ah! from the soul itself must issue forth
A light, a glory, a fair luminous cloud
Enveloping the Earth——
And from the soul itself must there be sent
A sweet and potent voice, of its own birth,
Of all sweet sounds the life and element!

Given this opposition, it is entirely logical that Coleridge should object to the stanza in which the leech-gatherer repeats his tale for its sudden 'transition . . . to a style not only unimpassioned but undistinguished'. It is also logical that he should take issue with Wordsworth's proposition in the preface to *Lyrical Ballads* that the best poetic language consists of 'a selection of the real language of men'[28]—in which Wordsworth is at one with Johnson in the *Preface to Shakespeare*: 'The dialogue of this authour is often so evidently determined by the incident which produces it, and is pursued with so much ease and simplicity, that it seems scarcely to claim the merit of fiction, but to have been gleaned by diligent selection out of common conversation.'[29] In Shakespeare Johnson found 'a stile which never becomes obsolete . . . probably to be sought in the common intercourse of life, among those who speak only to be understood, without ambition of elegance'[30] and this is closely paralleled by Wordsworth's discussion of those in rural life who 'being less under the influence of social vanity . . . convey their feelings and notions in simple and unelaborated expressions':

Such a language, arising out of repeated experience and regular feelings, is a more permanent, and a far more philosophical language, than that which is frequently substituted for it by Poets, who think that they are conferring

[28] *The Poetical Works of William Wordsworth*, ed. E. de Selincourt and Helen Darbishire (5 vols.; 1940–9), ii. 384. For Coleridge's attack, see *Biographia Literaria*, ii. 29–34, 38–43. Schlegel, too, was emphatic that *Poesie* precludes the language really spoken by men. He attributes the contrary view to the French criticism of the age of Louis XIV; see Schlegel, ii. 245, 270.

[29] *Yale*, vii. 63.

[30] Ibid. 70.

honour upon themselves and their art, in proportion as they separate themselves from the sympathies of men.[31]

Just so Johnson: 'Addison speaks the language of poets, and Shakespeare, of men.'[32] Clearly, Wordsworth's discussion of poetic language shares with Johnson certain convictions about the nature of poetry itself. By saying that, as a poet, he aspires to speak 'the real language of men', he declares his belief that it is not for anything in the process of poetic stylization that poetry matters, but for the reality of the human situations by which it is inspired and to which it refers: 'What is a Poet? To whom does he address himself? And what language is to be expected from him?—He is a man speaking to men . . .'.[33] The poet's special skill with language is not, in a strict sense, creative, but is good simply to articulate and to communicate feelings which do not themselves depend on poetry for their existence or their value. Coleridge's disagreement here is fundamental, as he had indeed suspected almost from the start; in 1802 he wrote to Sotheby:

Metre itself implies a *passion*, i.e. a state of excitement, both in the Poet's mind, & is expected in that of the Reader—and tho' I stated this to Wordsworth, & he has in some sort stated it in his preface, yet he has [not] done justice to it, nor has he in my opinion sufficiently answered it. In my opinion, Poetry justifies, as *Poetry* independent of any other Passion, some new combinations of Language, & *commands* the omission of many others . . . We have had lately some little controversy on this subject—& we begin to suspect, that there is, somewhere or other, a *radical* Difference [in our] opinions.[34]

Yet in the *Biographia* Coleridge is most unwilling to admit just how radical this difference is, and even while he dwells on his criticisms he minimizes their significance. Certain details in the *Lyrical Ballads* preface are misleadingly phrased, he suggests, and the poetry has occasional lapses into anticlimax, partly misguided in this by the imperfections of the theory, but these are represented as being minor, insignificant matters which should not be allowed to distract us from the true Wordsworthian elevation of sentiment and style. In taking issue with 'the real language of men' he does not openly engage with

[31] Wordsworth, *Poetical Works*, ii. 387.
[32] *Yale*, vii. 84.
[33] Wordsworth, *Poetical Works*, ii. 393.
[34] Coleridge, *Letters*, ii. 812 (no. 444: 13 July 1802).

Wordsworth's larger meaning at all, but, taking the phrase more narrowly to denote a stringent linguistic naturalism, chooses to concentrate his fire on that idea instead: on the technical point Coleridge's critique is overwhelming, but the more fundamental issue gets buried in the process, so that when in chapter XX Coleridge comes triumphantly to declare that much the greater part of Wordsworth's poetry does not conform even to the spirit of his theory, this being 'precluded by higher powers',[35] it is hard for us to recall how profoundly Wordsworth himself might wish to disagree. In fact, Coleridge's criticisms are radical in their implications, but covertly or unwillingly so; in the *Biographia* he effectively edits Wordsworth into a poet of the Coleridgean imagination, minimizing or suppressing the tension resulting from the equally Wordsworthian commitment to truth to nature, so that he acknowledges nothing problematic in including Wordsworth's 'perfect truth to nature' as third in the hierarchy of poetic virtues crowned by his 'gift of IMAGINATION'.[36] It is therefore interesting to note a conversation between them recorded by Crabb Robinson shortly after the publication of the *Biographia*, in which we see Wordsworth *forcing* the opposition of nature and imagination on to a reluctant Coleridge:

> Coleridge spoke of painting in that style of mysticism which is now his habit of feeling. Wordsworth met this by dry, unfeeling contradiction. The manner of Coleridge towards Wordsworth was most respectful, but Wordsworth towards Coleridge was cold and scornful. Coleridge maintained that painting was not an art which could operate on the vulgar, and Wordsworth declared this opinion to be degrading to the art. Coleridge illustrated his assertions by reference to Raphael's Madonnas. Wordsworth could not think that a field for high intellect lay within such a subject as a mother and child.

Robinson adds drily: 'Independently of the unfeeling manner, I thought Wordsworth substantially wrong. It was not so clear to me that Coleridge was right.'[37]

Crabb Robinson was right: it was an unhappy dichotomy. Clearly, Coleridge was uncomfortable to find himself opposing all that the Wordsworth of *Lyrical Ballads* held most dear. What he wanted was an approach that would reconcile this opposition, permitting him

---

[35] Coleridge, *Biographia Literaria*, ii. 77.   [36] Ibid. 121, 124.
[37] *Henry Crabb Robinson on Books and their Writers*, ed. Edith J. Morley (3 vols.; 1938), i. 214 f.

to say, in the words of Polixenes which he quotes in the *Biographia*, 'the art itself is nature'. Merely to speak of Wordsworth's 'fine balance of truth in observing, with the imaginative faculty in modifying the objects observed'[38] would not do; to make that idea of 'balance' something more than hopeful metaphor, what was needed was for the poet's imaginative vision to be a revelation, as well as a transmutation, of the objective world of experience. The great philosophical poem that Coleridge desiderated of Wordsworth was one that would show 'true Idealism necessarily perfecting itself in Realism, & Realism refining itself into Idealism'.[39] Only then could the cry go up with Leontes at the end of *The Winter's Tale*: 'If this be magic, let it be an art | Lawful as eating.'

For the theoretical reconciliation of these opposites Coleridge went to Schelling's philosophy of transcendental idealism, in the brief period of enthusiasm to which the *Biographia* bears witness; but even in the *Biographia* his embrace of Schelling is equivocal, and the resolution offered by transcendental idealism did not prove satisfying. This was not only because of the difficulties it presented to Coleridge's Christian beliefs. In theory, Schelling provides just what was needed; while retaining the principle of the mind's sovereign creativity, he appears to abolish the dualism of mind and nature by raising nature itself to its true dignity as the product and expression of imagination. 'What we call nature is a poem lying pent in a mysterious and wonderful script.'[40] Rewritten in the language of transcendental idealism, Polixenes's argument sounds like this:

The primal activity of imagination *is* the capacity of making poetry as its first level of activity, and *vice versa* what we call the capacity for making poetry is nothing other than the repetition of the activity of productive imagination raised to its highest power. What is active in both is one and the same, the one means by which we can bring together contradictions in our thought—the imagination.[41]

In Coleridge's terms, the primary imagination by which our experience of an 'external' world comes into being and the secondary imagination

---

[38] Coleridge, *Biographia Literaria*, i. 59.

[39] Coleridge, *Letters*, iv. 575 (no. 969: to William Wordsworth, 30 May 1815).

[40] *Schellings Werke*, ed. Manfred Schröter (13 vols.; Munich, 1946–59), ii. 628. For a lucid exposition of Coleridge's relation to transcendental idealism, see G. N. G. Orsini, *Coleridge and German Idealism* (Carbondale, Ill. 1969).

[41] Schelling, *Werke*, ii. 626.

by which we make and apprehend poetry are different manifestations of the same fundamental power. Poetry's fusion of subject and object enacts, according to Schelling, the primal identity of mind and world, so bringing to consciousness the foundations of all being; great art, far from setting the mind over against nature (Schelling's chief complaint against Fichte's system),[42] is 'the mediatress between, and reconciler of, nature and man':[43]

Every fine painting comes into being through the removal of what one might call the invisible partition that separates the real from the ideal world; it is in itself no more than the gateway to the world of imagination, from which come forth in their entirety those shapes and places which but glimmer imperfectly through the real. To the artist, nature is nothing other than that which it is to the philosopher, being only the ideal world as it appears under permanent restrictions, or only the imperfect reflection of a world that exists, not outside him, but within.[44]

Schlegel, who quotes that passage in his own lectures on aesthetics,[45] espoused transcendental idealism explicitly because it appeared to him to resolve the dualism bequeathed by Kant;[46] romantic art, according to Schlegel, is characterized by 'the striving to reconcile these two worlds of the spirit and the senses between which we feel ourselves divided, and to fuse them indissolubly together'.[47] But, although a transcendentalist may throw dualism out of the front door, it is always liable to seep back up through the floorboards: the ambiguity intrinsic to this way of thinking is precisely caught by the title of M. H. Abrams's study, *Natural Supernaturalism*. Even if we acknowledge a sense in which the vision of romantic art is 'natural', imitative of *natura naturans* if not *naturata*,[48] revealing the ideality of the very world in which we live, and even if we accept the metaphysic which that would seem to imply, there still remains a stubborn sense in which that vision is also 'supernatural', its specialness necessarily implying a (mere) world of phenomenal experience that is to be transfigured, transcended, rendered symbolic, or otherwise redeemed by the imaginative activity of the mind.

---

[42] See ibid. iii. 630.
[43] Coleridge, *Biographia Literaria*, ii. 253; cf. Schelling, *Werke*, supplementary vol. iii. 392.   [44] Schelling, *Werke*, ii. 628.
[45] Schlegel, ii. 81.   [46] See ibid. ii. 51 f., 72.   [47] Ibid. v. 26.
[48] The argument is put in these terms by Schelling (*Werke*, supplementary vol. iii. 393), Schlegel (ii. 90 f.), and Coleridge (*Biographia Literaria*, ii. 257).

Schelling cannot escape this ambiguity; in his essay 'On the Relation of the Fine Arts to Nature' he says of the artist:

He must therefore distance himself from the product or created entity, but only so that he may rise to the creative power itself and inwardly possess it. By doing this he goes over into the realm of pure ideas; he leaves behind the created entity in order to win it back again with a thousandfold profit and in this sense to return to nature.[49]

The stubborn question remains, Is the 'nature' to which we thus return the same nature that we left behind? Wellek believes not:

Both for Schelling and for Coleridge the distinctions between consciousness and being, form and matter prove after all insurmountable. Both of them merely postulate this synthesis as an ideal, both of them recognize the deficiencies of a Kantian dualism, but they never succeeded in carrying out this synthesis speculatively.[50]

Other, more sympathetic commentators preserve the careful ambiguity of Schelling's 'in this sense'. Korff, for example, writes of the doctrine of the first generation of German Romantics: 'It is precisely the "natural" world which is not the "true" one. The truth is rather to be found in the *Aufhebung* of the world of nature.'[51] *Aufhebung*—a term used by both Schelling and Schlegel for the 'poeticization' of nature—can mean 'preservation', 'elevation', and 'removal, dissolution, nullification'; all these meanings are held in suspension together. Muirhead summarizes Coleridge's view in a similar way: 'The world we meet in art is the world of sense, but it is the world of sense twice-born.'[52] A hostile commentator such as Wellek will regard this as mere self-contradiction, as the desire to have one's theoretical cake and eat it; a more appreciative reader will observe that this seeming contradiction is only the most fundamental of the

---

[49] Schelling, *Werke*, suppl. vol. iii. 401; paraphrased by Coleridge in his lecture 'Poesy or Art', in *Miscellaneous Criticism*, ed. T. M. Raysor (1936), 210.

[50] René Wellek, *Immanuel Kant in England, 1793–1838* (Princeton, NJ, 1931), 101.

[51] H. A. Korff, *Geist der Goethezeit: Versuch einer ideellen Entwicklung der klassisch-romantischen Literaturgeschichte*, 8th edn. (4 vols.; Leipzig, 1966), iii. 279.

[52] J. H. Muirhead, *Coleridge as Philosopher* (1930), 210. This ambiguity is recognized also in M. H. Abrams, *Natural Supernaturalism: Tradition and Revolution in Romantic Literature* (1971), 183 f.; E. D. Hirsch, Jun., *Wordsworth and Schelling: A Typological Study of Romanticism* (New Haven, Conn., 1960), p. 125; and R. W. Ewton, *The Literary Theories of August Wilhelm Schlegel* (The Hague, 1972), 68.

oppositions which the romantic imagination is called upon to resolve. But what is in any case clear is that to the question, 'Does such romantic theory exalt the mind at the expense of nature?', we can, at the level of theory, only ever get an ambiguous or equivocal reply.

To understand the true tendency of the romantic approach, then, and so to recognize more precisely the alternative priorities involved in Johnson's account, we need to turn from critical theory to critical practice, and to ask how, in practice, Schlegel and Coleridge read Shakespeare, and what happens to 'general nature' in the process. What we find is that Schlegel's adherence to Schelling's theory of art did not hinder him in the slightest from setting the reflecting mind decisively over above the motions of human life on which it reflects. To see into human nature with Shakespearean penetration, Schlegel believes, is necessarily to withdraw from it:

No-one has ever depicted as he has done the silent self-deception, the semi-conscious hypocrisy towards oneself with which even noble minds disguise the almost inevitable influence of egotistical drives in human nature. This secret irony in the characterization is something we admire for its infinite depth of penetration; but it is painful to all enthusiasm. For this is what one comes to when one has had the misfortune to see human nature through and through; there then remains only the choice between the melancholy truth that no virtue or greatness is altogether pure and genuine, and the dangerous error of supposing that the highest perfection might be attainable. Here I sense in the poet himself—even while he is exciting the most powerful emotions—a certain coldness: the coldness of a superior mind which has run through the circle of human existence and has survived the death of feeling.[53]

The spiritual detachment which Schlegel salutes in Shakespeare is something deeply incompatible with Johnson's response to human frailty and shortcoming—for which he too claims Shakespearean warrant—as also with Johnson's emphasis on the value and pleasure of participation. It is true that he, like Schlegel, found moments of 'coldness' in Shakespeare:

He no sooner begins to move, than he counteracts himself; and terrour and pity, as they are rising in the mind, are checked and blasted by sudden frigidity.[54]

---

[53] Schlegel, vi. 136.   [54] Yale, vii. 74.

But he marked such moments down as faults or lapses from the power that made Shakespeare a classic; how far he was from regarding them as the marks of a 'superior mind' can be gauged from his response to the ironic detachment that he found in the metaphysical poets:

They never enquired what on any occasion they should have said or done, but wrote rather as beholders than partakers of human nature; as beings looking upon good and evil, impassive and at leisure; as Epicurean deities making remarks on the actions of men and the vicissitudes of life, without interest and without emotion.[55]

The difference between Johnson and one kind of romantic response to Shakespeare is there clear-cut: the 'superiority' for which Johnson attacks the metaphysicals is precisely that which Coleridge, like Schlegel, can be found celebrating in Shakespeare. It is very much in terms of 'beholding' rather than 'partaking' that Coleridge characterizes the qualities of poetic genius manifest in *Venus and Adonis*:

It is throughout as if a superior spirit more intuitive, more intimately conscious even than the characters themselves, not only of every outward look and act, but of the flux and reflux of the mind in all its subtlest thoughts and feelings, were placing the whole before our view; himself meanwhile unparticipating in the passions, and actuated only by that pleasureable excitement, which had resulted from the energetic fervor of his own spirit in so vividly exhibiting, what it had so accurately and profoundly contemplated.[56]

Very noticeable there is Coleridge's concern to bring out both poet's and reader's 'unparticipation' in the poem's sexuality, or what he calls 'the unpleasing nature of the subject'.[57] The Coleridgean poetic imagination turns 'Bodies to spirit by sublimation strange', even, it seems, when the bodies in question are those of Venus and Adonis; in the *Biographia* he stresses with approval how 'Shakespeare has here represented the animal impulse itself, so as to preclude all

---

[55] Samuel Johnson, *Lives of the English Poets*, ed. G. B. Hill (3 vols.; 1905), i. 20.

[56] Coleridge, *Biographia Literaria*, ii. 15.

[57] Coleridge, *Biographia Literaria*, ii. 16. For Coleridge's difficulty in accepting sexuality, see Norman Fruman, *Coleridge: The Damaged Archangel* (1972), 365–420, esp. pp. 370–3. Fruman's commentary is perhaps malevolent, but Lockridge, a more sympathetic commentator, also speaks of Coleridge's 'profound repulsion by sexuality' (*Coleridge the Moralist*, p. 81).

sympathy with it', and in his notes on the poem he speaks of
Shakespeare's 'thinking faculty and thereby perfect abstraction from
himself; he works exactly as if of another planet, as describing
the movements of two butterflies.'[58] This liberation from animal
impulse is achieved by means of 'the poet's ever active mind', which
draws us up from the dangerous world of the flesh into its ceaseless
play of imagery and reflection, or what Coleridge elsewhere notes
as Shakespeare's 'endless activity of thought, in all the possible
associations of thought with thought, thought with feelings, or with
words, or of feelings with feelings, and words with words'.[59] Thus
the reader of *Venus and Adonis*, according to Coleridge in the
Biographia, 'is forced into too much action to sympathize with
the merely passive of our nature'. For the mode of response which
this precludes, one needs to think of Johnson's pleasure in the *repose*
of the mind that Shakespeare confers, and of his belief that too much
purely mental activity gets in the way of emotions coming from a
deeper, less conscious seat of self. 'Attention has no relief; the
affections are never moved.'[60] Coleridge and Johnson understand
the psychology of imaginative response similarly here, but come to
opposite conclusions; there are some affections in which Coleridge
thinks it well not to participate. Hence his Shakespeare can be praised
for writing 'as if of another planet', whereas for Johnson, as for
Wordsworth, the true poet writes as 'a man speaking to men'.[61]

As has already been pointed out, it was only with one part of his
mind that Coleridge read Shakespeare for his '*aloofness*' from those
states of human feeling 'of which he is at once the painter and the
analyst'.[62] Schlegel is in this respect both more consistent and more
thoroughgoing; tragedy, comedy, and Shakespeare's mingling of the
two are separately discussed, and each is read in such a way as to
make for the liberation of the mind from its participation in the world
of nature. For tragedy, Schlegel draws upon Kant's theory of the

---

[58] Coleridge, *Biographia Literaria*, ii, 16; *Shakespearean Criticism*, i. 193.

[59] Coleridge, *Biographia Literaria*, ii, 16; *Shakespearean Criticism*, i, 192.

[60] Johnson, *Lives of the Poets*, i. 55.

[61] Part of this difference in emphasis is due to the differing context of contemporary
taste. Johnson stresses how Shakespeare comes home to the reader partly in order
to distinguish him from the ideal represented by Addison's *Cato*: Coleridge stresses
his aloofness from ordinary life partly in order to distinguish him from Richardson
and Kotzebue. Such positions are not *necessarily* opposed. However, the difference
in question here goes beyond what could be explained in those terms.

[62] Coleridge, *Biographia Literaria*, ii. 16.

sublime. According to this, the sublime arises when the perception of man's apparent helplessness before the forces to which he may be subjected within the phenomenal world calls out in response the realization of the unconditioned and indestructible freedom of the transcendental self. The significance of this theory in Schlegel's hands is vividly conveyed by his student and patroness, Madame de Staël, in her account of Kant in *De l'Allemagne*:

Le pouvoir du destin et l'immensité de la nature sont dans une opposition infinie avec la misérable dépendance de la créature sur la terre; mais une étincelle du feu sacré dans notre sein triomphe de l'univers, puisqu'il suffit de cette étincelle pour résister à ce que toutes les forces du monde pourroient exiger de nous.

Le premier effet du sublime est d'accabler l'homme; et le second, de le relever. . . . Personne ne sauroit définir ce qui est, pour ainsi dire, au sommet de notre existence; *nous sommes trop élevés à l'égard de nous-mêmes, pour nous comprendre*, dit St. Augustin.[63]

For Schlegel, what is desperate or terrible in the situation of the tragic protagonist serves to intimate that *there is a world elsewhere* (to recall Coriolanus's cry as he 'banishes' the populace of Rome), a world in which the spirit rises indomitable over all that can befall it in its phenomenal aspect. Even the ending of *King Lear* cannot altogether quench that response in Schlegel: 'The poet shows us here that, to be established in its full extent, this faith in Providence requires a larger space than our dark earthly life.'[64]

This firm division between higher and lower realms of our being is preserved in Schlegel's approach to comedy. Human frailty, folly, and vice, if taken at all seriously, are felt to be damaging to the ideality of literature, and must therefore appear in comedy as essentially trivial things, the laughable manifestations of our lower, animal nature, without connection with or bearing on our higher powers of mind:

The imperfections of people and the incongruous relationships into which they fall are, when represented in comedy, no longer the objects of our disapproval or of our sorrow; instead, these strange contrarieties serve to entertain the understanding and to delight the fancy. The comic poet must, therefore, exclude anything that could arouse moral indignation at the conduct or true sympathy with the situation of his characters, as this would

[63] Madame de Staël Holstein, *De l'Allemagne* (3 vols.; Paris, 1810: repr. London, 1813), iii. 88 f.   [64] Schlegel, vi. 178.

certainly cause us to fall back into an attitude of seriousness. He must present their irregular conduct as arising from the dominance of what is sensual in their characters, and what happens to them must be depicted as merely ludicrous distresses which can have no damaging consequences.[65]

It is this general view of comedy that leads Schlegel to prefer Molière's farces to *Le Misanthrope*: he speaks of Molière's misguided attempt, probably influenced by Boileau, 'to unite what by their very natures cannot be united, dignity and merriment'.[66] It is plain from this why Schlegel could not subscribe to Johnson's defence of Shakespeare's mingling of comic and serious as evoking the true mingled nature of things. For the German critic, it is precisely the value of such 'mingled' effects that they function as a form of romantic irony, weakening rather than strengthening our sense of the claims of reality upon us; at such moments, Schlegel sees Shakespeare as a kind of Prospero:

In this way he enters into a sort of secret understanding with those select few among his readers or spectators who possess true insight into things; he shows them that their objections have been anticipated and conceded in advance; that he himself is not tied down to the represented object but floats freely above it; and that, if he chose differently, he could annihilate without compunction the beautiful and irresistibly attractive piece of illusion which he himself conjured up.[67]

'Be chearful, Sir: Our revels now are ended.' Yet Prospero's hymn to the insubstantiality of life, we may recall, is associated with a notably tense resistance to the all-too-substantial intrusions of Caliban upon the ideal scheme of things, and Schlegel, in his discussion of comedy, manifests what may be thought a very similar tenseness:

The comic poet—seeing that his task requires him always to be sailing close to the wind—must, above all, take care not to allow what is mean and base in human nature any opportunity of expressing itself. If the sense of shame which normally forces such ignoble tendencies back behind the bounds of decency is once overcome by the sight of others' participation in them, then our inherent sympathy with what is vile will soon break out with unrestrained insolence.[68]

The sense of general nature is precisely that which Schlegel's comic poet must avoid at all costs: if comedy necessarily deals with 'the

---

[65] Ibid. v. 42 f.   [66] Ibid. vi. 87.
[67] Ibid. 137.   [68] Ibid. v. 37.

imperfections of people', then let it be careful to observe the divide that separates such imperfections from our nobler and more serious selves, let it not presume to implicate *us* in the exhibition of folly by which we are to be diverted. Unlike Johnson on Falstaff, Schlegel believes that there are truths about our frail and fallen human nature which comedy must exclude or conceal.

Yet Schlegel, no less than Johnson, finds Falstaff to epitomize his ideal of comedy. It is worth pausing to compare the accounts they each give, partly because comedy provides the natural touchstone for what the mind may forfeit in making claims for its own superior powers, and partly because the comparison is in this case peculiarly revealing, Schlegel having almost certainly used Johnson's note as the basis for his own remarks:

Falstaff is the most agreeable and entertaining good-for-nothing ever depicted. His contemptible qualities are not disguised: a lascivious and slovenly old man, enormously fat and constantly with an eye to his own comforts as regards food, drink, and sleep; forever in debt and with few scruples as to how he comes by his money; a cowardly soldier and a lying braggart, a flatterer who speaks ill of his friends behind their backs, despite all this at no point does he arouse our indignation or dislike. We see that his tender care for himself is without any admixture of malice towards others: it is simply that he doesn't wish to be disturbed in the peaceful enjoyment of his sensuality, and this he obtains by his quickness of mind.[69]

The structure of the thought here—a piling up of Falstaff's despicable qualities, then the remarking of how notwithstanding he is a far from repulsive figure—is the same as in Johnson's note (see above, p. 48), and what is being said is broadly similar. Yet two differences are crucial. Firstly, Schlegel has softened Falstaff into the most harmless of rogues; his description has nothing corresponding to these phrases of Johnson's: '. . . always ready to cheat the weak, and prey upon the poor; to terrify the timorous and insult the defenceless. At once obsequious and malignant . . .'. And, secondly, Schlegel's account completely omits Johnson's very vigorous emphasis on Falstaff's power of attraction; whereas Johnson speaks of Hal as positively 'seduced by Falstaff', for example, Schlegel declares that 'what is ignoble touches him without leaving a mark'.[70] These changes mean that the force of the truth at which Johnson marvels—that *such* a

[69] Ibid. vi. 190 f.   [70] Ibid. 189.

contemptible figure should be such a *delightful* companion—entirely disappears: Schlegel's Falstaff is a creature too low in the scale of being to be felt as seriously immoral, dangerous, or seductive, and the statement that despite his contemptible qualities he never arouses our indignation or dislike expresses a cool, perhaps somewhat complacent, sense of superiority. By contrast, Johnson's feeling for Falstaff as his fellow creature—'mon semblable, mon frère'[71]—not only causes him to feel profoundly Falstaff's power to seduce, it also involves an intensely pleasurable generosity of response that breaks out in his use of the second person, and of the old form of that person: 'But Falstaff unimitated, unimitable Falstaff, how shall I describe thee?' '*Thou*', Johnson states in the *Dictionary*, 'is used only in very familiar or very solemn language'; to inferiors, and in 'addresses of worship'. Falstaff—'Thou compound of sense and vice; of sense which may be admired but not esteemed, of vice which may be despised, but hardly detested'—requires the full range of the word's implication.

Such generosity of response is absent also from Coleridge's account, although with a difference, since Coleridge, unlike Schlegel, does take seriously Falstaff's moral depravity. But in Coleridge, as not in Johnson, the movement towards morally engaged judgement seems to have been a movement away from participation and fellowship. In conversation with Crabb Robinson, Coleridge spoke of how Shakespeare 'delighted in portraying characters in which the intellectual powers were found in a preeminent degree, while the moral faculties were wanting, at the same time that he taught the superiority of moral greatness.' Along with Iago and Richard III, Coleridge instanced Falstaff, whom he found 'content to be thought both a liar and a coward in order to obtain influence over the minds of his associates. His aggravated lies about the robbery are conscious and purposed.'[72] What must have been a very similar conversation was recorded by Collier, and the same view of Falstaff as motivated throughout by his desire for power, a hypocrite even in his pleasures, appears in the report of the lectures at Bristol in 1813.[73] For the relevant lecture some of Coleridge's own notes also survive:

[71] See Baudelaire's poem, 'Au Lecteur'.
[72] Coleridge, *Shakespearean Criticism*, ii. 165 f.
[73] See ibid. ii. 237 f., and *Coleridge on Shakespeare*, p. 30.

. . . in his most impressive and in his own favourite characters the subordination of the moral to the intellectual being. . . . The first introduction of
Falstaff, the conscious intentionality of his wit, so that when it does not
flow of its own accord, its absence is felt, and effort visibly employed to
recall it; and the pride gratified in the power of influencing a prince of the
blood, the heir apparent, by means of it.[74]

In that thought about Shakespeare's delight in characters in whom
the moral faculties are subordinated to the intellectual, Coleridge
was drawing on Johnson's note on Parolles:

Parolles has many of the lineaments of Falstaff, and seems to be the character
which Shakespeare delighted to draw, a fellow that had more wit than virtue.
Though justice required that he should be detected and exposed, yet his 'vices
sit so fit in him' that he is not at last suffered to starve.[75]

But what is absent from Coleridge's portrait of Falstaff is anything
corresponding to Johnson's sense that the vices of such a character
'sit so fit in him' that he wins our liking, although not our approval,
so that, like Hal on the battlefield at Shrewsbury, we feel that we
could 'better spare a better man'. There is a great difference between
Coleridge's saying that in *Henry IV* Shakespeare teaches 'the
superiority of moral greatness' and Johnson's finding the moral of
the play to be that no such moral superiority is possible—'neither
wit nor honesty', he says, ought to think themselves safe with a
companion like Falstaff. Johnson's Falstaff is so dangerous because
we cannot help but warm to him even while we see him for what
he is; Coleridge, by contrast, can and does refrain from such
dangerous sympathy, as witness his finding in Falstaff's displays of
wit 'conscious intentionality', 'labour', 'effort visibly employed'.[76]
Where such intentionality is felt, our pleasure drains away. Falstaff's
preposterous lies about the Gad's Hill affair, for example, lose much
of their power to please if they are seen as part of a deep game that
he is playing for influence over Hal, as unequivocally 'conscious
and purposed', rather than being felt to flow from his absolute
irresponsibility to any truths or facts which contradict his desires
of the moment—an irresponsibility at once childlike and ruthless,
and one which, although itself clearly willed (because rejoiced in)
by Falstaff, is at the same time so fundamental to his nature as to

---

[74] Coleridge, *Shakespearean Criticism*, i. 206 f.   [75] *Yale*, vii. 399.
[76] Coleridge, *Shakespearean Criticism*, ii. 238.

baffle any attempt to bring the charge of downright insincerity to bear. We know that in the 1818 course of lectures Coleridge allowed Falstaff wit but denied him humour,[77] and despite the fragmentary nature of the evidence it does seem that he consistently drove at the moral issue in a way that ruled out being *pleased* by Falstaff. One recalls Carlyle's impression of Coleridge in later life:

In general he seemed deficient in laughter; or indeed in sympathy for concrete human things either on the sunny or on the stormy side. One right peal of concrete laughter at some convicted flesh-and-blood absurdity . . . how strange would it have been in that Kantean haze-world, and how infinitely cheering.[78]

This is not to suggest that Coleridge did not relish the comedy of the Falstaff scenes: rather that for him the comedy was all at Falstaff's expense, conferring on us a viewpoint simply superior to Falstaff's powers of attraction. How one feels about this depends in part on how one takes the tricky matter of Hal's relationship to Falstaff. Johnson believed Hal positively 'seduced', but Coleridge found him to come out the easy winner of all his contests; he speaks of 'the defeat of mere intellect by a noble feeling, the Prince being the superior moral character who rises above his insidious companion', and of 'the ease with which Prince Henry parries his shaft'.[79] Such a reading aligns itself with Hal's opening soliloquy, in which he assures both himself and us of his command of the situation and of the latent nobility of his proceeding—although that soliloquy can also be read rather differently: Johnson was disinclined to take it at face value, and found it to give 'a natural picture of a great mind offering excuses to itself, and palliating those follies which it can neither justify nor forsake'.[80] But whether or not Coleridge's reading is the more convincing one, there is, arguably, a price to be paid for embracing it: we lose our hold on nature. To banish plump Jack in the wrong way is to banish all the world; we may say of Coleridge's reading what Falstaff says of Hal, that his grace says that which his flesh rebels against.

There is at least one place in the Shakespeare criticism where Coleridge himself seems to be aware of what may be jeopardized

---

[77] See Coleridge, *Miscellaneous Criticism*, pp. 50, 111.
[78] Thomas Carlyle, *The Life of John Sterling* (1851), p. 74.
[79] Coleridge, *Shakespearean Criticism*, ii. 238, 166.
[80] *Yale*, vii. 458.

by an approach to Shakespeare that allows so much to the free creative powers of the mind. That place is his characterization of Hamlet; 'a person in whose view the external world, and all its objects, were comparatively dim and of no interest in themselves, and which began to interest only when they were reflected in the mirror of his mind.'[81] It is this predisposition, Coleridge believes, that makes for Hamlet's alienation from the world of action: 'His thoughts, images, and fancy far more vivid than his perceptions . . . hence great, enormous, intellectual activity, and a consequent proportionate aversion to real action.'[82] Many readers have noted an element of self-identification there; Coleridge described himself to Godwin as a man whose 'unhealthy & reverie-like vividness of *Thoughts*, & . . . diminished Impressibility from *Things*' had rendered his ideas, wishes, and feelings 'to a diseased degree disconnected from *motion* & *action*'.[83] What may be more precisely observed is how this Hamlet's ceaseless conversion of things into thoughts, external experience into internal meditation, is reflected in the manner of much of Coleridge's critical writing. With its continual speculative movement from what Shakespeare writes to how Shakespeare writes, from the product to the process, from the dramatic achievement to the conditions and implications of that achievement, this carries the assumption that the main interest of the plays resides in a significance of which the life represented in them can be only a sign, of little intrinsic interest until taken up into the life of the mind and seen as the product of that life. Critical understanding, Coleridge's manner often suggests, is virtually to be identified with a maximum of self-consciousness; the endeavour is to perceive the very quicksilver in the mirror that Shakespeare holds up to nature. And in this Coleridge has much in common with Hamlet, as he describes him:

It is the nature of thought to be indefinite, while definiteness belongs to reality. The sense of sublimity arises, not from the sight of an outward object, but from the reflection upon it; not from the impression, but from the idea. Few have seen a celebrated waterfall without feeling something of disappointment: it is only subsequently, by reflection, that the idea of the waterfall comes full into the mind, and brings with it a train of sublime

---

[81] *Coleridge on Shakespeare*, p. 124.
[82] Coleridge's *Shakespearean Criticism*, i. 34.
[83] Coleridge, *Letters*, ii. 782 (no. 432: to William Godwin, 22 Jan. 1802).

associations. Hamlet felt this: in him we see a mind that keeps itself in a state of abstraction, and beholds external objects as hieroglyphics. His soliloquy, 'Oh that this too, too solid flesh would melt,' arises from a craving after the indefinite: a disposition or temper which most easily besets men of genius; a morbid craving for that which is not.[84]

Moreover, in his ceaseless desire to transmute outward impressions into the more satisfying ideas of the mind, Coleridge's Hamlet resembles not only the critical intelligence that can thus describe him but also Coleridge's Shakespeare, in whom, as we have seen, 'meditation' predominates over 'observation', and 'materials' are subordinated to 'Ideas'. 'The poet, or original philosopher' Coleridge defines as one in whom the images of the mind 'become a satisfying world of themselves';[85] by this criterion Hamlet, with his 'prodigality of beautiful words, which are, as it were, the half embodyings of thoughts, that make them more than thoughts, give them an outness, a reality *sui generis*, and yet retain their correspondence and shadowy approach to the images and movements within',[86] is a philosopher poet manqué, whose 'great, enormous, intellectual activity' recalls what Coleridge identifies in *Venus and Adonis* as 'the poet's ever active mind'.

But, whereas in *Venus and Adonis* Coleridge speaks of that imaginative activity with unqualified approval, it is remarkable that in Hamlet he should have described that same predominance of mind—a disposition 'which most easily besets men of genius'— as *morbid*. He might easily have found in Hamlet's 'aversion to externals'[87] and 'craving after the indefinite' a noble idealism tragically at odds with the condition of earthly life (as Friedrich Schlegel had done).[88] Instead, by diagnosing morbidity in Hamlet, and drawing from the play the moral necessity of 'a due balance between the real and the imaginary world',[89] Coleridge offers an implicit

---

[84] Coleridge, *Shakespearean Criticism*, ii. 224.

[85] Ibid. i. 73.   [86] Ibid. 35.   [87] Ibid.

[88] See his letter to August Wilhelm, 19 June 1793, repr. in *Shakespeare in Germany 1740–1815*, ed. Roy Pascal (Cambridge, 1937), 128. Friedrich carried this view over into his general account of Shakespeare, where he firmly distinguishes the real Shakespeare whose craving after the indefinite is expressed in the lyrical and idyllic passages scattered throughout his work from the professional dramatist obliged grimly to hold up his mirror to the real; see lecture xii of his *Geschichte der alten und neuen Literatur*, in *Kritische Friedrich—Schlegel—Ausgabe*, ed. E. Behler (Munich, 1958–), vi. 291 f.

[89] Coleridge, *Shakespearean Criticism*, i. 34; see also *The Friend*, i. 452–5.

critique of his own general account of the imagination, or at least reveals more of its implications than he allows himself to do elsewhere. This is not to suggest that Coleridge here positively undermines that account: what is morbid in life may very well not be morbid as art. But what his notes on Hamlet do strongly suggest, with a quasi-confessional honesty entirely characteristic of Coleridge at his most illuminating, is the necessary cost of the romantic reading of Shakespeare in terms of participation in general nature; they define one aspect of the polarity that exists between the romantic reading and that of Johnson:

Reasons why *taedium vitae* oppresses minds like Hamlet's: the exhaustion of bodily feeling from perpetual exertion of mind; that all mental form being indefinite and ideal, realities must needs become cold.[90]

The Defiant Imagination—Lear—Audience Identification and Dramatic Illusion

In both Schlegel and Coleridge, the emphasis on the free creativity of the imagination is intertwined with, and partly supported by, the philosophical idealism to which they were both attracted. The romantic reading of Shakespeare does not, however, depend on idealist thought, and in certain respects its implications appear more clearly when it stands free of its philosophical scaffolding. Hazlitt was a man entirely sceptical of any notion of the transcendental, and who emphatically did not look to Shakespeare for effects of aloofness and irony;[1] his account of Shakespeare is remarkable for the directness and carelessness of theory with which it evokes his experience of the plays, and for its willingness to locate the roots of imaginative experience in the familiar passions of human life. Yet all this does not make Hazlitt a Johnsonian; his opposition to Johnson's Shakespeare was vigorous and unequivocal, and he regarded Schlegel's lectures on Shakespeare as 'by far the best account which has been given of the plays'.[2]

In his review of Schlegel's lectures on the drama, this is what Hazlitt makes of the distinction between the classical and the romantic in poetry:

---

[90] Coleridge, *Shakespearean Criticism*, i. 35.
[1] The exception that proves the rule concerns the peculiarly problematic *Troilus and Cressida*; see Hazlitt, iv. 225.   [2] Ibid. xvi. 59.

The two principles of imitation and imagination . . . are not only distinct, but almost opposite. For the imagination is that power which represents objects, not as they are, but as they are moulded according to our fancies and feelings. . . . This language is not the less true to nature because it is false in point of fact; but so much the more true and natural, if it conveys the impression which the object under the influence of passion makes on the mind. . . . When Lear calls upon the Heavens to avenge his cause, 'for they are old like him,' there is nothing extravagant or impious in this sublime identification of his age with theirs; for there is no other image which could do justice to the agonising sense of his wrongs and his despair!

The great difference, then, which we find between the classical and the romantic style, between ancient and modern poetry, is, that the one more frequently describes things as they are interesting in themselves,—the other for the sake of the associations of ideas connected with them . . . Florimel, in Spenser, where she is described sitting on the ground in the Witch's hut, is not classical, though in the highest degree poetical and romantic: for the incidents and situation are in themselves mean and disagreeable, till they are redeemed by the genius of the poet, and converted, by the very contrast, into a source of the utmost pathos and elevation of sentiment. . . . Even Lear is not classical; for he is a poor crazy old man, who has nothing sublime about him but his afflictions, and who dies of a broken heart.[3]

The function of true poetry, it would seem, is to supply things with the imaginative interest which in themselves they lack. Hazlitt expounds this view at some length in his lecture 'On Poetry in General',[4] written immediately after the book on Shakespeare, and this unJohnsonian distinction between art which is imaginative (therefore poetic) and inferior art which is merely representational recurs throughout his criticism, although the terms in which it is expressed vary according to the context. Prose can be the foil to poetry:

The poet spreads the colours of fancy, the illusions of his own mind, round every object, *ad libitum*; the prose-writer is compelled to extract his materials patiently and bit by bit, from his subject.[5]

Scott's novels are contrasted to Shakespearean drama on similar grounds:

---

[3] Ibid. 63, 61. Hazlitt uses the same formulation in the conclusion to his own *Lectures on the Literature of the Age of Elizabeth*: see Hazlitt, vi. 348–50.

[4] See ibid. v. 2–4.

[5] Ibid. xii. 9.

Sir Walter is an imitator of nature and nothing more; but I think Shakespear is infinitely more than this. The creative principle is every where restless and redundant in Shakespear . . . the colouring, the form, the motion, the combination of objects depend on the pre-disposition of the mind, moulding nature to its own purposes.[6]

Scott's own poetry is found deficient in 'that power in true poetry that lifts the mind from the ground of reality to a higher sphere',[7] and something of this deficiency is also observed in Chaucer, who 'attended chiefly to the real and natural', in contrast to Shakespeare, who exhibited 'not only what things are in themselves, but whatever they might seem to be, their different reflections, their endless combinations'.[8] Chaucer, Hazlitt declares, 'described external objects with the eye of a painter',[9] and the implied opposition of the imaginative art of poetry to the imitative art of painting is explicit in the lecture 'On Poetry in General',[10] and is also invoked, in *The Spirit of the Age*, against Crabbe:

A taste for that sort of poetry, which leans for support on the truth and fidelity of its imitations of nature, began to display itself much about that time . . . in consequence of the direction of the public taste to the subject of painting. . . . Painting is essentially an imitative art. . . . Thus an admirer of Teniers or Hobbima might think little of the pastoral sketches of Pope or Goldsmith; even Thomson describes not so much the naked object as what he sees in his mind's eye . . . but the adept in Dutch interiors, hovels and pig-styes must find in Mr. Crabbe a man after his own heart.[11]

Within painting itself, the same opposition reappears as a distinction between the 'picturesque' and the 'ideal',[12] or between the manner of Hogarth and the 'grand style':

There is a mighty world of sense, of custom, of every-day action, of accidents and objects coming home to us, and interesting because they do so; the gross, material, stirring, noisy world of common life and selfish passion, of which Hogarth was absolute lord and master: there is another mightier world, that which exists only in conception and in power, the universe of thought and sentiment, that surrounds and is raised above the ordinary world of reality.[13]

What these passages exhibit is the familiar romantic dualism of mind and world, albeit one in which the 'lower' term—'the gross,

[6] Ibid. 340, 343.   [7] Ibid. xi. 59.   [8] Ibid. iv. 226; see also vi. 240.
[9] Ibid. iv. 226.   [10] See ibid. v. 10 f.   [11] Ibid. xi. 165 f.
[12] Ibid. viii. 320 f.   [13] Ibid. vi. 146.

material . . . world of common life'—is apprehended with a more evident generosity of spirit than is apparent in either Schlegel or Coleridge.

It should be said, however, that Hazlitt does not always speak of great art in these unJohnsonian terms. What impresses him so enormously in Titian's portraits is the artist's power to represent 'the hidden soul' of his subject.[14] This is perception 'less by the eye than by the mind', but it is *perception* nevertheless: Hazlitt thinks of Titian as engaged in a disciplined attention to the world of which he is part, rather than as projecting a 'mightier world' of thought and sentiment on to 'the ordinary world of reality'. Such a passage, in which the essential criterion applied is that of fidelity to nature, is by no means unique in Hazlitt: the same man who when reviewing Schlegel declares 'the two principles of imitation and imagination' to be 'almost opposite', is equally capable of making a point against Shelley by asserting that both painting and poetry 'are true and unsophisticated, because they are conversant with real objects . . . and please by the truth of imitation only'.[15] Several other passages could be cited in which the context—often that of the more obviously mimetic art-forms, such as painting and theatrical performance— allows expression to that part of Hazlitt which seems always to have sought in great art just representations of nature.[16]

But when he is writing of Shakespeare Hazlitt's prevailing view is that nature can hold little interest for us until modified by the imaginative activity of the mind. In the Schlegel review he implies that if Lear *were* only 'a poor crazy old man . . . who dies of a broken heart' the play would lose most of its power; just so Lamb had argued that Lear cannot be represented in the theatre because he there becomes not the sublime figure of our imaginations but 'an old man tottering about the stage with a walking-stick, turned out of doors by his daughters in a rainy night'. Such a spectacle, Lamb believed, 'has nothing in it but what is painful and disgusting. We want to take him into shelter and relieve him. That is all the feeling which the acting of Lear ever produced in me.'[17] Nothing could be more contrary to the mode of response that led Johnson to find 'domestic'

---

[14] Ibid. xii. 288.
[15] Ibid. 245.
[16] See ibid. iv. 73–6; v. 69 f.; viii. 7–10, 82 f.; xii. 161 f., 334 f.
[17] *The Works of Charles and Mary Lamb*, ed. E. V. Lucas (7 vols.; 1903–5), i. 107 ('On the Tragedies of Shakspeare').

tragedy more powerful than 'imperial', and to argue that 'Lear would move our compassion but little, did we not rather consider the injured father than the degraded king'.[18] Johnson's compassion for Lear in the middle scenes of the play depends on his looking through the impassioned sublimity of Lear's fantasies to the injured human nature from which they spring, whereas for Lamb, when we are away from the theatre and responding as we ought, 'we see not Lear, but we are Lear,—we are in his mind, we are sustained by a grandeur which baffles the malice of daughters and storms.'[19] Hazlitt thought so highly of Lamb's argument as to quote it virtually entire as the conclusion to his own account of *King Lear*.[20] He too supposes the properly imaginative reader to *identify* with Lear's passion. Just as Lamb denies that in Lear's speeches in the storm we have any sense of 'corporal infirmities and weakness, the impotence of rage',[21] so for Hazlitt there can be nothing 'extravagant or impious' in Lear's identification of his cause with that of the heavens, since 'there is no other image which could do justice to the agonising sense of his wrongs and his despair'—where the definite article ('*the* agonising sense') merges Lear's sense of his situation with our own as though there could be no distinction between them. By contrast, Johnson's description of the play's emotional power presupposes a reader standing sufficiently back from Lear's feelings to perceive, and be gripped by, the rapidly shifting dramatic relations between things:

There is perhaps no play which keeps the attention so strongly fixed; which so much agitates our passions and interests our curiosity. The artful involutions of distinct interests, the striking opposition of contrary characters,

---

[18] *Yale*, viii. 705. For Johnson's preference of the domestic to the imperial see *Yale*, viii. 745; *Yale*, iii. 319 (*Rambler* no. 60); and Jean H. Hagstrum, *Samuel Johnson's Literary Criticism* (Minn., 1952), 141–3.   [19] Lamb, *Works*, i. 107.
[20] See Hazlitt, iv. 270 f. He also borrows Lamb's phrasing (Lear's 'sublime identification of his age' with that of the heavens) in the Schlegel review (xvi. 63) and again in 'On Poetry in General' (v. 4). See Roy Park, 'Lamb, Shakespeare, and the Stage', *Shakespeare Quarterly*, 33 (1982), 164–77, for Lamb's implied opposition of the quasi-redemptive imagination to the meanness of real life as known to the reason; it may be that Schlegel's book prompted thoughts in Hazlitt which he already had, in germ, from Lamb. An example not mentioned by Park is Lamb's note on Heywood (*Works*, iv. 95): 'Heywood is a sort of *prose* Shakspeare. His scenes are to the full as natural and affecting. But we miss *the Poet*, that which in Shakspeare always appears out and above the surface of *the nature* . . . Shakspeare makes us believe, while we are among his lovely creations, that they are nothing but what we are familiar with, as in dreams new things seem old: but we awake, and sigh for the difference.'
[21] Lamb, *Works*, i. 107.

the sudden changes of fortune, and the quick succession of events, fill the mind with a perpetual tumult of indignation, pity, and hope.[22]

The Johnsonian reader is powerfully moved, but (or because) he does not merge with Lear; his *attention* is fixed; the way in which Shakespeare does show him 'a poor crazy old man', and shows him what it means to be a poor crazy old man, is felt to need no further imaginative heightening. This sense of a common humanity is not possible when the reader's inwardness with the protagonist extends to the point of imaginative self-identification, so that 'we see not Lear, but we are Lear'. Hazlitt strongly identifies with Falstaff, for example, and is able to speak of him with a warmth which one misses in Schlegel and Coleridge: we like the 'knaves and fools' in *Henry IV*, he says, 'because they like themselves, and because we are made to sympathise with them'.[23] But just as in Coleridge judgement drove out sympathy, so such sympathy as this drives out judgement: Hazlitt is 'not offended but delighted' by Falstaff, he energetically denies that we can 'object to the character of Falstaff in a moral point of view', and he 'never could forgive' his rejection by Hal.[24] If the function of comedy is to render vice and folly ridiculous, then Shakespeare's comic Muse is 'too good-natured and magnanimous';[25] magnanimity for Hazlitt means the identification of oneself with another and as such cannot accommodate the judgement inherent in ridicule:

The imperfect and even deformed characters in Shakespeare's plays, as done to the life, by forming a part of our personal consciousness, claim our personal forgiveness, and suspend or evade our moral judgment, by bribing our self-love to side with them. Not to do so, is not morality, but affectation, stupidity, or ill-nature.[26]

If this evokes Shakespeare's magnanimity, it does so on the cheap: for how can *forgiveness* exist, Johnson might reasonably ask, where the moral judgement is evaded or suspended? And thus to identify oneself with Lear would be to buy passion at the price of knowledge; Lear is a man who 'hath ever but slenderly known himself'.

Audience identification with Shakespeare's characters—if such a thing were possible—would, then, work against general nature. This suggests the rationale for Johnson's seemingly perverse assertion

[22] *Yale*, viii. 702 f.   [23] Hazlitt, vi. 33.   [24] Ibid. iv. 279, 285.
[25] Ibid. vi. 35; see also iv. 313 f.   [26] Ibid. vi. 33.

about dramatic illusion: 'The truth is, that the spectators are always in their senses, and know, from the first act to the last, that the stage is only a stage, and that the players are only players.'[27] Johnson does not mean by this that while watching *King Lear*, for example, we are at leisure to admire the skill of the actors; he clearly admits the operation of some form of suspension of disbelief. The blinding of Gloucester seems to him 'an act too horrid to be endured in dramatick exhibition, and such as must always compel the mind to relieve its distress by incredulity'; the action in Smith's *Phaedra and Hippolitus* causes him to invoke the '*incredulus odi*. What I cannot for a moment believe, I cannot for a moment behold with interest or anxiety'.[28] Moreover, the analogy by which he explains his own understanding of drama's power to move us allows an essential function to the imagination:

The reflection that strikes the heart is not, that the evils before us are real evils, but that they are evils to which we ourselves may be exposed. If there be any fallacy, it is not that we fancy the players, but that we fancy ourselves unhappy for a moment; but we rather lament the possibility than suppose the presence of misery, as a mother weeps over her babe, when she remembers that death may take it from her.[29]

The mother who weeps over her child is imagining what she would feel were it to die, even while she sees the child in life and health before her. Yet—and this is for Johnson the crucial emphasis—there is nothing imaginary or fictive about what she then feels, although she has necessarily come to it by an act of imagination; her child, truly, is mortal, and its death is felt not as a supposed, illusory presence but as a real possibility of the here and now: what the mother would feel for the child in such a case is in truth part of what she does feel for the living child in any case, even though she may not often 'remember' the whole of what she feels. The act of imagination is indispensable; but it ends in 'the stability of truth'. 'Imitations produce pain or pleasure, not because they are mistaken for realities, but because they bring realities to mind.'[30]

This principled subordination of imaginative creation to 'realities' is the corner-stone of Johnson's entire approach. In 1765 it already seemed a somewhat grudging attitude. To reject the neoclassical

[27] *Yale*, vii. 77.
[28] Ibid. viii. 703; Johnson, *Lives of the Poets*, ii. 16.
[29] *Yale*, vii. 78.   [30] Ibid.

doctrine of the unities as inappropriate to Shakespeare was by then commonplace, and for some readers this called out a half-serious inclination to celebrate Shakespeare's power over the imagination as a liberation from all limit:

> When Shakespeare leads the mind a dance,
> From France to England, hence to France,
> Talk not to me of time and place;
> I own I'm happy in the chace.
> Whether the drama's here or there,
> 'Tis nature, Shakespeare, every where.
> The poet's fancy can create,
> Contract, enlarge, annihilate . . [31]

Thus wrote Robert Lloyd in 1760. In 1762 the widely influential Lord Kames put forward a similar view:

The spectator, once engaged, is willing to be deceived, loses sight of himself, and without scruple enjoys the spectacle as a reality. . . . After an interruption of the representation, it is no more difficult for a spectator to imagine a new place, or a different time, than, at the commencement of the play, to imagine himself at Rome, or in a period of time two thousand years back.[32]

It is the deep appeal of that mode of response that Johnson is concerned to resist; his assertion that 'the spectators are always in their senses' is as much normative as descriptive, and its provoking literal-mindedness is polemical:

Delusion, if delusion be admitted, has no certain limitation; if the spectator can be once persuaded, that his old acquaintance are Alexander and Caesar, that a room illuminated with candles is the plain of Pharsalia, or the bank of Granicus, he is in a state of elevation above the reach of reason, or of truth, and from the heights of empyrean poetry, may despise the circumscriptions of terrestrial nature.[33]

The energy with which Johnson invokes the hypothetical case—'if delusion be admitted'—reveals him to be concerned with wrong practice as well as wrong theory. Such a state of elevation is, for the solitary reader, by no means the practical impossibility that it is for the audience in the theatre; it is in fact precisely what the

---

[31] From Robert Lloyd, 'Shakespeare: An Epistle to Mr Garrick', quoted in Brian Vickers (ed.), *Shakespeare: The Critical Heritage* (6 vols.; 1973–81), iv. 420.
[32] Henry Home, Lord Kames, *Elements of Criticism*, 11th edn. (1840), 408, 415.
[33] *Yale*, vii. 77.

romantic reader goes to Shakespeare for, so that Schlegel was able to read Johnson's argument perfectly oblivious to its irony:

Johnson, a critic who is otherwise a strict upholder of the rules, makes the very just objection that if our imagination once goes so far as to transport us back through eighteen hundred years to Alexandria . . . the next step, that of jumping from Alexandria to Rome, is much easier. The ability of the mind to fly with the rapidity of lightning over immeasurable expanses of time and space is acknowledged in ordinary life; and shall poetry, whose function is in all respects to lend wings to the mind . . . alone be compelled to give up this general prerogative?[34]

It is the possibility of the romantic response that gives Johnson's implicit argument its point. To be carried away by the genius of Shakespeare, to believe oneself in the presence of Caesar, or to identify oneself so completely with the passion of Lear as to be unable to judge its extravagance, is perfectly possible (for the reader if not for the audience) and indeed confers upon the mind an exhilarating sense of greatly extended power and freedom, but such a state of mind is 'above the reach of reason, or of truth'; poetry which affects one in that way forfeits the power to bring realities to mind. Wholly to identify oneself with a creation of the imagination is a species of insanity; we may assume that what Johnson said of actors he believed equally true of audiences:

Talking of [acting] one day to Mr. Kemble, he said, 'Are you, Sir, one of those enthusiasts who believe yourself transformed into the very character you represent?' Upon Mr. Kemble's answering that he had never felt so strong a persuasion himself: 'To be sure not, Sir,' said Johnson, 'the thing is impossible. And if Garrick really believed himself to be that monster Richard the Third, he deserved to be hanged every time he performed it.'[35]

On one point Hazlitt agreed with Johnson: in the theatre, the thing is impossible. The theatre audience is always in its senses. But, whereas Johnson saw nothing wrong in this, and indeed was keen to deny the reader any privileged status—'a play read, affects the

---

[34] Schlegel, vi. 26. Schlegel is not the only distinguished critic to have misread Johnson here; see J. H. Adler, 'Johnson's "He that imagines this" ', *Shakespeare Quarterly*, 11 (1960), 225–8.

[35] *Boswell's Life of Johnson. Together with Boswell's Journal of a Tour to the Hebrides and Johnson's Diary of a Journey into North Wales*, ed. G. B. Hill, rev. edn. L. F. Powell (6 vols.; 1934–50), iv. 243 f.

mind like a play acted'[36]—Hazlitt, following Lamb, believed that the essence of Shakespeare was lost when the plays were put on stage: 'Poetry and the stage do not agree well together. . . . That which was merely an airy shape, a dream, a passing thought, immediately becomes an unmanageable reality.'[37] The Shakespearean imagination was, for Hazlitt, incompatible with the conditions of the theatre, where the audience is obliged literally to see as well as to imagine. No doubt, the manner in which the plays were produced in the Regency theatre played its part in this judgement. But in some cases at least it has also to do with Hazlitt's wish to keep his sympathy uncontaminated by any complicating perception. We have seen how he follows Lamb in wishing not to perceive Lear's 'infirmities and weakness'; Hamlet is another case in point:

We do not like to see our author's plays acted, and least of all, HAMLET. There is no play that suffers so much in being transferred to the stage. Hamlet himself seems hardly capable of being acted. . . . Mr. Kean's . . . manner is too strong and pointed. He throws a severity, approaching to virulence, into the common observations and answers. There is nothing of this in Hamlet. He is, as it were, wrapped up in his reflections, and only *thinks aloud*. There should therefore be no attempt to impress what he says upon others by a studied exaggeration of emphasis or manner; no *talking at* his hearers. There should be as much of the gentleman and scholar as possible infused into the part, and as little of the actor. A pensive air of sadness should sit reluctantly upon his brow, but no appearance of fixed and sullen gloom. He is full of weakness and melancholy, but there is no harshness in his nature. He is the most amiable of misanthropes.[38]

Kean's performance would seem to have suggested a certain lack of absolute sincerity and spontaneity in Hamlet's relations with others, a certain irritable self-consciousness which goes together with something approaching 'harshness' and 'virulence'. The presence of destructive impulses in Hamlet which flare out from time to time was a question that had been frequently raised by the end of the eighteenth century—Johnson, for example, speaks of the 'useless and wanton cruelty' of his treatment of Ophelia[39]—and it is significant that Hazlitt's argument that Hamlet cannot be acted comes directly

---

[36] *Yale*, vii. 79. It is true that Johnson finds 'imperial tragedy' to be always less powerful in the theatre than on the page: but by 'imperial tragedy' he means *Cato*. Shakespeare wrote no such plays.

[37] Hazlitt, iv. 247; see also v. 221 f., 231.

[38] Ibid. iv. 237.   [39] *Yale*, viii. 1011.

out of his repudiation of the notion that there is anything morally questionable about Hamlet's 'want of refinement': 'He may be said to be amenable only to the tribunal of his own thoughts, and is too much occupied with the airy world of contemplation, to lay as much stress as he ought on the practical consequences of things.'[40] Thus, Hazlitt's argument is that Hamlet's predilection for 'the airy world of contemplation' at the expense of 'the practical consequences of things' should be ours as well, preferring the 'airy shapes' of poetry to the 'unmanageable realities' of the stage, and that in this way what might otherwise seem morally questionable in Hamlet's behaviour will no longer appear so. This, again, amounts to self-identification with the protagonist; just as Lamb wrote, 'We see not Lear, but we are Lear', so Hazlitt writes, 'It is *we* who are Hamlet'.[41]

Hazlitt would not, I think, have denied that to respond to Shakespeare as he does is necessarily to be cut off from any normative sense of truth to nature; for him, as we have already seen, the question of whether or not there is extravagance or impiety in Lear's invocations of the gods simply cannot come up when we are fully engaged with the poetry. Schlegel and Coleridge are able to get back to the notion of truth in so far as they believe the excited imagination to be a transcendental organ of knowledge, but for Hazlitt, who rejects their transcendentalism, the impassioned imagination is imprisoned in—and only therefore uplifted by—its own subjectivity:

Poetry . . . is strictly the language of the imagination; and the imagination is that faculty which represents objects, not as they are in themselves, but as they are moulded by other thoughts and feelings, into an infinite variety of shapes and combinations of power. . . . The imagination, by thus embodying and turning them to shape, gives an obvious relief to the indistinct and importunate cravings of the will.[42]

The only truth to nature which Hazlitt can claim for Shakespeare is truth to feeling, but this fans out into an unrestricted plurality of illusion and desire. The special kind of feeling of which Macduff speaks:

[40] Hazlitt, v. 186. The connection of ideas in Hazlitt's original *Morning Chronicle* review becomes somewhat obscured in *Characters of Shakespear's Plays* through the insertion of extra material.
[41] Ibid. iv. 232.
[42] Ibid. v. 3 f., 8.

MALCOLM. Dispute it like a Man.
MACDUFF. I shall do so,
          But I must also feel it as a Man

—feeling which, arising from the very heart of human nature, is not
a 'craving of the will' but rather something which 'brings realities
to mind'—is not acknowledged by Hazlitt's account; instead, Hazlitt
sees the activity of the impassioned imagination very much as a matter
of 'disputing it', as the mind's countermovement against things as
they are in themselves—almost, one might say, as the mind's revenge.
Poets and artists, Hazlitt believes, frequently become such because
of their 'original poverty of spirit and weakness of constitution. As
a general rule, those who are dissatisfied with themselves, will seek to
go out of themselves into an ideal world.'[43] The pleasure of poetry
is the gratification of the will to power, and the sense of internal
power is generally aroused in response to a situation of external
weakness, suffering, or ennui: 'The sense of power has a sense of
pleasure annexed to it. . . . The resistance of the will to outward
circumstances, its determination to create its own good or evil, is
also a part of the same constitution of the mind.'[44] Thus, in the
review of Schlegel the incidents and situation in Spenser are seen as
'in themselves mean and disagreeable, till they are redeemed by the
genius of the poet, and converted, *by the very contrast*, into a
source of the utmost pathos and elevation of sentiment' (my italics).
And the power and sublimity of Lear—both the character and the
play—is entirely a matter of the resistance of the will to outward
circumstances:

Lear's injuries are without provocation, and admit of no alleviation or
atonement. They are strange, bewildering, overwhelming: they wrench
asunder, and stun the whole frame . . . The action of the mind, however,
under this load of disabling circumstances, is brought out in the play in
the most masterly and triumphant manner: it staggers under them, but it
does not yield. The character is cemented of human strength and human
weaknesses (the firmer for the mixture):—abandoned of fortune, of nature,
of reason, and without any energy of purpose, or power of action left,—
but sustained, reared to a majestic height out of the yawning abyss, by the
force of the affections, the imagination, and the cords of the human heart—it

[43] Ibid. iv. 58; see also xi. 308.
[44] Ibid. xii. 309. See John Kinnaird, 'Hazlitt and the "Design" of Shakespearean
Tragedy', *Shakespeare Quarterly*, 28 (1977), 22–39, esp. 31 f.; and, by the same
author, *William Hazlitt: Critic of Power* (New York, 1978), 112.

stands a proud monument, in the gap of nature, over barbarous cruelty and filial ingratitude.[45]

Hazlitt there has made his own Lamb's thought about a sustaining grandeur in Lear's mind 'which baffles the malice of daughters and storms'. Richard II's speeches at the moment of his fall similarly exemplify 'how far feeling is connected with the sense of weakness as well as of strength, or the power of imbecility, and the force of passiveness'.[46] And he praises Shakespeare's dramatization in his heroines of 'the sense of weakness leaning on the strength of its affections for support'[47]—most notably with regard to Cleopatra: 'She had great and unpardonable faults, but the grandeur of her death almost redeems them. She learns from the depth of despair the strength of her affections.'[48] The strength of those affections consists, in the final act, almost entirely in a kind of 'disputing it', in the resistance of her will and her passions to outward circumstances:

> CLEOPATRA. Think you, there was, or might be, such a man
>   As this I dreamt of?
> DOLABELLA.   Gentle Madam, no.
> CLEOPATRA. You lye, up to the hearing of the Gods . . .

Cleopatra never takes in the death of her husband as Macduff does take in the death of his wife and children: what is painful in the reality of her situation becomes a springboard for the transcending power of her imagination, and for her reckless, exhilarated awareness that this is so. And for Hazlitt, the right way of reading Shakespeare is one which, in this situation, goes all the way with Cleopatra: 'If poetry is a dream, the business of life is much the same. If it is a fiction, made up of what we wish things to be, and fancy that they are, because we wish them so, there is no other nor better quality.'[49] Just as Lear and Cleopatra rise above what is painful, pitiful, culpable, or terrible in their actual situations by the grandeur of their imaginative response—a response which is a kind of denial—so, for Hazlitt, our response to Shakespearean drama is characterized by this same movement of mind. If this involves a denial of realities, it is not in any simple sense escapist or unconscious of that which it denies: our under-consciousness of a sense in which Lear *is* 'a poor crazy old man, who has nothing sublime about him but his afflictions'

[45] Hazlitt, xviii. 332.   [46] Ibid. v. 224.
[47] Ibid. iv. 180.   [48] Ibid. 230.   [49] Ibid. v. 3.

is crucial to the passion with which we identify our own consciousness with the strenuous sublimity of his. Hazlitt elicits this recognition from us through his distinctively personal use of the essay form to give semi-dramatic expression to the check and flow of his thinking, so that his very assertion of what we do not respond to is felt as an integral part of the experience which the poetry affords. 'My desolation does begin to make | A better life' (Cleopatra); Hazlitt wishes us to feel something courageous, at root, in that impulse of the mind to deny its circumstances:

> The thing of courage,
> As rowz'd with rage, with rage doth sympathize;
> And, with an accent tun'd in self-same key,
> Returns to chiding fortune.

On two separate occasions he quotes those lines (from *Troilus and Cressida*, I. iii) as illustrating the effect of Shakespeare upon the reader.[50] The protagonist's imagination is kindled by passion; the reader's imagination kindles in sympathy; both repudiate—with 'rage'—what is given: 'The tragic poet . . . strengthens our yearnings after imaginary good, and lends wings to our desires, by which we, "at one bound, high overleap all bound" of actual suffering.'[51] It is Milton's Satan who high overleaps all bound when he enters Paradise; the point of Hazlitt's allusion lies in his association of the power of poetry with 'the resistance of the will to outward circumstances, its determination to create its own good or evil', which recalls the Satanic assertion that

> The mind is its own place, and in it self
> Can make a Heav'n of Hell, a Hell of Heav'n.[52]

Such a way of reading Shakespearean tragedy rests on a dualism of external reality and the world of the mind like that in Schlegel; but the significant difference between Hazlitt's account of our response to *King Lear* and Kant's theory of the sublime is that for Hazlitt the resulting feeling of internal grandeur, power, and desire for good can have reference to nothing beyond itself, being a merely psychological phenomenon generated in contradiction of the known reality. Hazlitt's awareness of this sometimes gives his account of

---

[50] Ibid. 52, 71.   [51] Ibid. xi. 167. See also iv. 271 f.
[52] *Paradise Lost*, i, ll. 254 f.

poetry a certain desperation, a quasi-tragic force of its own. This appears most plainly in his essay on *Coriolanus*, where he argues that we are bound to side in imagination with the 'mere pride and self-will' of Coriolanus against the just grievances of the people because 'the language of poetry naturally falls in with the language of power. The imagination is an exaggerating and exclusive faculty: it . . . seeks the greatest quantity of present excitement by inequality and disproportion.'[53] What most appeals to the imagination's love of power will necessarily be a distortion of the truth as judged by the understanding, a preference, in political terms, of 'might before right'.[54] Elsewhere he speaks, similarly, of 'that innate love of inequality and injustice, which is the favourite principle of the imagination',[55] and entertains the idea, half seriously at least, that the political apostasy of the Lake poets is only what is to be expected from imaginative writers.[56] In a political context, where justice depends on seeing things as they are in themselves and not as they are coloured by the mind, the unwelcome implications of Hazlitt's general account of the imagination are most obviously present to him; he admires the manner and power of Burke's prose, for example, as cordially as he detests its content and its influence. But, even when he is writing on poetry without reference to such concerns, the pessimism which underlies his view of the imagination sometimes makes itself felt:

Poetry . . . is 'the stuff of which our life is made.' The rest is 'mere oblivion,' a dead letter: for all that is worth remembering in life, is the poetry of it. Fear is poetry, hope is poetry, love is poetry, hatred is poetry; contempt, jealousy, remorse, admiration, wonder, pity, despair, or madness, are all poetry. Poetry is that fine particle within us, that expands, rarefies, refines, raises our whole being: without it 'man's life is poor as beast's'.[57]

Hazlitt there refers, of course, to lines of Lear's, in which Lear recoils from what he feels to be the unbearable consequences of seeing his situation as in itself it really is:

> O, reason not the need; our basest beggars
> Are in the poorest thing superfluous.
> Allow not nature more than nature needs,
> Man's life is cheap as beasts'.

[53] Ibid. iv. 214 f. [54] Ibid. 215. [55] Ibid. viii. 115; see also xiii. 51.
[56] See ibid. iv. 151–3; viii. 150–2; xi. 37 f., 79 f. [57] Ibid. v. 2.

Part of the reason that *King Lear* meant so much to Hazlitt—he thought it 'the best of all Shakespear's plays . . . the one in which he was the most in earnest'[58]—may have been the frequency and intensity in that play of the thought that human life, once stripped of its 'accommodations', is revealed to be something so poor and mean as to revolt the imagination. It is because nature as it is in itself gives the mind nothing on which it could repose that the imagination meets in us so desperate a need. For most of the play, Lear cannot bear to think of himself as 'a poor crazy old man', and no more can we, according to Hazlitt, find anything of pleasure or value in seeing our own human nature reflected in such a one; hence, we fly to the poetry of passion, as Lear does in the storm, we dispute the facts of the situation with all the sublimity of which the imagination is capable, and life appears worth living—or, if not quite that, then at least 'worth remembering'—once more.

Individuals or Species?

The significance of the main point on which Hazlitt chooses to take issue with Johnson can now be brought out. Pope had written that 'every single character in *Shakespear* is as much an Individual, as those in Life itself; it is as impossible to find any two alike'.[1] Johnson disputed this, praising Shakespeare's characters precisely because they are, in general, not individuals but species. Hazlitt regards this as proof positive of Johnson's incompetence to read Shakespeare; he opens his significantly titled *Characters of Shakespear's Plays* by quoting the relevant passage from Pope and attacking Johnson as 'the didactic reasoner' whose province is 'to take cognizance of those results of human nature which are constantly repeated and always the same':

Thus he says of Shakespear's characters, in contradiction to what Pope had observed, and to what every one else feels, that each character is a species, instead of being an individual. He in fact found the general species or *didactic* form in Shakespear's characters, which was all he sought or cared for; he did not find the individual traits, or the *dramatic* distinctions which

---

[58] Ibid. iv. 257.
[1] *The Works of Mr William Shakespear*, ed. Alexander Pope (6 vols.; 1723–5), vol. i, p. iii.

Shakespear has engrafted on this general nature, because he felt no interest in them.[2]

Part of what Hazlitt intends by this is not in contradiction with Johnson at all; this is the idea of individuality as it appears in his criticism of Shelley in *Prometheus Unbound*, whose descriptions are not given 'vividly and individually, so that any general results from what he writes must be from the aggregate of well-founded particulars: to embody an abstract theory, as if it were a given part of actual nature, is an impertinence and indecorum.'[3] In so far as Hazlitt is using 'individual' in antithesis to 'abstract', the difference between himself and Johnson is merely one of terminology; Johnson is applying essentially the same criterion when he contrasts *Othello* with *Cato*.[4]

But Hazlitt is also using 'individual' in antithesis to 'general', and it is on this point that the real disagreement with Johnson turns. Johnson of course recognizes that Shakespeare's characters are individualized and differentiated: 'Characters thus ample and general were not easily discriminated and preserved, yet perhaps no poet ever kept his personages more distinct from each other.'[5] But Johnson's priorities are the reverse of Hazlitt's: what we read Shakespeare for, according to Johnson, is the apprehension of general nature, the revelation of our common humanity in the actions and feelings of these individual men and women. 'Shakespeare has no heroes; his scenes are occupied only by men, who act and speak as the reader thinks that he should himself have spoken or acted on the same occasion'.[6] For Hazlitt, however, the 'general species' is merely the 'didactic form'—a concept, an abstraction: what matters above all is the absolute individual distinctness of each one of Shakespeare's characters:

We have already observed that Shakespear was scarcely more remarkable for the force and marked contrasts of his characters than for the truth and subtlety with which he has distinguished those which approached the nearest to each other. For instance, the soul of Othello is hardly more distinct from that of Iago than that of Desdemona is shewn to be from Aemilia's; the ambition of Macbeth is as distinct from the ambition of Richard III as it is from the meekness of Duncan; the real madness of Lear is as different from the feigned madness of Edgar as from the babbling of the fool; the

---

[2] Hazlitt, iv. 176.   [3] Ibid. xii. 246.
[4] See *Yale*, vii. 84.   [5] Ibid. 64.   [6] Ibid.

contrast between wit and folly in Falstaff and Shallow is not more characteristic though more obvious than the gradations of folly, loquacious or
reserved, in Shallow and Silence; and again, the gallantry of Prince Henry
is as little confounded with that of Hotspur as with the cowardice of
Falstaff, or as the sensual and philosophic cowardice of the Knight is with
the pitiful and cringing cowardice of Parolles. All these several personages
were as different in Shakespear as they would have been in themselves . . .
We shall attempt one example more in the characters of Richard II. and
Henry VI. . . . [7]

Hazlitt's difference of emphasis here is so great as to represent a
radically different way of reading: the concomitant of such attention
to the individuality and singularity of each character is that we cannot
relate to such a figure (he is so absolutely himself), we can only
identify our consciousness with his. In an essay written at about the
same time as the bulk of his Shakespeare criticism, Hazlitt brings
out the implications of 'our always imperceptibly connecting the idea
of the individual with man':

The springs that move the human form, and make it friendly or adverse
to me, lie hid within it. There is an infinity of motives, passions, and ideas
contained in that narrow compass, of which I know nothing, and in which
I have no share. Each individual is a world to himself, governed by a
thousand contradictory and wayward impulses. I can, therefore, make no
inference from one individual to another; nor can my habitual sentiments,
with respect to any individual, extend beyond himself to others. [8]

In reading Shakespeare, we escape from this isolation within the
personal self only by exchanging our own consciousness for that of
another: 'we see not Lear, but we are Lear'. To understand how great
a compliment Hazlitt is here paying Shakespeare one needs to be
aware of the importance of the concept of disinterestedness in his
thinking ever since the early *Essay on the Principles of Human Action*:
the only act of the mind which escapes an exclusive self-referentiality
is that by which 'the mind identifies itself with something so as to
be no longer master of itself',[9] producing a state in which there is
no reference whatsoever back to the self. For Johnson, by contrast,
when we go out of ourselves we do not leave ourselves behind; the
alternative to self-centredness is not projective self-identification but
relationship. The great virtue of Dryden's prose is that in it Dryden

---

[7] Hazlitt, iv. 293 f.; see also iv. 192 f., 311; v. 50, 185, 204–6.
[8] Ibid. iv. 19.   [9] Ibid. xii. 328.

is 'always *another and the same*'; when we are most moved by Lear, it is because we find ourselves in Lear, and Lear in ourselves: 'The reflection that strikes the heart is not, that the evils before us are real evils, but that they are evils to which we ourselves may be exposed.' The Johnsonian reader or spectator is 'always in his senses'. But this is only possible when we are principally struck by the way that Shakespeare's characters are human beings like ourselves. Hazlitt is impressed rather by their distinctness, their individuality, and so he chooses to dwell on the way that they act, not according to nature, but each according to the law of his own nature; his closeness to that side of Pope's individualistic thinking which Johnson disliked appears in his readiness to speak of the 'ruling passion' of particular characters. Hamlet's 'ruling passion is to think, not to act'; Iago is 'the dupe and victim of his ruling passion—an insatiable craving after action of the most difficult and dangerous kind'; in creating character 'Shakespear seizes only on the ruling passion, and miraculously evolves all the rest from it'.[10] Hazlitt's essay 'On Personal Character' begins by quoting Pope on the ruling passion and goes on to assert the primacy and inveteracy of individual character as the determining influence on a man's life;[11] and in his Shakespeare criticism he frequently employs the same idea without actually using Pope's phrase: 'Cleopatra's whole character is the triumph of the voluptuous, of the love of pleasure and the power of giving it, over every other consideration.'[12] We can put Johnson into dialogue with Hazlitt by noting his objections to Pope's theory in the *Life*:

Of any passion thus innate and irresistible the existence may reasonably be doubted. Human characters are by no means constant; men change by change of place, of fortune, of acquaintance . . . This doctrine is in itself pernicious as well as false; its tendency is to produce the belief of a kind of moral predestination or overruling principle which cannot be resisted.[13]

---

[10] Ibid. iv. 235, 207; xii. 343.

[11] Ibid. xii. 230–41, esp. 230–2.   [12] Ibid. iv. 229.

[13] Johnson, *Lives of the Poets*, iii. 174. A similar thought lies behind Johnson's illustrating 'Individuality' in the *Dictionary* by the following quotation from Arbuthnot's *Memoirs of Scriblerus* (ch. vii): 'Crambe would tell his instructor, that all men were not singular; that individuality could hardly be predicated of any man; for it was commonly said that a man is not the same he was, and that mad men are beside themselves'. Crambe is, of course, a fool; his reasoning is merely verbal; but Warburton annotated this passage with a closely parallel quotation from Locke ('. . . we say such an one *is not himself*, or is *besides himself*'), suggesting that there may indeed be a kind of truth in what Crambe says. (See John Locke, *An Essay Concerning Human*

For Johnson, what makes us into distinctive characters is superficial by comparison with that general human nature which we all have in common. His note on Constance in *King John* illustrates how he habitually looked for generality rather than differentiation in Shakespeare's men and women:

> To me, and to the State of my great Grief,
> Let Kings assemble.

In *Much Ado About Nothing*, the father of Hero, depressed by her disgrace, declares himself so subdued by grief that 'a thread may lead him.' How is it that grief in Leonato and Lady Constance, produces effects directly opposite, and yet both agreeable to nature. Sorrow softens the mind while it is yet warmed by hope, but hardens it when it is congealed by despair. Distress, while there yet remains any prospect of relief, is weak and flexible, but when no succour remains, is fearless and stubborn; angry alike at those that injure, and at those that do not help; careless to please where nothing can be gained, and fearless to offend when there is nothing further to be dreaded. Such was this writer's knowledge of the passions [14]

A reader who saw Constance and Leonato primarily as individuals would refer this difference to their difference of character; by such a reading, what makes Constance respond to affliction as she does is that unique and irreducible quiddity of self that distinguishes her from Leonato, and indeed from everyone else in the world— or, put another way, it is through the individuality of her response that Shakespeare creates a distinct, vivid, living character. Constance herself certainly appears to feel her experience as intensely individual, unique, incomparable: 'To me, and to the State of my great Grief . . .'—the first person pronouns carry tremendous emphasis, enforcing the sense of a single, isolated self whose relations with the world have been ruptured or negated; the feeling comes from the maddened and desperate ego, as indeed all sense of oneself as a uniquely differentiated individual must be the claim or creation of the ego. To respond to Constance as to an individual would thus be to identify one's consciousness of her with her own self-consciousness, and the effect of this would be something like that sense of sublimity and awesome internal power which Hazlitt finds in Lear's not dissimilar frenzy in the storm, which 'cannot be brought to conceive of any other cause of misery than that which has bowed it down, and absorbs all other sorrow in its own'.[15] Johnson's manner of response, by contrast, implies the need for a distinction between such egotistical consciousness and a 'deeper' seat of self—between the mind and the heart: Johnson is relatively unsympathetic to Constance's sense of something *majestic* in her situation in order to respond instead to her not as an individual but as a species. Her 'hardening of the mind' into a posture of agonized defiance can then be seen as the natural expression of insupportable grief, such as the reader feels that he himself, under such circumstances, would undergo. By doing this, Johnson is able to see Constance, without sentimentality, as his fellow-creature.

Leopold Damrosch has remarked that, given Johnson's insistence on 'truth to real life', his lack of interest in character criticism is 'the greatest of all the paradoxes in Johnson's criticism of Shakespeare'.[16] His assumption, evidently, is that in real life it is our 'character' which most fundamentally constitutes and expresses what we are. When one sees that Johnson does not subscribe to this assumption, and that for him the truth of real life comes when we are released from the absoluteness of the individual self, the paradox imputed to him disappears. This is a necessary point to make, since the twentieth-century attack on the inadequacy of character criticism in Shakespeare studies is sometimes supposed equally to have swept the board of all accounts of Shakespeare that insist on his truth to real life. But when we perceive *nature* our main interest cannot be in the psychology of the individual.

Supernatural Creation—Caliban and Prospero

Schlegel, like Hazlitt, takes Pope's side against Johnson on the question of whether Shakespeare's characters are individuals or species, and his way of praising Shakespeare's power of individual characterization brings out a further aspect of the romantic reading which Johnson's stress on general nature is, already in 1765, concerned to oppose. The point is this: in so far as each of Shakespeare's characters is a pure individual, 'a world to himself' as Hazlitt puts

---

[15] Hazlitt, v. 5.
[16] Leopold Damrosch, Jun., *Samuel Johnson and the Tragic Sense* (Princeton, NJ, 1972), 241.

it, Shakespeare's power to embody these figures can no longer be described as representational, since there is no real original to be represented; instead, it must be seen as freely creative, not as following nature but as creating a new nature with each new character. Shakespeare's men and women, that is to say, are creations of the same kind as his witches and fairies:

In the final analysis, a man acts as he does because that is the man he is. And just *how* each man is, is what Shakespeare reveals to us with extraordinary immediacy: he demands and obtains our belief even in that which is strange and deviant from the ordinary course of nature. His gift for characterization is perhaps the most comprehensive that there has ever been. . . . This Prometheus does not form human beings alone, he opens the gates to the magical world of spirits, calls up ghosts, has witches practise their foul mischiefs, peoples the air with sportive fairies or sylphs; and although these beings exist only in the imagination, they possess such truth that, even though they be such misshapen and monstrous abortions as Caliban, Shakespeare still compels in us the conviction that were such beings to exist, they would behave just as they do in the plays.[1]

On this point, Schlegel is doing little more than summarizing a thought about Shakespeare which had been in the air since at least the beginning of the eighteenth century, when Rowe declared:

Certainly the greatness of this Author's Genius do's no where so much appear, as where he gives his Imagination an entire Loose, and raises his Fancy to a flight above Mankind and the Limits of the visible World. . . . I am very sensible that he do's in this Play [*The Tempest*] depart too much from that likeness to Truth which ought to be observ'd in these sort of Writings; yet he do's it so very finely, that one is easily drawn in to have more Faith for his sake, than Reason does well allow of.[2]

Where an eighteenth-century critic responds to the pull of the romantic reading of Shakespeare he is likely to place special emphasis on the supernatural scenes and figures in the plays as the salient examples of how Shakespeare's art does something more than represent nature. Rowe finds *The Tempest* 'as perfect in its Kind, as almost any thing we have of his', and goes on:

His Magick has something in it very Solemn and very Poetical: And that extravagant Character of *Caliban* is mighty well sustain'd, shews a wonderful

---

[1] Schlegel, vi. 130.
[2] *The Works of Mr William Shakespear*, ed. Nicholas Rowe (6 vols.; 1709), vol. i, p. xxiii f.

Invention in the Author, who could strike out such a particular wild Image, and is certainly one of the finest and most uncommon Grotesques that was ever seen. The Observation, which I have been inform'd three very great Men concurr'd in making upon this Part, was extremely just. *That Shakespear had not only found out a new Character in his* Caliban, *but had also devis'd and adapted a new manner of Language for that Character.*[3]

This was to become a commonplace. Addison believed that 'it shews a greater Genius in *Shakespear* to have drawn his *Calyban*, than his *Hotspur* or *Julius Caesar*: The one was to be supplied out of his own Imagination, whereas the other might have been formed upon Tradition, History and Observation.[4] Theobald agreed, as did Joseph Warton; Hurd distinguished poetry which, following nature, seeks to 'touch the affections and interest the heart', from 'the more sublime and creative poetry' which addresses itself to imagination as opposed to experience and deals in the impossible and the marvellous; and Mrs Montagu devoted one chapter of her popular essay to Shakespeare's 'Praeternatural Beings' and to 'his peculiar felicity, in those fictions and inventions, from which poetry derives its highest distinction'.[5] To this way of thinking, the power of Shakespeare's supernatural figures to grip the imagination seemed to imply a radical qualification of the notion that Shakespeare's greatness lay in his power to represent nature: Caliban, surely, lies outside general nature: Shakespeare's success in giving this monster convincing dramatic life cannot depend on bringing realities to mind: the reader, as Rowe had observed, 'is easily drawn in to have more Faith . . . than Reason does well allow of'. Under pressure from ideas of this kind, 'nature'—where the term is retained at all—begins to become not that which Shakespearean drama represents but that which it *creates*: thus Warburton writes:

These two first Plays, The *Tempest* and the *Midsummer-night's Dream*, are the noblest Efforts of that sublime and amazing Imagination, peculiar to

[3] Ibid.

[4] The *Spectator*, ed. Donald F. Bond (5 vols.; Oxford, 1965), ii. 586 f. (no. 279).

[5] *The Works of Shakespeare*, ed. Lewis Theobald (7 vols.; 1733), i. 44 n.: the *Adventurer* (2 vols.; 1753–4), facsimile repr. ed. D. D. Eddy (2 vols.; 1978), ii. 157 (no. 97); Richard Hurd, *Moral and Political Dialogues: With Letters on Chivalry and Romance*, 3rd edn. (3 vols.; 1765), iii. 306, 305; Elizabeth Montagu, *An Essay on the Writings and Genius of Shakespear, Compared with the Greek and French Dramatic Poets: With Some Remarks upon the Misrepresentations of Mons. de Voltaire* (1769), 133.

Shakespear, which soars above the Bounds of Nature without forsaking Sense: or, more properly, carries Nature along with him beyond her established Limits.[6]

According to Charles Churchill, Shakespeare, 'passing Nature's bounds, was something more'.[7] While there may be an element of conscious extravagance in these expressions, in an essay by George Colman published four years before Johnson's Shakespeare the essential ideality of Shakespeare's art is defended against 'the chastised notions of our modern Criticks' with entire seriousness:

To create, is to be a Poet indeed; to draw down Beings from another sphere, and endue them with suitable Passions, Affections, Dispositions, allotting them at the same time proper employment; 'to body forth, by the Powers of Imagination, the forms of things unknown, and to give to airy Nothing a local Habitation and a Name,' surely requires a Genius for the Drama equal, if not superior, to the delineation of personages, in the ordinary course of Nature. Shakespeare, in particular . . . 'appears to have disdained to put his Free Soul into circumscription and confine,' which denied his extraordinary talents their full play, nor gave scope to the Boundlesness of his Imagination. His Witches, Ghosts, Fairies, and other Imaginary Beings, scattered through his plays, are so many glaring violations of the common table of Dramatick Laws. What then shall we say? Shall we confess their Force and Power over the Soul, shall we allow them to be Beauties of the most exquisite kind, and yet insist on their being expunged? . . . Our Old Writers thought no personage whatever, unworthy a place in the Drama, to which they could annex what may be called a *Seity*; that is, to which they could allot Manners and Employment peculiar to itself. The severest of the Antients cannot be more eminent for the constant Preservation of Uniformity of Character, than Shakespeare; and Shakespeare, in no instance, supports his Characters with more exactness, than in the conduct of his Ideal Beings.[8]

Colman's reading of Shakespeare effectively denies 'general nature' as Johnson understands it: he stresses the individuality or 'seity' of each character, he asserts the supremacy of the creative 'Free Soul' over circumscription and confine, and he finds Shakespeare's power to create supernatural figures 'equal, if not superior' in artistic merit to the power to represent life as it is.

---

[6] *The Works of Shakespear*, ed. William Warburton (8 vols.; 1747), i. 3 n.

[7] *The Poetical Works of Charles Churchill*, ed. D. Grant (1956), 10 (*Rosciad*, l. 270).

[8] George Colman, *Prose on Several Occasions* (3 vols.; 1787), ii. 116–18.

And Caliban was only the thin end of the wedge. For if the magic of Shakespeare's art can make us accept the reality of so unnatural a creature as Caliban, should we not find the same process at work in our response to the 'unnatural' actions and sentiments of, say, an Othello? That is the argument put forward by William Guthrie in his *Essay upon English Tragedy* (not dated, but thought to have been published in 1747). Why is it, Guthrie inquires, that a student of literature, who has been persuaded by French criticism 'that all poetry is or ought to be an imitation of nature', will find that Shakespeare entirely fails this test?

Shall I attempt to give the reason of this? It is not Shakespear who speaks the language of nature, but nature rather speaks the language of Shakespear. He is not so much her imitator, as her master, her director, her moulder. Nature is a stranger to objects which Shakespear has rendered natural. Nature never created a Caliban till Shakespear introduced the monster, and we now take him to be nature's composition. Nature never meant that the fairest, the gentlest, the most virtuous of her sex, should fall in love with a rough, blustering, awkward Moor; she never meant that this Moor, in the course of a barbarous jealousy, and, during the commission of a detestable murder, should be the chief object of compassion throughout the play. Yet Shakespear has effected all this; and every sigh that rises, every tear that drops, is prompted by nature.

Nature never designed that a complication of the meanest, the most infamous, the most execrable qualities should form so agreeable a composition, that we think Henry the fifth makes a conquest of himself when he discards Jack Falstaff. Yet Shakespear has struck out this moral contradiction, and reconciled it to nature.[9]

It is not at all clear what Guthrie means by Shakespeare's reconciling such contradictions to nature. His phrasing is ambiguous; he tries not to abandon altogether the idea of truth to nature while responding to the attraction of the romantic reading, rather as Polixenes tries to persuade Perdita that the art itself is nature. Yet the implication of his describing Shakespeare as nature's 'director' and 'moulder' seems to be that Shakespeare draws us so completely into the imaginative world of each play that we respond to such non-natural figures as Caliban, Othello, and Falstaff as though they were natural, having left behind (or transcended) that faculty of judgement which

---

[9] William Guthrie, *An Essay upon English Tragedy: With Remarks upon the Abbé de Blanc's Observations on the English Stage* [1747], 11 f.

could say yea or nay to the question of their truth. That with one
part of his mind, at least, Guthrie was drawn to such a romantic
view can be seen from the way that, like Colman, he immediately
goes on to praise the absolute individuality and distinctness of each
of Shakespeare's characters:

To what perfection has our heaven-instructed Englishman brought this
excellency? . . . His fools are as different from one another as his heroes.
But above all, how has he varied guilty ambition in a species so narrow of
itself, that it seems impossible to diversify it! For we see Hamlet's father-in-
law, Macbeth, King John, and King Richard, all rising to royalty by
murdering their kindred kings. Yet what a character has Shakespeare affixed
to every instance of the same species. Observe the remorse of the Dane, how
varied it is from the distraction of the Scot: mark the confusion of John,
how different from both; while the close, the vigilant, the jealous guilt of
Richard is peculiar to himself.[10]

Peculiar to himself, indeed:

> I have no brother, I am like no brother;
> And this word *Love*, which grey-beards call divine,
> Be resident in men like one another,
> And not in me: I am myself alone.

Thus Richard describes himself in the penultimate scene of *Henry VI:
Part Three*. Yet the passage which Johnson remarks as 'truly
tragical'[11] is that in which Richard awakens from his troubled
dreams on the eve of Bosworth and his feeling for his lost participation
in human nature returns upon him:

> All several sins, all us'd in each degree,
> Throng to the bar, all crying, *guilty! guilty!*
> I shall despair—there is no creature loves me:
> And if I die, no soul shall pity me.
> Nay, wherefore should they? since that I myself
> Find in myself no pity to myself?

'His scenes are occupied only by men, who act and speak as the
reader thinks that he should himself have spoken or acted on the
same occasion'; Richard's feelings here are certainly immediately
distinguishable from those of Macbeth, yet they have, also, their
similarity:

---

[10] Ibid. 12 f.   [11] *Yale*, viii. 631.

And that, which should accompany old age,
As honour, love, obedience, troops of friends,
I must not look to have . . .

This is similar enough for Guthrie's placing of the emphasis on the difference rather than the similarity to be a matter of critical choice rather than critical necessity.

It is against his contemporaries' choice of such readings that Johnson applies his weight. He does this in a number of different ways. His insistence that the reader or spectator be 'always in his senses', with its virtual corollary that Shakespeare's characters are not best described as individuals, has already been discussed. There is also some point to the brevity with which he dismisses attacks on Shakespeare's violations of the *bienséances*, and in the fact that he does so explicitly in the name of general nature: Shakespeare's 'adherence to general nature has exposed him to the censure of criticks, who form their judgments upon narrower principles'.[12] Several of Johnson's contemporaries—for example, both Colman and Guthrie in the passages already quoted—were inclined to make much of the inadequacy of such rigidly neoclassicizing censure in order to gain momentum for their argument that Shakespeare goes beyond the merely natural. This, Johnson says in effect, is to pay Voltaire too high a compliment. It is not that Shakespeare soars above nature, but that Voltaire's criteria cannot rise to it; Shakespeare's offences against a narrowly conceived neoclassical code of what is to be deemed 'natural' do not have the general significance that the romantically inclined reader may wish to find in them. (The popularity of Mrs Montagu's consciously important defence of Shakespeare against Voltaire, published four years after Johnson's edition, suggests how far Johnson was here resisting the expectations of his readers.)

But no less significant, given his contemporaries' enthusiasm for the supernatural in Shakespeare, is Johnson's firm insistence that 'even where the agency is supernatural the dialogue is level with life'.[13] This is a firmness enforced by a number of his notes. Ariel's song to Ferdinand had been described by Gildon as a 'senseless piece of trifling', but Warburton had disputed this, arguing for its important function in Prospero's plan to marry Ferdinand to

[12] Ibid. vii. 65.   [13] Ibid. 64.

Miranda, and Joseph Warton had found it 'exceedingly solemn and striking', conveying 'information in words not proper for any but a SPIRIT to utter'.[14] Johnson's note sets itself deliberately against any such response as Warton's:

I know not whether Dr. Warburton has very successfully defended these songs from Gildon's accusation. Ariel's lays, however seasonable and efficacious, must be allowed to be of no supernatural dignity or elegance, they express nothing great, nor reveal any thing above mortal discovery.

The reason for which Ariel is introduced thus trifling is, that he and his companions are evidently of the fairy kind, an order of beings to which tradition has always ascribed a sort of diminutive agency, powerful but ludicrous, a humorous and frolick controlment of nature, well expressed by the songs of Ariel.[15]

Johnson's general observation on *A Midsummer Night's Dream* similarly points out that the fairies belong to a long tradition of folklore and were moreover 'much in fashion' in Shakespeare's day: *ex nihilo nihil fit*.[16] And at the beginning of *Macbeth* he gives a long note on the prevalence of belief in witchcraft at the time, designed to demonstrate that Shakespeare's contemporaries could have found the scenes with the witches 'awful and affecting' while remaining very much in their senses; Johnson deploys his learning to show how scenes of 'witchcraft or enchantment' would have required no special suspension of disbelief, not only for a Jacobean audience, but for most of mankind throughout history.[17] Similarly, in *Hamlet* he is careful to point out that the reality of ghosts has been 'in all ages credited'.[18] In these notes he is addressing not only the enlightenment rationalist who might suppose such scenes primitive or ridiculous—the Voltaire who speaks of the witches' incantations in *Macbeth* as 'ces puérilités'[19]—but also the romantically minded reader inclined to see Shakespeare's fairies and witches as the pure creations of the free poetic imagination, existing independently of the opinions, feelings, and experiences natural to mankind.

[14] For Gildon and Warburton see *The Plays of William Shakespeare*, ed. Samuel Johnson (8 vols.; 1765), i. 25 n.; and for Warton the *Adventurer*, ii. 137 (no. 93).
[15] *Yale*, vii. 124.   [16] Ibid. 160.
[17] Ibid. viii. 752–5 (first pub. in the 1745 *Miscellaneous Observations on the Tragedy of Macbeth*).
[18] *Yale*, viii. 969.
[19] *Voltaire on Shakespeare*, ed. T. Besterman (Geneva, 1967), 90.

The most significant of these notes, however, is on Caliban. We have seen that the observation that 'the character of Caliban . . . stands before us with a language and manners of its own' (as Hazlitt repeated it)[20] was current throughout the eighteenth century, and that this idea of Caliban as the quintessential individual whose creation could not depend on Shakespeare's knowledge of man had become, by the time of Johnson's edition, a focus for the thought that Shakespeare's genius lay in his power of creation rather than representation. It was this notion of which Johnson, in 1784 consciously swimming against the tide, attempted to disabuse Fanny Burney:

'There is nothing so little comprehended among mankind as what is genius. They give to it all, when it can be but a part. Genius is nothing more than knowing the use of tools; but there must be tools for it to use: a man who has spent all his life in this room will give a very poor account of what is contained in the next.'

'Certainly, sir; yet there is such a thing as invention? Shakspeare could never have seen a Caliban.'

'No; but he had seen a man, and knew, therefore, how to vary him to a monster.'[21]

In Johnson's view—also very firmly stated in the *Preface*—[22] the greatest power of genius counted for nothing without a wide experience and knowledge of life. Such scepticism as to the absoluteness of 'invention' might seem a rather negative (and ungenerous) position, but its positive aspect is there in Johnson's willingness to see Caliban as a kind of man (albeit a man 'varied' to a monster) and is more strongly present in one of his notes on *The Tempest*. The immediate context is Caliban's cursing of Prospero:

Whence these criticks derived the notion of a new language appropriated to Caliban I cannot find: They certainly mistook brutality of sentiment for uncouthness of words. Caliban had learned to speak of Prospero and his daughter, he had no names for the sun and moon before their arrival, and could not have invented a language of his own without more understanding than Shakespeare has thought it proper to bestow upon him. His diction is indeed somewhat clouded by the gloominess of his temper and the

[20] Hazlitt, v. 48.
[21] *Diary and Letters of Madame D'Arblay*, ed. Charlotte Barrett (6 vols.; 1904–5), ii. 271.
[22] See *Yale*, vii. 87 f.

malignity of his purposes; but let any other being entertain the same thoughts and he will find them easily issue in the same expressions.[23]

Together with the coolness about original creation goes the power to accept Caliban's 'brutality of sentiment' within the pale of humanity: for Johnson to suggest with such straightforwardness that the reader 'entertain the same thoughts' and test the naturalness of Caliban's language by reference to his own feelings, is to reclaim Caliban for general nature, to respond to him not as a monster but as a being essentially like Shakespeare's other men and women, 'who act and speak as the reader thinks that he should himself have spoken or acted on the same occasion'. It is hardly too much to say that Johnson here shows himself strongly and easily able to do what, at the end of *The Tempest*, Prospero achieves only with difficulty:

> This thing of darkness I
> Acknowledge mine.

Arguably, such a strenuous impulse of acknowledgement is central to the play as a whole. If the power of art in *The Tempest* sometimes seems capable of redeeming our frail and fallen human nature, transforming the world we know into a brave new world of harmony and love, it is in the tensions of Prospero's relationship with Caliban that we feel what is problematic in the aspiration to such a high spiritualizing power, and it is Prospero's recollection of Caliban as his own that marks a limit to what his art can do, cutting short the 'most majestic vision' of the masque and revealing it as illusion.

This, however, implies too large a claim for Johnson's note; if his firmness with the idea of Caliban as a supernatural creation has implications central to *The Tempest* as a whole, he himself seems not to have been aware of these. Impressive though it is, his acceptance of Caliban's 'brutality of sentiment' as human is somewhat too easy, too unstrenuous; he nowhere shows himself sensitive to *The Tempest*'s immense potential attraction for a romantic reading of Shakespeare. It was one of only four plays for which he failed to provide a general observation in the 1765 edition (the others were *The Comedy of Errors*, *Much Ado*, and *The Merry Wives of Windsor*), and the note which he supplied in 1773 is striking only for its vapidity:

---

[23] Ibid. 123.

Whatever might be Shakespeare's intention in forming or adopting the plot, he has made it instrumental to the production of many characters, diversified with boundless invention, and preserved with profound skill in nature, extensive knowledge of opinions, and accurate observation of life. In a single drama are here exhibited princes, courtiers, and sailors, all speaking in their real characters. There is the agency of airy spirits, and of an earthly goblin. The operations of magick, the tumults of a storm, the adventures of a desart island, the native effusion of untaught affection, the punishment of guilt, and the final happiness of the pair for whom our passions and reason are equally interested.[24]

Johnson could hardly say less about *The Tempest*, or sound more like Dick Minim, than in those bored and mechanically assembled phrases, written with so little critical purpose that the absence of a verb in the final sentence is hardly felt to matter. Without trying to infer too much from what is simply not there, one may suspect that *The Tempest* left Johnson at a loss, or cold, or both.

However, such indifference, while hardly a mark of critical intelligence, itself acquires a certain point in the light of the high regard in which the romantic critics held the play. What is entirely absent from Johnson's response is the kind of enthusiasm for *The Tempest* already epitomized in two essays contributed by Joseph Warton to the *Adventurer* in 1753:

The poet is a more powerful magician than his own PROSPERO: we are transported into fairy-land; we are wrapt in a delicious dream, from which it is misery to be disturbed; all around is enchantment!
    —The isle is full of noises,
    Sounds, and sweet airs, that give delight and hurt not.[25]

In brief compass, Warton's essays on the play bring together various elements of the romantic reading of Shakespeare—response to the power of dramatic illusion as to a kind of dream that transports the reader out of reality; a strong emphasis on Shakespeare's 'preservation of the consistency of his characters' as distinct individuals; and praise for the 'creative imagination' and 'creative power' which could produce 'characters the most new and singular that can well be conceived'.[26] Warton does not himself suppose that such praise could be incompatible with a full appreciation of Shakespeare's 'strokes of nature and passion', which he recognizes as Shakespeare's

[24] Ibid. 135.   [25] The *Adventurer*, ii. 138 (no. 93).
[26] Ibid. 134 (no. 93).

other principal mode of excellence; but the way in which *The Tempest* pulls *against* general nature can be felt in the manner that he chooses to conclude. Having spoken of the 'awful solemnity' of Prospero's character, he draws attention to one part of Prospero's behaviour that 'deserves to be particularly pointed out': the moment when Prospero remembers Caliban's plot against his life:

He appears to be greatly moved; and suitably to this agitation of mind, which his danger has excited, he takes occasion, from the sudden disappearance of the visionary scene, to moralize on the dissolution of all things:

> ——These our actors,
> As I foretold you, were all spirits; and
> Are melted into air, into thin air.
> And, like the baseless fabric of this vision,
> The cloud-capt towers, the gorgeous palaces,
> The solemn temples, the great globe itself,
> Yea, all which it inherit, shall dissolve;
> And, like this unsubstantial pageant faded,
> Leave not a rack behind——

To these noble images he adds a short but comprehensive observation on human life, not excelled by any passage of the moral and sententious EURIPIDES:

> ——We are such stuff
> As dreams are made on; and our little life
> Is rounded with a sleep![27]

For Prospero there, the thought of 'the dissolution of all things' and its accompanying intuition of an essential insubstantiality permeating the very fabric of physical life hold a kind of comfort, a kind of beauty. If Warton is right, and there is moral nobility and wisdom in this, then the sense of general nature surely cannot be sustained. We have no note of Johnson's on Prospero's speech, but we do have his acrid comment on the comparable lines in *Measure for Measure* in which the Duke endeavours to persuade Claudio that death is only sleep: 'a sentence which in the Friar is impious, in the reasoner is foolish, and in the poet trite and vulgar.'[28] In that play, however, the voice of nature makes itself clearly heard in reply, not only in Claudio:

> Ay, but to die, and go we know not where;
> To lye in cold obstruction, and to rot . . .

---

[27] Ibid. 161 f. (no. 97).   [28] *Yale*, vii. 193.

and in Barnardine:

> I swear, I will not die to-day for any man's persuasion

but also in that same speech of the Duke's, as the warmth of
Johnson's engagement amply testifies:

> Thou hast nor youth, nor age;
> But as it were an after-dinner's sleep,
> Dreaming on both.

This is exquisitely imagined. When we are young we busy ourselves in
forming schemes for succeeding time, and miss the gratifications that are
before us; when we are old we amuse the languour of age with the recollection
of youthful pleasures or performances; so that our life, of which no part
is filled with the business of the present time, resembles our dreams after
dinner, when the events of the morning are mingled with the designs of the
evening.[29]

There, the Duke's meditation on the vanity of life is itself intimately
grounded in human experience; to appreciate its force is, paradoxically, to be drawn into a deeper and fuller sense of life, a
lived sense of how life eludes us. What is conveyed is not the
wearisomeness of life and desirability of death but on the contrary
the ineradicably human foolishness of the way human beings live
and love their lives; hence, Claudio's expression of the fear of death,
when it comes, is felt to complement quite as much as to rebut what
the Duke is saying here. (The idea of 'an after-dinner's sleep' as an
image of our life is, after all, far from unattractive.) None of this
is true of the lines Johnson read with such indignation:

> Thy best of Rest is sleep,
> And that thou oft provok'st; yet grosly fear'st
> Thy death, which is no more.

The thought here invokes what is merely an idea, a purely speculative
analogy between sleep and death unsupported by anything known
in experience. Without the kind of specificity and reality of reference
that Johnson finds in the image of life as 'an after-dinner's sleep' the
commonplace that death is a kind of sleep remains poetically inert,
fails to find the passes of the mind: what is 'foolish' in the reasoner
is for that very reason 'trite and vulgar' in the poet. Instead of

---

[29] Ibid.

reflecting on some known or knowable quality of life, we are invited
to form an idea about death, which we do not know. And this is
true also of Prospero's speech in *The Tempest*. What knowable
reality is brought to mind by those images of universal dissolution?
Our personal mortality—the 'rounding' of our 'little life' in the sleep
of death—is not, truly, the end of the world. There is no sense of
a Christian eschatology. What *is* potently suggested is our experience
of masque, or more generally our sometimes poignant sense of the
transience of theatrical experience: but our lives do not end with
the play we are watching; that very sense of poignancy marks a
transition, not an extinction, in our consciousness of things. We must
say, I think, that the poetry of Prospero's speech does not call realities
to mind but creates its own reality; the experience to which it refers
has no existence beyond the experience created in the mind of the
reader by Shakespeare's genius with language. The art itself is nature.

That is, it replaces nature. For it is worth recalling once more that
at this moment in the play Prospero is finding it extremely difficult
to acknowledge the thing of darkness which is Caliban as his own;
his meditation on the insubstantiality of human life is an attempt
to calm his beating mind, to detach himself from the actuality of
life by a spiritual discipline of the imagination and so to rise to a
kind of Schlegelian irony—'the coldness of a superior mind which
has run through the circle of human existence and has survived the
death of feeling'. Warton, who finds nobility in this, is, significantly,
equally unwilling to acknowledge Caliban as his own: he asserts that
Shakespeare could have had 'no assistance from observation or
experience' in creating such 'a prodigy of cruelty, malice, pride,
ignorance, idleness, gluttony and lust', and the only passage in the
play to which he objects is that which suggests to him Caliban's
participation in humanity:

I ALWAYS lament that our author has not preserved this fierce and implacable
spirit in CALYBAN, to the end of the play; instead of which, he has, I think,
injudiciously put into his mouth, words that imply repentance and understanding:
>   —I'll be wise hereafter
> And seek for grace. What a thrice double ass
> Was I, to take this drunkard for a God,
> And worship this dull fool?[30]

---

[30] The *Adventurer*, ii. 157 f., 160 (no. 97).

Schlegel's repudiation of Caliban is more pointed still; this is how he concludes his own description of Caliban's 'rooted malignity':

The whole depiction of this monster has the most inconceivably profound implications; yet, despite its loathsomeness, it is not hurtful to our feelings, since the honour of human nature is not threatened by it.[31]

Be cheerful, sir: despite appearances, Caliban has no claim on us: we are such stuff as dreams are made of, and when the mind realizes its power to render insubstantial the external world it comes into its true inheritance. So Prospero tells himself, and when the romantic critics read Shakespeare in sympathy with such a thought they found his art to confer something very like the freedom of imagination which Prospero there desiderates. For it was *The Tempest* more than any other play that generated the romantic account of dramatic illusion as a dream-like state in which situation, action, and event lose their reference to the real world and are subjected to the plastic power of the mind. Schlegel's description of poetic illusion as 'a voluntary waking dream'[32] may well be indebted to the essay which Ludwig Tieck had prefixed to his version of *The Tempest*, and which Schlegel had reviewed; there Tieck says of our experience in dreaming:

In this unceasing confusion we lose the standard by which we normally judge of the truth of things; there is nothing real to hold our attention, and so we lose all recollection of reality in the uninterrupted activity of our imagination. . . . All this which the imagination perceives when we are dreaming has been realised by Shakespeare in *The Tempest*. . . . Here nothing takes us back to the real world.[33]

And it was as part of his discussion of *The Tempest* that Coleridge opposed Johnson's account of dramatic illusion with his own:

In what this consists I cannot better explain than by referring you to the highest degree of it; namely, dreaming. It is laxly said that during sleep we take our dreams for realities, but this is irreconcilable with the nature of sleep, which consists in a suspension of the voluntary and, therefore, of the comparative power. The fact is that we pass no judgement either way; we simply do not judge them to be unreal, in consequence of which

---

[31] Schlegel, vi. 161.   [32] Ibid. ii. 283.
[33] Ludwig Tieck, *Kritische Schriften* (4 vols.; Leipzig, 1848–52), i. 44 f. Schlegel's brief review is to be found in his *Sämmtliche Werke*, ed. E. Böcking (12 vols.; Leipzig, 1846–7), xi. 16–20.

the images act on our minds, as far as they act at all, by their own force as images.[34]

'In Xanadu did Kubla Khan . . .' The images of dissolution in Prospero's speech, too, work upon the imagination purely 'by their own force as images', and the substantial world of our experience melts away while we read. Such poetry (and there is a great deal of it in the last plays), referring the mind to nothing outside itself, as Coleridge recognizes, carries with it its own truth. But Coleridge also goes on to observe one main difference between dreaming and dramatic illusion with regard to this 'suspension of the voluntary and, therefore, of the comparative power'; in our response to drama, such suspension is itself a voluntary act, taking place 'with the consent and positive aidance of our own will. We *choose* to be deceived.'[35] Johnson—like Prospero? like Shakespeare, finally?—chooses not to be: although with far less awareness than either of what is given up by such a choice.

*Organic Unity—Wordplay—*Romeo and Juliet

No one finds fault with their experience while they are dreaming, when 'the comparative power', as Coleridge puts it, is suspended, and 'we pass no judgement either way'. The single most striking difference between Johnson and the romantic critics, and that which marks him out most clearly as their antagonist, is his assertion that Shakespeare is an immensely careless and uneven writer, whose faults of language and dramatic structure are 'sufficient to obscure and overwhelm any other merit', whose plots are 'so carelessly pursued, that he seems not always fully to comprehend his own design', and who 'never has six lines together without a fault'.[1] It was against this view that Schlegel and Coleridge, in particular, felt the essence of their critical mission to lie: Coleridge declared:

[34] Coleridge, *Shakespearean Criticism*, i. 116; see also ibid. ii. 258, and *Biographia Literaria*, ii. 107.

[35] Coleridge, *Shakespearean Criticism*, i. 116. Not only is the suspension of the voluntary and comparative power licensed by the will, it is also informed by an awareness of the difference between the artistic representation and the thing represented (e.g. *Shakespearean Criticism*, i. 181), which would seem to imply an underlying or residual power of comparative judgement. This may be self-contradictory, as Badawi thinks (*Coleridge: Critic of Shakespeare*, pp. 56 f., 62–4), but there is nothing psychologically implausible in the idea of a state of mind that connives at its own unconsciousness.

[1] *Yale*, vii. 71; ibid.; Boswell, *Life of Johnson*, ii. 96.

In all the successive courses delivered by me . . . it has been and it still remains my object to prove that in all points from the most important to the most minute, the judgement of Shakespeare is commensurate with his genius— nay, that his genius reveals itself in his judgement, as in its most exalted form.[2]

And the Schlegels wrote in the *Athenäum*:

There is no modern poet more 'correct' than Shakespeare in the original and nobler sense of the word—that is, where it means that the innermost and smallest parts of the work are deliberately shaped and developed in all their relations with one another according to the spirit of the whole. Similarly, too, Shakespeare is systematic as no other writer is.[3]

By these lights, the primary task of the critic of Shakespeare is to become sensitive to these patterns of significance, to apprehend the seminal principle or idea out of which everything in the play can then be seen to grow, 'swiftly grasping the myriad separate circumstances of the play in all their enormously complicated interrelationships at the one point of contact which they all have in common'.[4] To see a play or passage as an organized whole in this way is to create a perspective in which the specific faults and the general carelessness remarked by Johnson disappear in the unity of the living organism.

No aspect of the romantic account of Shakespeare has been more influential than this. Most sixth-formers now studying Shakespeare learn to believe that Shakespeare is a writer of unwavering artistic conscience, that the play set for their special study is a flawless diamond, and that the aim of their study is to discover how every element of the text contributes to the meaning of the whole. However, the diversity of defensible unifying readings of particular plays which we by now know to be possible encourages the inference that any one unifying interpretation is rarely *necessitated* by the text; it would seem that the multiple suggestiveness and exploratory open-endedness of Shakespeare's art can often accommodate a number of diverse readings, permitting different aspects of a play to appear as its organizing principle accordingly as they are nominated such. The idea that Shakespeare's plays are organic unities is not in fact

---

[2] Coleridge, *Shakespearean Criticism*, i. 114.
[3] *Athenäum*, ed. A. W. and F. Schlegel (3 vols.; Berlin, 1798–1800), i. 246. See also Schlegel, vi. 144.
[4] Schlegel, i. 92; see also vi. 128.

a testable hypothesis but a postulate of inquiry, a postulate that can certainly yield interesting consequences, but which is nevertheless a methodological option rather than a demonstrable truth of a kind to render untenable Johnson's reading of the plays. It is salutary to note that Goethe, with every opportunity of learning from Schlegel of the organic unity of Shakespeare's art, still preferred to think otherwise:

The basis of all works of art must be a unity of thought, a vital structuring of the relationship of parts to whole that works through oppositions to a coherent identity. It is this which the French have grasped in a mechanical way in their drama, and which Shakespeare does not possess, so that in this respect his pieces are worthless despite all their poetic power.[5]

Shakespeare is lacking in unity, the Schlegels can say what they like.[6]

Indeed, the account of Shakespeare as a careless, faulty, and uneven writer has from the very beginning been advanced not dogmatically but deliberately, made in the awareness of a different way of reading him by which all his geese become swans:

I remember, the Players have often mentioned it as an honour to Shakespeare, that in his writing, (whatsoever he penn'd) hee never blotted out line. My answer hath beene, Would he had blotted a thousand. Which they thought a malevolent speech. I had not told posterity this, but for their ignorance, who choose that circumstance to commend their friend by, wherein he most faulted.[7]

Johnson's emphasis in the Preface on Shakespeare's faults is similarly combative:

It must be at last confessed, that as we owe every thing to him, he owes something to us; that, if much of his praise is paid by perception and judgement, much is likewise given by custom and veneration. We fix our eyes upon his graces, and turn them from his deformities, and endure in him what we should in another loath or despise. . . . I have seen, in the book of some modern critick, a collection of anomalies, which shew that he has corrupted language by every mode of depravation, but which his admirer has accumulated as a monument of honour.[8]

---

[5] Goethes Gespräche, ed. von Biedermann, 2nd edn. (5 vols.; Leipzig, 1909), ii. 320.

[6] Ibid. 344; see also ii. 241.

[7] Ben Jonson, ed. C. H. Herford and Percy and Evelyn Simpson (11 vols.; 1925–52), viii. 583 ('Timber: or Discoveries').

[8] Yale, vii. 91.

Read one way, Shakespeare is the most uneven of writers; read differently, he becomes one of the most perfect. Arguably, neither way of reading imposes itself as a necessity. If this be so, the appropriate question to ask (as throughout this chapter) becomes, not 'Is it Johnson or Schlegel who is, in general, right about Shakespeare?', but 'What is involved in choosing to read Shakespeare in one way rather than the other?'

Before taking a specific focus for this question, some general points can be made. What is at issue between Schlegel and Johnson is not only whether or not Shakespeare's plays are perfect wholes, but also how much it matters. For Johnson it does not finally matter very much: all Shakespeare's carelessness, however deplorable in itself, cannot jeopardize his claim to classic status. Johnson is entirely comfortable with the thought that Shakespeare's highest powers are displayed in brief, relatively concentrated bursts—that the unit of Shakespearean greatness is not the play but the scene:

He has scenes of undoubted and perpetual excellence, but perhaps not one play, which, if it were now exhibited as the work of a contemporary writer, would be heard to the conclusion.

In some of his happier scenes [he has carried both character and dialogue] to the utmost height.

What he does best, he soon ceases to do.[9]

If Schlegel had believed this to be true, he would have found relatively little left to praise; for him it is the demonstrable unity of Shakespearean drama, more than anything else, which constitutes its greatness. This is because the idea of organic unity is taken by Schlegel, as by Coleridge, to imply an organizing power of the mind—in Coleridge's terms, an 'esemplastic' or 'methodizing' power—of transcendental origin, superior to the welter of circumstance and sensation which would otherwise determine our experience of the world. In the *Critique of Judgement* Kant defined an organism as a body all the parts of which can be described as reciprocally both end and means: the leaves of a tree function for the sake of its roots, and the roots for the sake of its leaves. An organism, therefore, Kant argued, cannot be adequately described in terms of the mechanism of causality which is the category of explanation normally appropriate to the world of phenomena, but irresistibly suggests the idea of

[9] Ibid. 91, 87, 74.

purpose or ends, an idea normally reserved for the supersensible realm of the practical reason.[10] The importance of the organic is thus that it stands as a bridge between the phenomenal and the supersensible realm, being an area of our phenomenal experience which calls the higher powers of the mind into play.[11] Coleridge speaks in the *Biographia* of 'the high spiritual instinct of the human being impelling us to seek unity',[12] and similarly in the 'Essay on Method' what immediately distinguishes the conversation of 'the man of superior mind' is 'the habit of foreseeing, in each integral part . . . the whole that he then intends to communicate': Coleridge goes on to suggest that this 'methodizing' power, supremely active in Shakespeare's creation of character, can involve nothing less than a transcendence of the temporal condition of earthly life.[13] Schlegel, too, recognizes in the power to perceive and create unity in diversity the expression of the transcendental self: 'The principle of self-originating activity, which may be called the ego or the personal principle, and which is opposed to all animal dependence on forces outside itself, is able to realize itself only through its striving to bring connection and unity into existence.'[14] The organic unity of Shakespeare's plays is, so to speak, their transcendental guarantee.

Schlegel's statement that such an organizing principle 'is opposed to all animal dependence on forces outside itself' brings out a further point of the organic analogy: an organism may be thought of as 'self-originating' and essentially autonomous, not caught in the web of natural causality but wholly explicable in terms of its own purposes. As Coleridge puts it in the *Biographia*: 'Nothing can permanently please, which does not contain in itself the reason why it is so, and not otherwise.'[15] The implication of this is most clearly expressed in *Aids to Reflection*: 'Whatever originates its own acts, or in any sense contains in itself the cause of its own state, must be *spiritual*, and consequently *supernatural*: yet not on that account necessarily *miraculous*.'[16] On this 'supernatural' principle, the reason why, say, Lear treats Cordelia as he does is to be referred to the play's formal dynamics and thematic patterning and internal imaginative logic,

---

[10] See Kant, *Werke*, v. 447–54, 466 f. (*Kritik der Urteilskraft*, paras. 64 f., 71).
[11] See ibid. 244, 264–6 (*Kritik der Urteilskraft*, intro.: sects. ii, ix).
[12] Coleridge, *Biographia Literaria*, ii. 56.
[13] See Coleridge, *The Friend*, i. 449 f.   [14] Schlegel, ii. 237.
[15] Coleridge, *Biographia Literaria*, ii. 9.
[16] Coleridge, *Aids to Reflection*, p. 166.

not to the question of whether a truth of old age or of parent–child relationship has there been caught and communicated.[17] Just as Hazlitt regards each of Shakespeare's *characters* as a unique individual whose truth lies in his self-consistency, 'a world to himself', so Schlegel regards each *play* as a heterocosm, 'a foreign world' where the poet rules 'according to his own laws'.[18] For the Johnsonian reader, however, there is only one world: the crucial point of Johnson's insistence on Shakespeare's faults is not that they matter very greatly in themselves, but that the reader's or spectator's grip on reality should be such as to make him aware of them. What antagonizes the romantic critics is not in itself the proposition that Shakespeare has faults—Coleridge and Hazlitt themselves find many things in the plays problematic—but Johnson's 'inappropriate' bringing of a daylight standard of truth and nature to imaginative experience, his combative refusal to suspend 'the comparative power' and dream the dream of art, to enter into the world of the play on its own terms.

Nowhere is this more striking to a modern reader than in Johnson's exasperation with the irresponsibility of Shakespeare's freedom of imagination, which he found always liable to free wheel away from even the most intensely realized dramatic situation. In a note written in 1745, Johnson believed that the clause, 'as, it is said | *Anthony's* was by *Caesar*' must have been an unShakespearean interpolation in this speech by Macbeth:

> There is none but he,
> Whose Being I do fear: and, under him,
> My Genius is rebuk'd; as, it is said,
> *Anthony's* was by *Caesar*. He chid the Sisters,
> When first they put the name of King upon me,
> And bade them speak to him . . .

I cannot but propose the rejection of this passage, which I believe was an insertion of some player, that . . . has . . . weakened the author's sense by the intrusion of a remote and useless image into a speech bursting from a man wholly possess'd with his own present condition, and therefore not at leisure to explain his own allusions to himself.[19]

---

[17] For an enlightening discussion of the theoretical implications of this difference in approach, see A. D. Nuttall, *A New Mimesis: Shakespeare and the Representation of Reality* (1983), esp. pp. 71–85.

[18] Schlegel, ii. 87; see also vi. 128.

[19] *Yale*, vii. 24 f.

For the 1773 edition, however, Johnson added: 'This note was
written before I was fully acquainted with Shakespeare's manner,
and I do not now think it of much weight.'[20] Fuller acquaintance
with Shakespeare had revealed to Johnson how often 'remote and
useless images', generated by an excessively lively play of mind
that overflows the reality with which it is engaged, break the
imaginative contact between reader and dramatic situation and so
disrupt the experience of nature. It is this tendency of Shakespeare's
imagination that produces what Johnson calls 'harsh' figures of
speech—'Unthread the rude eye of rebellion', 'Just death, kind umpire
of men's miseries'[21]—as well as the ubiquitous quibbles which are
allowed to disfigure some of the finest things in the plays:

> What! old acquaintance! could not all this flesh
> Keep in a little life? Poor *Jack*! farewel!
> I could have better spar'd a better man.
> Oh, I should have a heavy miss of thee,
> If I were much in love with Vanity.
> Death hath not struck so fair a Deer to day,
> Though many a dearer in this bloody fray.

There is in these lines a very natural mixture of the serious and the ludicrous
produced by the view of Percy and Falstaff. I wish all play on words had
been forborn.[22]

It is not that Johnson has any general objection to what is unAugustan
in the energy of Shakespeare's handling of language when in full
career; 'that fulness of idea, which might sometimes load his words
with more sentiment than they could conveniently convey, and that
rapidity of imagination which might hurry him to a second thought
before he had fully explained the first'[23] are qualities which Johnson
plainly finds very attractive. Nor does he seriously object to the
Shakespearean dance of quibble and conceit in passages of comedy
and exuberance; this is but part of that natural disposition for comedy
which affords Johnson such delight.[24] What does draw his serious

---

[20] Ibid. viii. 776.   [21] See ibid. vii. 427; viii. 571.
[22] Ibid. vii. 489.   [23] Ibid. 54.
[24] Of *Love's Labour's Lost* Johnson wrote: 'In this play, which all the editors have
concurred to censure, and some have rejected as unworthy of our poet, it must be
confessed that there are many passages mean, childish, and vulgar . . . But there are
scattered, through the whole, many sparks of genius; nor is there any play that has
more evident marks of the hand of Shakespeare' (*Yale*, vii. 287).

criticism is Shakespeare's propensity to play with words and ideas
even at moments of pathos or of high dramatic intensity:

What he does best, he soon ceases to do. He is not long soft and pathetick
without some idle conceit, or contemptible equivocation. He no sooner begins
to move, than he counteracts himself; and terrour and pity, as they are rising
in the mind, are checked and blasted by sudden frigidity.[25]

In *Richard II*, for example, Johnson finds that Richard's speech,
'What must the King do now? . . .' is blemished by the passage where
Richard comes to 'play the wanton with his woes' and to imagine
the sighs and tears of Aumerle and himself blowing down the
corn and fretting out a pair of graves in the earth: 'Shakespeare is
very apt to deviate from the *pathetick* to the *ridiculous*. Had the
speech of Richard ended at this line ['May hourly trample on their
Sovereign's head'] it had exhibited the natural language of submissive
misery.'[26] Johnson records a similarly chequered response to the
scene with Richard and Bolingbroke in which Richard sends for
the mirror, a scene absent from the first three quartos. 'Part of the
addition is proper, and part might have been forborn without much
loss. The authour, I suppose, intended to make a very moving
scene.'[27] Presumably, Richard's histrionics with the buckets and the
mirror did not much please Johnson, any more than Richard's conceit
of the fire in V. i.:

> For why? the senseless brands will sympathize
> The heavy accent of thy moving tongue,
> And in compassion weep the fire out;
> And some will mourn in ashes, some coal-black,
> For the deposing of a rightful King.

The poet should have ended this speech with the foregoing line, and have
spared his childish prattle about the fire.[28]

It might be replied that the nearness to bathos in these passages is
functional, that the effect of 'childish prattle' expresses the weakness
of Richard's tendency to self-pity and of his flight from reality into
self-dramatization. But Johnson is able to make just the same
complaint of expressions used by Posthumus and by Enobarbus at
moments of the most unself-regarding intensity of feeling:

[25] Ibid. 74. [26] Ibid. 443. [27] Ibid. 446. [28] Ibid. 449.

> If you will take this audit, take this life,
> And cancel those cold bonds.

This equivocal use of 'bonds' is another instance of our authour's infelicity in pathetick speeches.[29]

> Throw my heart
> Against the flint and hardness of my fault,
> Which, being dried with grief, will break to powder,
> And finish all foul thoughts.

The pathetick of Shakespeare too often ends in the ridiculous. It is painful to find the gloomy dignity of this noble scene destroyed by the intrusion of a conceit so far-fetched and unaffecting.[30]

Like Enobarbus, both Romeo and Juliet die with a conceit and a quibble on their lips. In order now to focus more precisely on the difference between an approach that finds Shakespeare to be a faulty and careless writer and one that finds almost all his plays to be marvels of artistic organization, it is illuminating to compare in detail Johnson's adverse criticisms of *Romeo and Juliet* with a more purely favourable view: specifically, with an early essay by Schlegel on the play. In that essay Schlegel gave what was to be his fullest demonstration of the organicism of Shakespeare's art, a demonstration by which he was still prepared to stand when he published the Vienna lectures on the drama:

In an essay on *Romeo and Juliet* written several years ago I went through all the scenes in order and demonstrated the internal necessity of each with regard to the whole; I showed the reason that that particular circle of characters and relationships had been assembled around the two lovers; I explained the significance of the scattered passages of humour and justified the occasions when the poetical colours had been heightened. From all this the conclusion appeared to me inescapable that, with the exception only of a few witticisms that have lost their point or that are foreign to our present taste . . . nothing could be taken away, nothing added, nothing otherwise arranged without mutilating and distorting the complete and perfect work. I would be prepared to do the same for all the more mature plays of Shakespeare.[31]

The continuing influence of that approach to Shakespeare—new when Schlegel propounded it—can be conveniently illustrated from the Arden *Romeo and Juliet*, published in 1980. There one may read

---

[29] Ibid. viii. 905.   [30] Ibid. 862.   [31] Schlegel, vi. 128 f.

that 'the two modes of tragedy and comedy are opposed, so generating the central dynamic of the action, but there are subterranean connections between them which make an antithetical structure complex like a living organism'. One learns that 'Mercutio is drawn magnetically to Tybalt as is Romeo to Juliet; his diversion of the quarrel to himself is ironically comparable to a rival lover's act of seduction'; one is alerted to 'the recapitulation of tragic leitmotivs' and 'the insistent patterning of the action'; one realizes that the Nurse's mention of an earthquake on the day that Juliet was weaned 'probably makes a subliminal contribution to our sense of instability and violence', and that Romeo's 'He jests at scars that never felt a wound' is 'an ironic anticipation of later events'.[32] In such a reading of the play the spirit of Schlegel's seminal early essay lives on.

That essay was largely concerned to rebut the dissatisfactions expressed by Johnson, and it is certainly true that Johnson finds *Romeo and Juliet* to be rich in what he regards as Shakespeare's characteristic faults. Not that this gets in the way of his very strong general praise: he finds the play to be 'one of the most pleasing of our author's performances', allows the catastrophe to be 'irresistibly affecting', praises the portrayal of the nurse as 'one of the characters in which the author delighted', and speaks with especial warmth of the 'wit, gaiety and courage' of Mercutio and the 'airy sprightliness' of the young men generally. Then, however, comes the concluding paragraph:

His comick scenes are happily wrought, but his pathetick strains are always polluted with some unexpected depravations. His persons, however distressed, 'have a conceit left them in their misery, a miserable conceit.'[33]

Johnson's tone makes it clear how far Shakespeare's favourite vice is from alienating his pleasure: but the fault found is, notwithstanding, a substantial one. Although he recognizes that the death of the lovers is 'irresistibly affecting', he does not believe that the pathos it inspires goes very deep; its relative shallowness of draught is felt in the freedom of Shakespeare's mind to play with words and ideas even at the most moving moments of the play. 'In tragedy he is always struggling after some occasion to be comick':[34] the dramatic

---

[32] *Romeo and Juliet*, ed. Brian Gibbons (Arden edn., 1980), 62 f., 69, 50, 63, 61, 127 n.

[33] *Yale*, viii. 956 f.   [34] Ibid. vii. 69.

situation in *Romeo and Juliet* is never felt to become so serious as to take up all the slack, all the exuberant, excessive, energetic play of mind that constitutes Shakespeare's disposition for comedy. There are two notes that illustrate this finding directly. One refers to the moment when Juliet misunderstands the nurse as saying that Romeo, not Tybalt, has been killed:

> Hath *Romeo* slain himself? say thou but, I;
> And that bare vowel, I, shall poison more
> Than the death-darting eye of cockatrice.
> I am not I, if there be such an I,
> Or these eyes shot, that make thee answer, I;
> If he be slain, say I; or if not, No;
> Brief sound determine of my weal or woe.

Johnson refers in passing to the 'meanness' of the last four lines and says that they 'hardly deserve emendation'.[35] The second note is on this exchange between Lady Capulet and Juliet:

> —God pardon him! I do, with all my Heart:
>   And, yet, no Man like he doth grieve my Heart.
> —That is, because the Traitor lives.
> —I, Madam, from the Reach of these my hands—
>   Would, none but I might venge my Cousin's Death!

Juliet's equivocations are rather too artful for a mind disturbed by the loss of a new lover.[36]

The mental activity communicated by passages like these, Johnson feels, suggests a Juliet who is excited rather than distressed by her situation; they express an elasticity and buoyancy of mind quite unlike the slow, stunned, groping movements with which the mind might struggle to accept a real pain forced on it by events outside its control; they are disposed, that is, to comedy rather than tragedy. And so Johnson proposes his distinction between the 'comick scenes' and the 'pathetick strains'; he refuses to see the play as an organic unity, but questions whether the unhappy ending is connected to the comic scenes by any convincing internal logic:

> My bosom's Lord sits lightly on his throne,
> And, all this day, an unaccustom'd spirit
> Lifts me above the ground with chearful thoughts.

---

[35] Ibid. viii. 949.   [36] Ibid. 951.

These three lines are very gay and pleasing. But why does Shakespeare give Romeo this involuntary cheerfulness just before the extremity of unhappiness? Perhaps to show the vanity of trusting to those uncertain and casual exaltations or depressions, which many consider as certain foretokens of good and evil.[37]

Perhaps . . . but Johnson is plainly not convinced; he does his best to propose a connection between the comedy and the tragedy while remarking its implausibility. This, too, must be what lies behind his speculation about Juliet:

> But, gentle nurse,
> I pray thee, leave me to myself to-night;
> For I have need of many Orisons.

Juliet plays most of her pranks under the appearance of religion; perhaps Shakespeare meant to punish her hypocrisy.[38]

This startling note is there primarily to offer a hypothesis as to how the tragic ending might have been intended to grow out of the scenes of love and humour and 'airy sprightliness'. It is a hypothesis in which Johnson shows that he has little confidence: if Juliet's crimes are nothing more than 'pranks', they will hardly seem to merit death.[39] By the time we come to the final speeches of the Friar and the Prince, speeches whose function is to draw the whole of the play together and to make us feel that the tragic consequences of the feud have been from the beginning inseparably intertwined with the feelings of the lovers, Johnson believes that Shakespeare has lost his grip on his play: 'It is much to be lamented that the poet did not conclude the dialogue with the action, and avoid a narrative of events which the audience already knew.'[40] These last hundred lines, Johnson feels, are superfluous and frigid; they counteract the pathos of what has gone before, and also exemplify Shakespeare's recurrent weakness for effects of false dignity and solemnity: 'narration in dramatick poetry is naturally tedious . . . Shakespeare found it an encumbrance, and instead of lightening it by brevity, endeavoured to recommend it by dignity and splendour'.[41] The attempt at 'dignity and splendour' at the end of *Romeo and Juliet* is to be felt less in the language than

---

[37] Ibid. 954.   [38] Ibid. 953.

[39] It should be said that in the *Dictionary* Johnson defines 'prank' as 'a frolick; a wild flight; a ludicrous trick; a wicked act'; but the OED confirms that this last meaning was already obsolete in Johnson's day.

[40] *Yale*, viii. 956.   [41] Ibid. vii. 73.

in the duration and position of such a scene, in its formal claim to bring out and to dwell on the *significance* of all that we have seen. The pathos is too lightweight and the comedy too lively, Johnson implies, for such a self-consciously significant conclusion to be in keeping.

Against this account of Johnson's, Schlegel finds all the diversity of *Romeo and Juliet* to grow out of a single organizing idea: the precious qualities of love and youth cannot but be transient and brief. This is the point of connection between love and death, between the comic and the tragic scenes, and also between Romeo and Mercutio:

The same richness of imagination which when joined to Romeo's depth of feeling gives birth in him to a romantic cast of mind, makes the clear-headed Mercutio into something of a young genius. In both of them life's rich abundance rises to a peak; in both of them, too, one senses the fleeting away of what is precious, the transient quality of all that is in blossom, for which the whole play is one gentle song of lamentation. Mercutio, like Romeo, is destined to die young.[42]

For Schlegel, the vitality of Romeo's love and Mercutio's high spirits is, from the beginning, saturated in the poignancy of transience. Such things are too beautiful to last; such blossoms could never turn into fruit. Schlegel is able to accept the transition to the final catastrophe as right and inevitable, as 'destined' by the playwright; Romeo's lightness of heart before he hears of Juliet's death is not problematic to him as it is to Johnson: 'This sudden surge of feeling is just one final flaring up of life—the "lightning before death" of which Romeo is himself later to speak.'[43] Schlegel's ability to experience the play as a unified whole also allows him to find much more in the ending than Johnson is prepared to do:

The reconciliation of the two heads of the families over the dead bodies of their children—the one drop of balm for the broken heart—only becomes possible through their understanding of how this thing has come about. The ill fortune and unhappiness of the lovers has its positive aspect after all: sprung from the hatred with which the play begins, as the wheel of events comes full circle it turns against its own source and chokes it up.[44]

---

[42] Schlegel, i. 133. Schlegel's essay on *Romeo and Juliet* takes over a number of ideas and phrases from his wife Caroline; see *Caroline: Briefe aus der Frühromantik*, ed. Erich Schmidt (2 vols.; Leipzig, 1913), i. 426–32.

[43] Schlegel, i. 129 f.   [44] Ibid. 135.

In his final appearance, the Prince, Schlegel finds, 'becomes a grand and solemn figure . . . He gathers suffering, guilt, and compassion around himself and views these things not only as an earthly judge, but as the spokesman of wisdom and humanity, speaking in a way worthy of this high and serious role.'[45]

How does Schlegel arrive at so different a reading from that of Johnson? Part of the answer is that he is prepared to collaborate imaginatively with selected aspects of the play in a way that Johnson is not. The ending certainly seems to be asking for just such a sense of significant finality as Schlegel describes, and the idea of the essential instability and transience of perfect fulfilment in youthful love is indeed suggested at various points in the play; yet the collaboration of the reader is required if those suggestions are to be promoted to become the organizing centre of our response. A critical choice is involved. For example, there are certainly lines in the balcony scene which support Schlegel's reading:

> Although I joy in thee,
> I have no joy of this contract to-night;
> It is too rash, too unadvis'd, too sudden,
> Too like the lightning, which doth cease to be,
> Ere one can say, it lightens.

Shall we allow this image to supply the ground-note of the whole scene, and ultimately—remembering perhaps Romeo's 'lightning before death'—of the whole play, so establishing the organic relation of the image to the scene, and of the scene to the catastrophe? If we do so, the love between Romeo and Juliet becomes already, here, touched with poignancy. Juliet's fears convey a premonitory *frisson*, and other passages suggesting that the feelings of the moment are too precious to endure will acquire an added charge:

> I am afraid,
> Being in night, all this is but a dream;
> Too flattering-sweet to be substantial.

Or shall we see Juliet's fearfulness in committing herself to another not as significant of anything beyond itself, but simply as a touch of nature which makes her feelings more real to us, her innocence, her hope, her fear, and her love not less but more substantial, more

---

[45] Ibid. 134.

fully and humanly present? If we do that, we shall find the lines quoted incomplete without those that follow, in which the human fear that such happiness cannot last leads naturally and without dramatic irony into the equally human hope and faith that it shall:

> Sweet, good night.
> This bud of love by summer's ripening breath
> May prove a beauteous flower, when next we meet.
> Good night, good night—as sweet Repose and Rest
> Come to thy heart, as that within my breast!

Both readings are tenable, yet each will tend to exclude or at least to subordinate the other. What is involved in Schlegel's reading is the willingness to favour the impulse of the mind to have unity and meaning in its experience; by giving a central emphasis to the suggestion of love's inevitable transience, he causes the rest of the play to organize itself around that suggestion, thus becoming intelligible as the product of a larger shaping and controlling activity of mind. Schlegel, unlike Johnson, chooses to see a significance in lines such as Juliet's, the assumption favouring such a choice being that the discovery of *significance* is a revelation of the higher, organizing powers of the mind: Schlegel would feel that his reading was to be preferred because it yields a better play. Yet from Johnson's point of view this is open to question: in so far as we collaborate in the creation of the autonomous imaginative world of the play—a world in which every event is primarily of interest to us for its significance in the pattern of the whole—we forfeit the ability to experience that world as an extension or reflection of our own. While Schlegel is able to find Juliet's lines significant, Johnson is able to find them natural. Schlegel is able to make more of Shakespeare in one way only because he makes less of him in another.

One particularly clear example of this 'collaboration' in the general design of the play is Schlegel's willingness to praise Shakespeare's presentation of Juliet's parents as tyrannical, vulgar, and wholly unsympathetic:

This gets Juliet out of any conflict between love and filial feeling, which would have been quite out of place here. . . . After an encounter like this Juliet could no longer have any respect for her parents; since she is forced into deceit, she does it with firmness of purpose and without any qualms of conscience.[46]

[46] Ibid. 130 f.

Schlegel finds Shakespeare's manipulation of our feelings in the interests of his heroine to be matter for positive commendation; 'it was most beautiful', as Coleridge put it, 'that the great characters he had principally in view are presumed innocent from all that could do them injury in our feelings concerning them'.[47] Any more critical note—a note, in fact, like that struck by Johnson's remark that 'Juliet plays most of her pranks under the appearance of religion'— would have broken the harmony of this particular and incommensurable imaginative world. Schlegel protested at the 'thick-skinned insensitivity' of Johnson's observation: he adduced Friar Lawrence's consistently secular sentiments as proof, if proof were needed, that in this play serious thoughts about the characters' religious lives are not in place.[48] Johnson, however, insists on applying the standards of real life, on retaining his sense of Juliet as a member of a family and a human being with responsibilities other than those to her lover; the deliberately insensitive tone in which he speaks of her 'pranks' (a word intended to remind us that she is a child) constitutes a recognition of how easy Shakespeare makes it for us to forget about these things here, and a refusal to collaborate in that way. In so far as we are allowed greater sympathy with the fathers of Desdemona and Cordelia, does Shakespeare not, from Johnson's point of view, get in more of the truth? Even Coleridge seems to have been troubled by how little of his imagination Shakespeare gives to the feelings of Juliet's family and household at what appears to them to be her death: 'As the audience knew that Juliet is not dead, this scene is, perhaps, excusable. . . . It is difficult to understand what *effect*, whether that of pity or laughter, Shakespeare meant to produce—the occasion and the characteristic speeches are so little in harmony.'[49] If Shakespeare had caused us to be moved by the grief of Juliet's parents at this point, our sympathy with her would have been not perhaps injured but certainly complicated.

Schlegel takes a similarly partisan view of Paris, whom he describes as a well-meaning *bon bourgeois* who, by his act in visiting Juliet's tomb, 'ventures timidly to the edge of what he might have read about in novels'. Without any real claim on our interest or sympathy, his dramatic function is simply to set off the infinitely more ardent feelings of Romeo.

[47] *Coleridge on Shakespeare*, p. 77.   [48] See Schlegel, i. 132.
[49] Coleridge, *Shakespearean Criticism*, i. 10.

And so I cannot question whether it was necessary that this honest soul should go to the sacrifice and that Romeo should spill blood for a second time. Paris is one of those people one praises while they are alive but does not mourn for over-much when they die.[50]

If Schlegel is right in saying that Paris's death means little or nothing to us, this, from Johnson's point of view, amounts to further evidence that in the 'pathetick strains' of *Romeo and Juliet* Shakespeare is less than fully engaged with his material. But for Schlegel this is a felicity of Shakespeare's art; Romeo's encounter with Paris is 'one of the many juxtapositions of ordinary life with the entirely individual and self-created existence of the lovers, by which Shakespeare makes us perceive the infinite distance that exists between the two.'[51] For Schlegel the world of 'ordinary life' is properly subordinate to the imaginative world of the play and, as a version or type of this, to the 'entirely individual and self-created' world of the lovers. A mere Paris can therefore easily be spared; what is most valuable in the love of Romeo and Juliet lies in its infinite distance from the claims and criteria of ordinary life.

In the *Preface* Johnson gives Shakespeare special praise precisely for *not* treating love in this way:

Upon every other stage the universal agent is love, by whose power all good and evil is distributed, and every action quickened or retarded. To bring a lover, a lady and a rival into the fable . . . to make them meet in rapture and part in agony; to fill their mouths with hyperbolical joy and outrageous sorrow; to distress them as nothing human ever was distressed; to deliver them as nothing human ever was delivered, is the business of a modern dramatist. For this, probability is violated, life is misrepresented, and language is depraved. But love is only one of many passions, and as it has no great influence upon the sum of life, it has little operation in the dramas of a poet, who caught his ideas from the living world, and exhibited only what he saw before him. He knew, that any other passion, as it was regular or exorbitant, was a cause of happiness or calamity.[52]

This is one of those passages in which Johnson's vehemence drives him beyond the mark; without the rhetorical leverage afforded him by 'every other stage' he would surely find it hard to defend the proposition that love has 'little operation' in Shakespeare's plays. The disintoxication is somewhat overdone; Johnson himself ends by

---

[50] Schlegel, i. 130.   [51] Ibid.   [52] *Yale*, vii. 63 f.

saying that love, like other passions, has the power to produce either happiness or calamity, in Shakespeare as in life. But, despite the over-emphasis, the main thought is clear enough: Johnson is expressing a vigorously sceptical sobriety about the claims of 'exorbitant' love, love which consumes all other considerations in its own heat, and about literature which colludes with those claims; and he finds his own scepticism to be upheld by Shakespeare's preference for 'the living world' over the hyperbolical ideas of the mind. The understanding of a right love is bound up with the understanding of a right art: just as Shakespeare's art is, despite its many minor infidelities, wedded to the living world before him, so it does not lend itself to the celebration of a passionate love that lacks any object in which it could credibly rest. The same analogy between different uses of the imagination and different kinds of love is drawn in the *Life of Dryden*; Johnson is describing how the predominance of intellectual power over 'quick sensibility' in Dryden leads to 'sentiments not such as Nature enforces, but meditation supplies':

With the simple and elemental passions, as they spring separate in the mind, he seems not much acquainted; and seldom describes them but as they are complicated by the various relations of society, and confused in the tumults and agitations of life.

What he says of love may contribute to the explanation of his character:

> Love various minds does variously inspire;
> It stirs in gentle bosoms gentle fire,
> Like that of incense on the altar laid;
> But raging flames tempestuous souls invade,
> A fire which every windy passion blows;
> With pride it mounts, or with revenge it glows.

Dryden's was not one of the 'gentle bosoms': Love, as it subsists in itself, with no tendency but to the person loved and wishing only for correspondent kindness, such love as shuts out all other interest, the Love of the Golden Age, was too soft and subtle to put his faculties in motion. He hardly conceived it but in its turbulent effervescence with some other desires: when it was inflamed by rivalry or obstructed by difficulties; when it invigorated ambition or exasperated revenge.

He is therefore, with all his variety of excellence, not often pathetick; and had so little sensibility of the power of effusions purely natural, that he did not esteem them in others. Simplicity gave him no pleasure.[53]

---

[53] Johnson, *Lives of the Poets*, i. 457 f.

Johnson is implicitly contrasting Dryden with Shakespeare at his best; the love of which he speaks—a love of the created being in all his or her creatureliness, absorbed in its object, filling the mind and stilling its restless desires—is one expression of the power of nature that animates Shakespeare's art, an art equally absorbed in the human life which it acts to represent. Firmly distinguished from such love is the 'turbulent effervescence' of passion kindled only by the sense of striving against obstruction, passion for which the object alone is not enough.

Johnson then goes immediately on to think specifically of Dryden's plays, and to relate the 'false magnificence' which fills them to this predominance in Dryden of complex mental activity over 'the genuine operations of the heart':

It was necessary to fix attention; and the mind can be captivated only by recollection or by curiosity; by reviving natural sentiments or impressing new appearances of things: sentences were readier at his call than images, he could more easily fill the ear with some splendid novelty than awaken those ideas that slumber in the heart.[54]

There one has something like the Shakespearean fondness for conceit and word-play. Not, of course, that Shakespeare works with 'sentences' rather than images, nor that he *needs* to resort to this inferior means of captivating the mind: but the teeming ingenuity with which Shakespeare 'impresses new appearances of things' with his conceits and his quibbles is, like that of Dryden, a power which dazzles rather than illuminates; it is an alternative to the power of 'reviving natural sentiments'. It follows that Johnson's disparagement of Shakespeare's 'faults' of language in passages of pathos or marked dramatic intensity is no incidental issue of linguistic decorum but involved with his most deeply felt priorities; the quibble, 'poor and barren as it is', was to Shakespeare 'the fatal Cleopatra for which he lost the world, and was content to lose it',[55] and for all their humour Johnson's paragraphs on that fatal infatuation are presented as the climax to his catalogue of Shakespeare's faults.

Johnson's proposition, then, is that to be moved and engaged by one of Shakespeare's 'miserable conceits' in *Romeo and Juliet*—for example, Juliet's last line:

---

[54] Ibid. 458 f.   [55] *Yale*, vii. 74.

> O happy dagger!
> This is thy sheath, there rust and let me die!

—is not compatible with participation in general nature. And the romantic reply to Johnson supports that proposition. For, Johnson and Schlegel are, broadly speaking, in agreement on the effect of Shakespeare's conceits upon the mind, and disagree only in how they value that effect: what Johnson deplores is what Schlegel extols, for Schlegel too invokes an analogy between the kind of imaginative activity that produces such conceits and a restless, Cleopatra-like, world-transcending love:

Love loses hold of any measure of reality in the moment of magic that picks out the one being in one's mind and elevates him or her above the rest of the world; love can rise up to the very limits of things on the wings of ardent imagination, without any consciousness of having gone astray. Love is the poetry of life. How could it not weave poetry around its object? The more remote and unlikely the images it calls up, the more ingenious its comparisons will appear . . . Hidden in the very nature of love are contradictions which mean that, even when most finely requited, it can never be resolved in a perfect harmony, and because of this it will always tend to express itself through antitheses.[56]

Love is the *Poesie* of life: just as Shakespeare is the free creator of the world of *Romeo and Juliet*, so the lovers freely create their imaginative experience, and their extravagance of metaphor stands doubly justified as the language of love and the language of poetry. To bring ideas into a connection striking for its unlikeliness—Juliet with her dead husband, thinking of her body as sheath to the rusting dagger—expresses the freedom of the mind to take apart the world as given in experience and to re-create its world in a new and unconditioned form, to 'impress new appearances of things'; the function of metaphor as Schlegel describes it in his more theoretical works is not to throw light upon the object about which it is employed but to render that object insubstantial, to dissipate the illusion of *Wirklichkeit* and so to approach the transcendental viewpoint from which the phenomenal world appears as such.[57] It is this which vindicates the poet's impulse

to draw comparisons not only between objects which are real to the senses, but also between what is known to the senses and what is not. That which

---

[56] Schlegel, i. 137 f.   [57] See ibid. ii. 83.

lies closest to hand will thus finally come to serve as a sign for the most sublime spiritual perception. Everything in language becomes in this way an image of everything else, and language itself thereby becomes an allegory of the pervasive mutual interpenetration of all things . . . A metaphor can in fact never be too bold.[58]

Plainly, Schlegel's defence of Shakespeare's 'faults' of language is closely bound up with his transcendentalism: too much so, most readers will feel, to stand as an acceptably general account of what is involved in disagreement with Johnson on this point. One need not be a transcendentalist, surely, to hold that the last lines of Romeo and Juliet are great and moving poetry? Yet, although it is true that Schlegel's commitment to system does rather limit the value of his criticism, it is also true that transcendentalism, in this context, is simply an attempt to give metaphysical habitation and a name to the specific quality of response that Shakespeare's play with words and ideas can excite in any appreciative reader. M. M. Mahood's classic study of Shakespeare's word-play, for example, has no philosophical axe to grind, and offers a subtler and more perceptive analysis than anything in Schlegel; yet in its fundamental tendency it has much in common with the state of feeling accommodated by Schlegel's transcendentalism. Mahood sees clearly that although the word-play at moments of pathos may sometimes have a certain psychological expressiveness, this is not its primary or most potent function: 'The vital word-play in Shakespeare's writings is that between the characters and their creator, between the primary meanings of words in the context of a person's speech and their secondary meanings as part of the play's underlying pattern of thought.'[59] Thus, the word-play in Juliet's final cry ('O happy dagger! | This is thy sheath, there rust and let me die!') contributes to the play's '*leitmotiv*' of 'Death as Juliet's bridegroom', since it yields a double conceit whereby the 'sheathing' of the dagger in Juliet's body is also an act of sexual penetration: '*Happy* implies not only "fortunate to me in being ready to my hand" but also "successful, fortunate in itself" and so suggests a further quibble on *die*. Death has long been Romeo's rival and enjoys Juliet at the last.'[60] Although the play on words and on ideas may not contribute to the pathos,

---

[58] Ibid. 241, 251. Much post-structuralist criticism exhibits an interestingly similar impulse.
[59] M. M. Mahood, *Shakespeare's Wordplay* (1957), 41.   [60] Ibid. 57 f.

it does offer us that other, very different, kind of interest. Mahood's analysis is meticulous and acute; that one can—if one wishes—respond to Shakespeare's word-play in this way is clear. What is also clear is that it was logical and proper for Johnson not to do so; Mahood's summary of the word-play's function drives general nature away from the centre of our experience:

It holds together the play's imagery in a rich pattern and gives an outlet to the tumultuous feelings of the central characters. By its proleptic second and third meanings it serves to sharpen the play's dramatic irony. Above all, it clarifies the conflict of incompatible truths and helps to establish their final equipoise.[61]

It holds together the play's imagery in a rich pattern. This is pure Schlegel in its move towards experiencing the play not as a representation of life but as a poetic symbol, a pattern of significances; what Romeo and Juliet do and say means something of which they themselves cannot be fully aware, and to appreciate this we need to step back from them, to adopt a more ironic mode of response: the word-play *serves to sharpen the play's dramatic irony* not simply by allowing us anticipations of what is to come, but by fundamentally altering the quality of the attention that we give to the action. 'Dramatic irony' is virtually a tautology for Mahood, who speaks of 'the ironic interplay between character and creator which is the essence of drama';[62] to make irony so central to our experience of Shakespeare recalls Schlegel's finding 'a secret irony in the characterization' and sensing 'in the poet himself—even while he is exciting the most powerful emotions—a certain coldness'. And entirely congenial to Schlegel's approach is Mahood's description of what an alertness to such ironic interplay makes possible: *it clarifies the conflict of incompatible truths and helps to establish their final equipoise.* Here, we may recall Schlegel on the 'contradictions hidden in the very nature of love'; the thought which underlies Schlegel's analysis of Shakespearean conceit and also word-play as formally antithetical constructions is that the products of the creative imagination so transcend our phenomenal experience that they are likely to appear to the understanding, or in the world, in the form of contradictions. Just so Mahood believes that 'it is the prerogative of poetry to give effect and value to incompatible meanings'.[63] He

[61] Ibid. 56.   [62] Ibid. 41.   [63] Ibid. 72.

makes this statement after observing how Romeo's dying pun on 'quick' ('Oh, true apothecary! | Thy drugs are quick') reaffirms 'the paradox of the play's experience': the poison is quickening, 'life-giving' medicine as well as being swiftly fatal: the lovers both lose and win, death is both the frustration and the fulfilment of their love. At the end, therefore, we feel neither satisfaction nor dismay but 'a tragic equilibrium which includes and transcends both these feelings'.[64] Although the word 'transcends' carries none of the metaphysical implication which it bears in Schlegel, it expresses much the same aspiration. What is transcended is the realm of nature—in which death is not an ambiguity. Haunting those metaphors of 'equipoise' and 'equilibrium' is the ghost of the transcendentalist's ideal: a condition of mind in which all the oppositions attendant upon our earthly life are found to be resolved in a higher unity.

'Transcends', used simply with reference to a feeling in the mind, can be a crucially vague term. For a more precisely illuminating description of what is happening in the mind when one of Shakespeare's 'miserable conceits' is experienced as great poetry, we need to turn to Coleridge. The essence of Coleridge's defence of Shakespeare's play with words and ideas in situations of pathos or high dramatic intensity is that such play is the proper expression of a heightened mental activity that overflows its immediate object. 'The passion that carries off its excess by play on words' is how he describes Gaunt's deathbed punning on his own name in *Richard II*,[65] and in another note he expands on this, justifying such word-play as Navarre's 'then grace us in the disgrace of death' by invoking 'the law of passion, which, inducing in the mind an unusual activity, seeks for means to waste its superfluity . . . making the words themselves the subjects and materials of that surplus action, and for the same cause that agitates our limbs, and forces our very gestures into a tempest in states of high excitement.'[66] Applied to certain of Shakespeare's characters, this account is irresistibly convincing. Richard II and Hamlet come immediately to mind as characters whose poetic conceits and self-conscious plays on words may readily be seen as generated by a nervous mental excitement which is a kind of 'excess' or 'superfluity', a way of responding to a situation in which they cannot find themselves and to which they cannot be reconciled.

[64] Ibid.   [65] Coleridge, *Shakespearean Criticism*, i. 135.
[66] Ibid. 86 f.

Remembering his strictures on Richard's 'childish prattle', one feels that Johnson could have learnt from Coleridge here. But Coleridge's thought is larger than an appeal to the criterion of psychological appropriateness, although it includes such an appeal; the 'passion' and 'high excitement' of which he speaks is not primarily Romeo's or Gaunt's or Navarre's, but a quality of the poetic imagination itself. '*Metre itself* implies a *passion*, i.e. a state of excitement, both in the Poet's mind, & . . . in that of the Reader',[67] as he wrote with reference to his disagreement with Wordsworth; the 'excess' of passion which overflows as conceit and word-play is our own as readers of Shakespeare's poetry, as well as being sometimes echoed in the psychology of particular characters.

To look at those particular cases, however, where Coleridge's account is, as psychological criticism, at its strongest, is to appreciate the point of Johnson's *general* resistance. Those characters whose 'unusual activity' of mind impels them to use language in this way are characters who strikingly do not feel themselves to share in general nature, characters whose intense inner life is so radically estranged from the world in which they live as to bring them to the verge of madness:

> I have been studying, how to compare
> This prison, where I live, unto the world;
> And, for because the world is populous,
> And here is not a creature but my self,
> I cannot do it; yet I'll hammer on't.
> My brain I'll prove the female to my soul,
> My soul, the father; and these two beget
> A generation of still-breeding thoughts;
> And these same thoughts people this little world;
> In humour, like the people of this world,
> For no thought is contented.

In an elaborate conceit, Richard muses on the nature of such conceits, on how they can create and people a little world of thoughts in place of that populous world of men of which he cannot feel himself to be part. The very strength of Coleridge's account of the dramatic appropriateness of conceit in such a passage as this clarifies the grounds of Johnson's coolness with regard to Shakespearean conceit generally; the passionate sense of not belonging in the world of men,

[67] Quoted in full above, p. 75.

finely and powerfully expressed in the language of Richard II and of Hamlet, is not the sense that Johnson wishes poetry to induce in the reader. 'These are but wild and whirling words, my lord', Horatio complains to Hamlet, but for Coleridge that unusual activity of mind which he analyses in Hamlet seems to be continuous with the power of *Shakespeare*'s poetic imagination,—that 'endless activity of thought, in all the possible associations of thought with thought, thought with feelings, or with words, or of feelings with feelings, and words with words'[68] which Coleridge regards not as the restless working of a mind for which the time is out of joint, a mind running too free and too fast to engage with the world in which it finds itself, but as the mark of the power, life, and freedom of the mind generally.

Coleridge's fullest and sharpest description of that special activity of mind is occasioned by lines in the first scene of *Romeo and Juliet* in which Romeo speaks of his love for Rosaline:

> Why then, O brawling love! O loving hate!
> O any thing of nothing first create!
> O heavy lightness! serious vanity! . . .

Of those lines Johnson had remarked that 'neither the sense nor occasion is very evident. He is not yet in love with an enemy, and to love one and hate another is no such uncommon state, as can deserve all this toil of antithesis.'[69] Coleridge, no doubt with Johnson's note in mind, mounted a remarkable defence. Our account comes from Collier:

Such passages as these Coleridge dared not declare to be absolutely unnatural, because there is an effort in the mind, when it would describe what it cannot satisfy itself with the description of, to reconcile opposites, and to leave a middle state of mind more strictly appropriate to the imagination than any other when it is hovering between two images: as soon as it is fixed on one it becomes understanding, and when it is waving between them, attaching itself to neither, it is imagination. . . . These were the grandest effects, where the imagination was called forth, not to produce a distinct form, but a strong working of the mind still producing what it still repels, and again calling forth what it again negatives, and the result is what the Poet wishes to impress, to substitute a grand feeling of the unimaginable for a mere image.[70]

[68] Coleridge, *Shakespearean Criticism*, i. 192.　　[69] *Yale*, viii. 940.
[70] *Coleridge on Shakespeare*, p. 82.

In the light of that fine analysis, let us look at part of Romeo's final speech, which we know that Coleridge very greatly admired, yet which also contains a number of quibbles and conceits of precisely the kind to provoke Johnson's exasperation:

> Ah dear *Juliet*,
> Why art thou yet so fair? shall I believe
> That unsubstantial death is amorous,
> And that the lean abhorred monster keeps
> Thee here in dark, to be his paramour?
> For fear of that, I still will stay with thee;
> And never from this Palace of dim night
> Depart again: Here, here will I remain,
> With worms that are thy chamber-maids; oh here
> Will I set up my everlasting Rest;
> And shake the yoke of inauspicious stars
> From this world-weary'd flesh. Eyes, look your last!
> Arms, take your last embrace! and lips, oh you
> The doors of breath, seal with a righteous kiss
> A dateless bargain to engrossing death.
> Come, bitter conduct! come, unsav'ry guide!
> Thou desp'rate pilot, now at once run on
> The dashing rocks my sea-sick, weary, bark.
> Here's to my love! Oh, true apothecary!
> Thy drugs are quick. Thus with a kiss I die.

The general power and beauty of those lines are not in question; Johnson acknowledged the catastrophe of *Romeo and Juliet* 'irresistibly affecting'. But he also found that the 'pathetick strains are always polluted by some unexpected depravations', and one can speculate as to which elements in the passage he would have found to detract from the pathos. Romeo sees the worms that will consume his wife's body as chambermaids attending upon her; he introduces a bawdy quibble with the idea of 'setting up his rest' with Juliet in death;[71] he speaks of his lips as 'the doors of breath' and also the seals for a legal contract with 'engrossing death', where 'engrossing', according to the Arden editor, carries the senses of '(i) purchasing in gross, in large quantities, (ii) writing a legal document, (iii) illegally monopolizing or amassing'; and he apostrophizes the poison he is about to drink as the despairing pilot of a ship labouring in heavy

---

[71] See the Arden *Romeo and Juliet*, p. 209 n.

seas. Finally, there comes what is perhaps a pun on 'quick'. One may reasonably suppose that some or all of these 'curious' thoughts seemed to Johnson too elaborate to grip the mind with the reality of bereavement and grief. But Coleridge found this passage to be 'the master-example how beauty can at once increase and modify passion',[72] and it is entirely possible to respond to the power of Romeo's speech in a way that makes Johnsonian reservations seem finically literal-minded, and to do so directly and immediately, without necessarily referring the images to their place in some underlying pattern of thought. If by their nervous energy Romeo's conceits convey the sense of being only half felt, of being projected from within rather than impressed by realities from without, this can serve to evoke the state of imaginative excitement that generates such swift and intricate connections of ideas as a way of discharging its own heady intensity. As Coleridge's analysis enables us to see, to respond to the power of Romeo's lines is to be drawn up into the surge and movement of the mind itself.

. . . passion, which, inducing in the mind an unusual activity, seeks for means to waste its superfluity . . .

. . . a strong working of the mind still producing what it still repels . . .

. . . the result is what the Poet wishes to impress, to substitute a grand feeling of the unimaginable for a mere image.

What is to be felt is, as Coleridge perceives, the very 'excess' of feeling; even Romeo's marvellously shuddery image of death as his rival for Juliet's love functions not as a window on to the reality—

> Ay, but to die, and go we know not where;
> To lye in cold obstruction and to rot
>
> I know, when one is dead, and when one lives;
> She's dead as earth!

—but as a mirror reflecting back upon the 'strong working of the mind' which produces it. Coleridge's defence of Shakespearean conceit and word-play in these terms is the stronger for addressing what is recognizably the same phenomenon as that which Johnson regards as a fault. Where Johnson finds that Shakespeare 'no sooner begins to move, than he counteracts himself',[73] Coleridge speaks of the mind 'hovering between two images . . . attaching itself to neither';

---

[72] Coleridge, *Shakespearean Criticism*, i. 11.   [73] *Yale*, vii. 74.

where Johnson observes that 'the equality of words to things is very often neglected',[74] Coleridge finds an 'excess' or 'superfluity' of mind. Johnson's strictures are encompassed within Coleridge's terms of praise, and by enabling us to feel what is powerfully attractive in such imaginative effects Coleridge helps us to understand their congeniality for Shakespeare as Johnson himself cannot, with his quizzical wonder at the 'malignant power' of a quibble over Shakespeare's mind.[75] Yet Coleridge's analysis also serves to clarify, rather than to dispel, the grounds of Johnson's resistance to such a mode of response, for that analysis clearly suggests how in such conceits nature is dissipated or consumed in the working of the mind, 'still producing what it still repels' in a way that recalls Orsino's feeling for the power of love, and imagination, at the beginning of *Twelfth Night*:

> O spirit of love, how quick and fresh art thou!
> That, notwithstanding thy capacity
> Receiveth as the sea, nought enters there,
> Of what validity and pitch soe'er,
> But falls into abatement and low price,
> Even in a minute; so full of shapes is fancy,
> That it alone is high fantastical.

The spirit of such love, like the spirit of a certain kind of poetry, is a genuinely creative force, quick and fresh with its own restless power and beauty: but it is also a spirit which causes its objects to fall into abatement and low price, consumed by an excess or superfluity of passion of which it is always possible for Viola to observe that, when put to the proof, its shows are more than will.

Conclusion: On the Necessity of Choosing

What follows is addressed to the reader who questions the usefulness of the relentlessly dichotomizing approach adopted in this chapter, where the findings of such fine critics as Johnson and Coleridge have been repeatedly pressed into positions of mutual exclusivity from which neither, it would seem, can fertilize the other. Such a reader may be inclined to believe that not 'either/or' but 'both/and' would be the more intelligent note to strike in dealing with an artist so fluid

---

[74] Ibid. 73.   [75] Ibid. 74.

and multiple-minded as Shakespeare. If no such synthesis is to be attempted, what moral for our own critical practice is to be drawn from the contemplation of these two antagonistic ways of reading? Each assuredly realizes an immensely interesting and attractive potential of Shakespeare's art; surely anything like a hard-edged choice between them could only be damaging to the wholeness and expansiveness of response that is every good reader's aim?

It would perhaps be a little facile to reply merely that we cannot choose but choose, and that 'both / and' is itself inescapably a choice that excludes quite as much as it comprehends. (Coleridge versus Wordsworth is a case in point; or we may reflect that the critic who attends to the simultaneous presence of two opposite meanings in a piece of Shakespearean word-play is forgoing the differently valuable experience of attending only to one.) But at the simplest level, the principle that criticism means choosing can hardly be denied. A Shakespeare play, like any work of literature, has existence only in the responses of its readers and auditors; by the act of relationship which accompanies or precedes all critical discrimination we each make the play what, for each of us, it is. Of course, in such an act of relationship our response is partly determined by its object: we cannot make of Shakespeare whatever we please. If in the moment of relationship we re-create the play, it also re-creates us: otherwise there is misreading. But although there are demonstrably such things as misreadings, this does not imply that there is a single right experience of the play; our response is never wholly determined by the words of the text, but necessarily involves an element of choice from amongst competing possibilities, be this at the level of how precisely to 'take' the protagonist, or of how to weigh and pace a particular line of verse. These are choices which, whether consciously or subliminally, we have to make; every reader of Shakespeare reads, in the final analysis, for the best Shakespeare he can get—his personal sense of what *is* the best informing all those finely interactive choices in relationship without which there could be no experience of the play at all. What results is, like most experience, both something given and something chosen; the dimension of choice is inescapable. And in a great critic such as Johnson or Coleridge or Hazlitt the choice to read a particular passage in one way rather than another is intimately part of a larger set of choices, each modifying and aspiring to congruence with all the others, which extends to considerations of what is the best

literature and best relation of one's literary experience to the rest
of life.

To recognize that the disagreements between Johnson and Coleridge
over specifics are involved in choices such as these, is to appreciate
that such disagreements require rather to be understood than to be
resolved. One is thereby enabled to make a more intelligent choice
for oneself, or at least to understand more clearly the implications
of the choices that one has, at some level, already made.

Yet this need not be a mere process of entrenchment, a simple
hardening of boundaries. Critical choice is most intelligent when
made *at* a boundary, when most alive to those possibilities which
it rejects; and this kind of intelligence is directly fostered by the way
that Shakespeare's plays themselves explore or exhibit those tensions
which oppose the romantic to the Johnsonian reading. The critical
debate can, often, properly be seen as part of the dramatic subject,
reflecting attitudes that are explored within the drama itself. And
where Shakespeare's drama does illuminate that debate, it invariably
illuminates and invigorates *both* sides of it. To enter into the relations
between the world and the spirit as these are mirrored in *Henry IV*,
or in *Hamlet*, or in the sensation of Shakespearean word-play; to
weigh the claims of imagination according to our apprehension of
Cleopatra's final act; to see Hazlitt's principles of reading in the light
afforded by our understanding of Lear, or Schlegel's in the context
of Prospero, is to feel how Shakespeare characteristically gives
'heaped measure, pressed down and running over' on all sides of the
question. If this makes the reader's act of choice unusually difficult,
it also allows it to be unusually meaningful, because it can be
undertaken with such sharp and intimate consciousness of what is
not being chosen, of the richness of those imaginative possibilities
that are sacrificed to what the reader believes, after all, to be the
main thing. Choice of this kind, undertaken not dogmatically
but deliberatively, so to speak, does not deny the extraordinarily
'open' quality of Shakespeare's art; indeed it depends upon the real
possibility of other ways of reading, other placings of the emphasis,
for its own vitality and value *as* choice. It implies dialogue, encounter,
and a process of definition through relationship: whereas the mis-
conceived endeavour at synthesis would be, paradoxically, quite
unShakespearean in its desire to hear only a single speaking voice.

4

JOHNSON AND TRAGEDY

If thou hast nature in thee, bear it not.
(The GHOST in *Hamlet*)

THERE are two different kinds of comment made by Johnson that could be thought to bear on the subject of tragedy in Shakespeare; these are sometimes run together as though they belonged to the same line of thought, but it is essential to distinguish clearly between them. On the one hand, there are some half-dozen notes on *Hamlet*, *Othello*, *King Lear*, and *Macbeth* that express feelings of intense strain, shock, and dismay· these notes raise questions at the very heart of Shakespearean tragedy. On the other, there are Johnson's notorious generalizations in the *Preface*:

In tragedy he often writes with great appearance of toil and study, what is written at last with little felicity; but in his comick scenes, he seems to produce without labour, what no labour can improve. . . . In his tragick scenes there is always something wanting, but his comedy often surpasses expectation or desire. . . . What he does best, he soon ceases to do. He is not long soft and pathetick without some idle conceit, or contemptible equivocation. He no sooner begins to move, than he counteracts himself; and terrour and pity, as they are rising in the mind, are checked and blasted by sudden frigidity.[1]

These generalizations are *not* directly related to the feelings expressed in those few crucial notes—which register anything but 'frigidity'. In the *Preface*, 'tragedy' and 'tragick scenes' are terms explicitly opposed to 'comick scenes' and 'comedy' and refer, not specifically to what we should now think of as Shakespeare's tragedies, but to all the passages in Shakespeare which one would describe as serious rather than comic. Wherever Shakespeare is not comic he is, in this sense, 'tragic'; Johnson's strictures refer not primarily to *Othello* and *King Lear* but equally to scenes in, for example, *Troilus and Cressida*, *Much Ado*, and *King John*.

[1] *Yale*, vii. 69, 74.

In making these general strictures, Johnson has two things in mind. One is Shakespeare's tendency, discussed above in connection with *Romeo and Juliet*, to disfigure passages of pathos by a too energetic play of mind that overflows as quibble and conceit. The other is what Johnson sees as Shakespeare's weakness in his attempts at 'amplification'; when in set speeches or passages of narration Shakespeare goes for 'dignity and splendour' the result is all too often 'a disproportionate pomp of diction' and/or 'a wearisome train of circumlocution'.[2] A small but entirely typical example is provided by Johnson's note on Camillo's lines in *The Winter's Tale*:

> Whereof the execution did cry out
> Against the non-performance

This is one of the expressions by which Shakespeare too frequently clouds his meaning. This sounding phrase means, I think, no more than 'a thing necessary to be done.'[3]

The equality of words to things is neglected: the expression is too big for the sense. On the frequency of such passages Johnson builds his proposition that Shakespeare's sureness of touch regularly fails him when he sets out to evoke grandeur through the grandeur of his language, by heightening his diction and his style. It is only with regard to 'the diction of common life' that Johnson is prepared to praise Shakespeare as 'one of the original masters of our language';[4] he cannot, one might say, do what Milton can do; where he tries to impress by the adoption of a high style, he goes against the natural tendency of his genius:

In tragedy his performance seems constantly to be worse, as his labour is more. The effusions of passion which exigence forces out are for the most part striking and energetick; but whenever he solicits his invention, or strains his faculties, the offspring of his throes is tumour, meanness, tediousness, and obscurity.[5]

A good deal could be said in support of those general observations, rightly understood, but the point to be made here is that, whatever one may think of them, they plainly have no very pressing relevance to the four great tragedies in Johnson's mind. This is clear from both

---

[2] Ibid. 73.   [3] Ibid. 290.
[4] *The Works of Samuel Johnson LLD* (11 vols.; Oxford, 1825), v. 40 (Preface to the *Dictionary*); *Yale*, vii. 70.   [5] *Yale*, vii. 72 f.

the warmth of his praise and the nature of his reservations. His pleasure in *Othello*, *King Lear*, and *Macbeth* is manifestly immense, and even *Hamlet*, which he seems to admire least of the four, possesses in its serious scenes a solemnity 'not strained by poetical violence above the natural sentiments of man'.[6] And those notes which register disruptions of that pleasure suggest not that Shakespeare lapses into tediousness and obscurity, but rather that at certain moments these four plays move us in ways so powerfully disturbing to our human nature as to be hardly endurable. Although few, those notes are of central significance to Johnson's response to tragedy, and it is they, and not the more general and far more relaxed faultfinding, which will provide the focus of inquiry in this chapter.

The question of what Johnson found so disturbing in Shakespeare's tragedies may be approached through a prior question: what did he see in Thomas Rymer—the critic who had, notoriously, found *Othello* to be 'plainly none other than a Bloody Farce, without salt or savour'?[7] Johnson must have known that he was making his general remarks doubly provocative by citing such a figure in their support: 'his disposition, as Rhymer has remarked, led him to comedy'.[8] This makes Rymer the only critic of Shakespeare other than Dryden to be named with approval in the critical portion of the *Preface*. In the *Life of Dryden*, too, it is Rymer with whom Dryden the critic is compared, and although Johnson dislikes Rymer's 'ferocity' of manner he admits the possibility that the arguments have some truth in them: 'Truth, if we meet her, appears repulsive by her mien and ungraceful by her habit.'[9] If Johnson was impressed by Rymer's criticism he was in distinguished company; Dryden himself thought *Tragedies of the Last Age* 'the best piece of criticism in the English tongue; perhaps in any other of the modern', and, while protesting at Rymer's one-sidedness and his tone, conceded of his attack on *Othello* that 'almost all the faults which he has discovered are truly there'.[10] And Pope is thus reported by Spence:

   [6] Ibid. viii. 1011.
   [7] *The Critical Works of Thomas Rymer*, ed. C. A. Zimansky (New Haven, Conn., 1956), 164.
   [8] *Yale*, vii. 69.
   [9] Johnson, *Lives of the English Poets*, ed. G. B. Hill (3 vols.; 1905), i. 413.
   [10] John Dryden, *Of Dramatic Poesy and Other Critical Essays*, ed. George Watson (2 vols.; 1962), i. 209 and ii. 178.

'Rymer, a learned and strict critic?'

'Aye, that's exactly his character. He is generally right, though rather too severe in his opinions of the particular plays he speaks of, and is on the whole one of the best critics we ever had.'[11]

Most modern commentators, however, have agreed in finding it 'self-evident that Rymer's attack . . . is not even superficially impressive'.[12] Despite T. S. Eliot's observation that 'he makes out a very good case',[13] Rymer is generally taken to be one of the 'fanatics of classicist dogma',[14] the source of whose findings on *Othello* need therefore not be sought in the play itself but can be explained as the result of his mechanical application of grotesquely inappropriate criteria: 'Rymer . . . holds that the demands of reason are formulated in the rules, and he exercises his own reason, not independently, but in the process of applying the rules. In all of this he is doing just what the French formalists advocated before him.'[15] The critics most frequently proposed in this connection are La Mesnardière and d'Aubignac, and, to a lesser extent, Rapin and Le Bossu.

But this explanation of Rymer's findings is open to considerable objections. Zimansky, his editor, raises two of the most serious of these, only to dismiss them again:

Two points of apparent disagreement between Rymer and his French sources must be noted. Rymer states categorically that the end of poetry is pleasure, while French formalists without exception insist that its end is instruction. In practice this matters little, since for tragedy Rymer immediately adds that it cannot please without profiting, while French critics add that it cannot profit without pleasing. A more important difference is Rymer's stress on common sense. French critics insisted on a previous knowledge of the rules and regarded poetry as an esoteric art, the beauty or even probability of which could be judged only by those properly instructed. La Mesnardière and D'Aubignac are more insistent here than are the later critics. But in practice the difference is slight, since common sense leads to knowledge of the rules and thence to good taste and sound judgment.[16]

---

[11] Joseph Spence, *Observations, Anecdotes, and Characters of Books and Men: Collected from Conversation*, ed. J. M. Osborn (2 vols.; 1966), i. 205.

[12] George Watson, *The Literary Critics: A Study of English Descriptive Criticism*, 2nd. edn. (1973), 40 f.

[13] T. S. Eliot, *Elizabethan Essays* (1934), 17 n.

[14] Patrick Cruttwell, *The Shakespearian Moment: And its Place in the Poetry of the 17th Century* (1954), 241.

[15] G. B. Dutton, 'The French Aristotelian Formalists and Thomas Rymer', *PMLA* 29 (1914), 168.   [16] *Critical Works of Thomas Rymer*, p. xxx.

When Zimansky says 'in practice' he appears to mean, 'in the theoretical development of this position, abstractly considered'. But in Rymer's actual critical practice his tone of colloquial ridicule insists on the empirical basis of his criticism, implicitly and explicitly appealing to a standard of natural human feeling in which all men share. Instead of reasoning from fixed formalist criteria, he frequently quotes passages as self-evidently too ridiculous, outrageous, or offensive for further comment to be necessary:

And certainly there is not requir'd much Learning, or that a man must be some *Aristotle*, and *Doctor* of *Subtilties*, to form a right judgment in this particular; common sense suffices; and rarely have I known the *Women-judges* mistake in these points, when they have the patience to think, and (left to their own heads) they decide with their own sense. But if people are prepossesst, if they will judg of *Rollo* by *Othello*, and one *crooked line* by another, we can never have a certainty.[17]

It is in the vigour of Rymer's prose, as well as in what he actually says, that the difference between himself and the earlier French critics makes itself felt. Admittedly, he is attracted by some of the rigidities of neoclassical doctrine, and having once declared war on a play he is not above throwing every missile that comes to hand; his criticism of the lack of Roman decorum in the characters in *Julius Caesar*, for example, Johnson does not hesitate to class among the 'petty cavils of petty minds'.[18] But such cavils as these play, on the whole, no part in Rymer's more serious critical purpose, as he himself is willing to acknowledge: 'I would not examin the *proportions*, the *unities* and *outward* regularities, the *mechanical part* of Tragedies: there is no talking of Beauties when there wants Essentials.'[19] On the change of scene in *Othello* from Venice to Cyprus he comments: 'Well, the absurdities of this kind break no Bones. They may make Fools of us; but do not hurt our Morals.'[20] It is not *Othello*'s offences against the *bienséances* which draw Rymer's most serious attack but its tendency to 'hurt our Morals' by 'turning all Morality,

---

[17] Ibid. 18. This has more in common with the appeal to 'the common reader' that Johnson makes at the end of the *Life of Gray* than with d'Aubignac's appeal to 'le sens commun et la raison naturelle', where 'il faut que cette raison naturelle. soit parfaitement instruite en ce genre d'image dont les hommes ont voulu se servir pour representer quelque action' (François Hédelin, Abbé d'Aubignac, *Le Pratique du théâtre*, ed. Hans-Jörg Neuschäfer (Munich, 1971), 68 f.).
[18] *Yale*, vii. 66.   [19] *Critical Works of Thomas Rymer*, p. 18.
[20] Ibid. 142.

good sence, and humanity into mockery and derision'.[21] The charge that *Othello* is a monstrous and shocking play, whose action is 'horrible' and 'unnatural', is pressed again and again, and it is noteworthy that there is nothing whatsoever resembling it in his earlier attacks on the Beaumont and Fletcher tragedies for their ludicrous absurdity; to this extent, at least, Rymer's invective against *Othello* is not undiscriminating with regard to its object.

If a special explanation for the vehemence of Rymer's demand for 'poetical justice' is felt to be necessary, this can be found elsewhere than in French neoclassical theory. In 1663, when Rymer was about twenty and probably still a student at Cambridge, his father and elder brother were seized and accused of preparing rebellion. Clarendon describes the father as being 'of the quality of the better sort of grand-jurymen, and held a wise man . . . he was discovered by a person of intimate trust with him . . . He was a sullen man, and used few words to excuse himself, and none to hurt any body else.' Rymer's brother confessed, and was amongst those who implicated the father; the brother was sentenced to imprisonment for life; the father was hanged, drawn, and quartered.[22] These events can hardly have been without influence on the man who was to demand that tragic poetry give us general truths about life more sustaining than what is thrown up by the contingencies of history, and to attack—with 'ferocity'—a play which seemed to him to do outrage to our human nature:

What instruction can we make out of this Catastrophe? Or whither must our reflection lead us? Is not this to envenome and sour our spirits, to make us repine and grumble at Providence; and the government of the World? . . . What can remain with the Audience to carry home with them from this sort of Poetry, for their use and edification? how can it work, unless (instead of settling the mind, and purging our passions) to delude our senses, disorder our thoughts, addle our brain, pervert our affections, hair our imaginations, corrupt our appetite, and fill our head with vanity, confusion, *Tintamarre*, and Jingle-jangle?[23]

But such special explanations are not, in fact, necessary. For, if one clears one's mind of the assumption that Rymer must have been too full of neoclassical theory to look at what was in front of him, it becomes surprisingly possible to see *Othello* through his eyes. He

---

[21] Ibid. 145.   [22] See ibid. p. xi.   [23] Ibid. 161, 164.

is, for example, the first of many critics to be troubled by Iago's lack
of any adequate motive for what he does:

But what is most intolerable is *Jago*. . . . *Desdemona* had never done him
harm, always kind to him, and to his Wife; was his Country-woman, a Dame
of quality: for him to abet her Murder, shews nothing of a Souldier, nothing
of a Man, nothing of Nature in it. The *Ordinary* of *New gate* never had
the like Monster to pass under his examination. Can it be any diversion
to see a Rogue beyond what the Devil ever finish'd? Or wou'd it be any
instruction to an Audience? . . . But the Poet must do every thing by
contraries: to surprize the Audience still with something horrible and
prodigious, beyond any human imagination. At this rate he must out-do
the Devil, to be a Poet in the rank with *Shakespear*.[24]

By the best neoclassical doctrine, Rymer was not obliged to condemn
such a figure as Iago; Le Bossu had interpreted Aristotle's requirement
that the characters in tragedy be good in such a way as to vindicate
the representation of an abhorrent and cruel Medea, or of a brutal,
unjust, and self-willed Achilles. Aristotle only disapproves of the
characterization of tragic characters as vicious, Le Bossu argued,
where their immoral acts are not a necessary part of the action, or
are not clearly related to their immorality of motive: where these
conditions are met, a character can be 'bon poëtiquement' although
'mauvais moralement'.[25] It is not, however, simply the fact of Iago's
immorality to which Rymer objects, but specifically its unnatural,
gratuitous quality; the play he makes with the idea of Iago as literally
diabolical is sufficiently attentive to what Shakespeare gives us to
be echoing a suggestion made several times in the course of the play
itself. In Shakespeare's play as in Rymer's response, the question of
whether such evil as is released by Iago has its root in human nature
takes us to the edge of the unthinkable, where we may uncertainly
perceive 'something horrible and prodigious, beyond any human
imagination':

> OTHELLO. Will you, I pray, demand that demy-devil,
>   Why he hath thus ensnar'd my soul and body?
> IAGO. Demand me nothing: What you know, you know.
>   From this time forth I never will speak word.

---

[24] Ibid. 134, 155 f.
[25] Le Bossu, *Traité du poëme épique* (2 vols.; Paris, 1675), ii. 50; for the general
argument see vol. ii, pp. 36–54.

'What you know, you know': Othello's question returns terribly upon
him. Iago's evil is so disturbing because we, like Othello, are denied
a frame of reference within which to comprehend and to contain
it; the prevailing atmosphere of the play is one of moral vertigo, in
which evil breeds with unnatural and horrible ease. What makes
Rymer angriest is how little all the characters have to assert *against*
the evil that engulfs them:

Of what flesh and blood does our Poet make these noble Venetians? the
men without Gall; the Women without either Brains or Sense? A Senators
Daughter runs away with this Black-amoor; the Government employs
this Moor to defend them against the Turks, so resent not the Moors
Marriage at present, but the danger over, her Father gets the Moor Cashier'd,
sends his Kinsman, Seignior *Ludovico*, to Cyprus with the Commission
for a new General; who, at his arrival, finds the Moor calling the Lady
his Kinswoman, Whore and Strumpet, and kicking her: what says the
Magnifico?

> LUD. *My Lord this would not be believ'd in* Venice,
> *Tho' I shou'd swear I saw't, 'tis very much;*
> *Make her amends: she weeps.*

The Moor has no body to take his part, no body of his Colour: *Ludovico*
has the new Governour *Cassio*, and all his Countrymen Venetians about
him. What Poet wou'd give a villanous Blackamoor this Ascendant? What
Tramontain could fancy the Venetians so low, so despicable, or so patient?
this outrage to an injur'd Lady, the *Divine Desdemona*, might in a colder
Climate have provoked some body to be her Champion: but the Italians
may well conclude we have a strange Genius for Poetry. In the next Scene
Othello is examining the supposed Bawd; then follows another storm of
horrour and outrage against the poor Chicken, his Wife . . .[26]

A strong case can be made that what Rymer is responding to in
Ludovico's lines—a paralysis of all strong natural feeling, a condition
of moral and emotional shock—is one of the recurrent notes of the
play. One thinks of Cassio's strange collapse on the loss of his
'reputation', or of the way in which even Desdemona is reduced to
a stunned and helpless passivity: it is peculiarly horrible to see such
a courageous and free spirit as Desdemona shows herself to be at
the beginning of the play (there is an obvious contrast with Ophelia)
so utterly unable to comprehend what is happening within Othello,
or to stand up against his treatment of her:

[26] *Critical Works of Thomas Rymer*, p. 157.

A Venetian Lady is to be the Fool. . . . Tho' she perceives the *Moor* Jealous of *Cassio*, yet will she not forbear, but still rings *Cassio, Cassio* in both his Ears.[27]

. . . But nothing is to provoke a Venetian; she takes all in good part; had the Scene lain in *Russia*, what cou'd we have expected more? With us a Tinkers Trull wou'd be Nettled, wou'd repartee with more spirit, and not appear so void of spleen.

> DESD.   *O good* Jago,
> *What shall I do to win my Lord agen?*
No Woman bred out of a Pig-stye, cou'd talk so meanly.[28]

In such passages as these Rymer's outrageously insensitive, sweeping, knockabout manner is there to make a serious point: *this* is the note we miss in *Othello*, he is all the time telling us, *this* unintimidated common sense, *this* indignation, *this* confidence of moral assertion, *this* sureness of reference to unshakeable human values. One might say that his commentary is intended to supply the same quality of uncompromised, downright humanity which Kent embodies at the beginning of *King Lear*, but which is largely absent from *Othello* until Emilia's outburst at the end, as Bradley has described it:

She is the only person who utters for us the violent common emotions which we feel, together with those more tragic emotions which she does not comprehend. . . . Her outbursts against Othello—even that most characteristic one,
> She was too fond of her most filthy bargain—
lift the overwhelming weight of calamity that oppresses us, and bring us an extraordinary lightening of the heart.[29]

Rymer, that is, could defend his outrageousness against Shakespeare as Kent defends his against Lear:

> Be *Kent* unmannerly,
> When *Lear* is mad. . . .
> . . . whilst I can vent clamour from my throat,
> I'll tell thee, thou dost evil.

For, it is Rymer's claim that the evil which engulfs Othello's imagination also taints the play as a whole:

---

[27] Ibid. 135.   [28] Ibid. 158.
[29] A. C. Bradley, *Shakespearean Tragedy: Lectures on* Hamlet, Othello, King Lear, Macbeth (1904), 241 f.

The foundation of the Play must be concluded to be Monstrous; And the constitition, all over, to be *most rank*,
> Foul disproportion, thoughts unnatural.

Which instead of moving pity, or any passion Tragical and Reasonable, can produce nothing but horror and aversion, and what is odious and grievous to an Audience.[30]

The objection immediately offers itself that it is the business of tragedy to present situations of 'foul disproportion'; it might well seem that in objecting to the action of *Othello* as unnatural Rymer is rejecting all tragedy worthy of the name. This is, however, not necessarily the case. In the course of savaging Beaumont and Fletcher's *King and No King* (in *Tragedies of the Last Age*), Rymer adduces Euripides' treatment of Phaedra's passion for Hippolytus as a contrast to the presentation of the supposedly incestuous love between Panthea and Arbaces in the modern play.[31] He emphasizes the intensity of Phaedra's horror at her own desires, her anguish of mind, and her extreme reluctance to speak; the situation in Euripides can be tragic, he argues, because the dark passion which possesses Phaedra is felt to be something distinct from her own natural feelings, a monstrous and alien force which inspires horrified resistance in its victim, and which therefore is never confused with the desperate struggling humanity which it invades, throws into blinding relief, and finally overwhelms. Panthea, by the same principle, cannot be a tragic figure because her 'drawling, yawning, yielding answer' to Arbaces—

> But is there nothing else
> That we may do, but only walk? methinks
> Brothers and Sisters lawfully may kiss
>
> (*A King and No King*, iv. iv. 151–3)

—shows her desire for him to be all too human, and this obscures the distinction on which tragedy depends between the horror of unnatural desire and the natural feelings of humanity that are violated by such desire. Rymer underlines his point by comparing Euripides' Phaedra to Seneca's, in whose willingness to force her love upon Hippolytus the decadence of modern tragedy is already apparent:

[30] *Critical Works of Thomas Rymer*, p. 150.
[31] Ibid. 48–57.

Now in this *Phedra* of *Seneca*, what one occasion of *pitty* have we? what ground for *terror*? and, above all, what *manners* have we? ask the generality of Women if they are mov'd and concern'd, if their hearts and good will go along and attend the thoughts and motions of this *Phedra*? will they not answer that they know no such Woman, that she is no way a kin to them, nor has any resemblance with their nature? . . . Nor can this be a cause of *terror*: for few Women would be apt to fancy that they could (in any circumstances) be so wicked as this *Phedra*. Each will say, were it my fate, or should I be curst to love where I ought not, I would certainly conceal my love, and strive with it, my thoughts, words, and actions, and all, my condition might be every way the same, or very like to that of *Phedra* in *Euripides*. But I could never speak or act at this impudent abominable rate, could never be transform'd to such a monster as this *Phedra* of *Seneca*.[32]

It follows that Rymer is not objecting to the unnatural and horrific in themselves as elements of tragedy but, on the contrary, is insisting that they be felt and acknowledged as such; indeed, he argues more than once that 'the violence of superior powers, of Demons and Furies, which we want language to express,—ἦ δεινά τις ἔρις Θεός: or some terrible goddess discord'[33] is likely to be essential to true tragic feeling. The central requirement is that we be able to find our own humanity in the protagonist, that we be allowed a clear, unambiguous, uncompromised sense of nature even while that nature, as embodied in the protagonist, is driven to unnatural action or held in the grip of unnatural desire.

It is from this position that Rymer finds Othello unacceptable as a tragic protagonist. Euripides' Phaedra responded to her incestuous desires with horror; but Othello is highly susceptible to evil suggestion and seems almost to welcome and caress his foul imaginations: '*Othello* shews nothing of the Souldiers Mettle: but like a tedious, drawling, tame Goose, is gaping after any paultrey insinuation, labouring to be jealous; And catching at every blown surmise.'[34] On this occasion, the appeal to decorum—to ideas of what is and is not in keeping for a soldier—does have its point: if Othello here behaved more like a soldier, he would also be acting more like a man. 'Othello's occupation's gone!' is a thought which seems to Rymer all too painfully true:

[32] *Critical Works of Thomas Rymer.* 56 f.
[33] Ibid. 30; see also pp. 48, 49–51, 73, 167.
[34] Ibid. 149.

Othello is made a Venetian General. We see nothing done by him, nor related concerning him, that comports with the condition of a General, or, indeed, of a Man, unless the killing himself, to avoid a death the Law was about to inflict upon him. When his Jealousy had wrought him up to a resolution of's taking revenge for the suppos'd injury, He sets *Jago* to the fighting part, to kill *Cassio*; And chuses himself to murder the silly Woman his Wife, that was like to make no resistance.[35]

Perhaps more tellingly, Rymer can no more find a full humanity in the way Othello speaks than in what he does. His account before the senate of his wooing is full of 'fustian Circumstance', and the first twenty lines earn the tart comment, 'All this is but *Preamble*, to tell the Court that He wants words'.[36] His way of expressing his anger when disturbed on his wedding-night gives Rymer the impression that '*Shakespears* Souldiers were never bred in a Camp, but rather had belong'd to some Affadavit-Office. . . . No Justice *Clod-pate* could go on with more Phlegm and deliberation'.[37] Of the 'volly of scoundrel filthy Language' with which he abuses Desdemona in IV. ii Rymer remarks simply, 'this is not to describe passion',[38] and his exclamations after the murder ('Oh heavy hour! . . .'), like the lines in which he bids farewell to his 'occupation', are merely 'sound All-sufficient'.[39] In these comments Rymer is clearly responding, however perversely, to something that really is in the play. Most modern readers would, I suspect, agree that the power and fascination of Othello's language has to do with the impression it makes of being a surface over depths; in its 'Phlegm and deliberation' it seems strangely—and, as the play gathers momentum, disturbingly—remote from the realities of feeling in which it has, or may be presumed to have, its source. It does not fall under Ben Jonson's dictum, '*Language* most shewes a man: speake that I may see thee':[40] in Othello's language the man, the core of human feeling, has been partially transmuted into something rich and strange, 'And smooth as monumental alabaster'. What that language 'shewes' as Othello prepares to kill Desdemona is a perversion or dislocation of natural feeling not wholly recognizable as human; Rymer's commentary is at its best here, in that his feeling

---

[35] Ibid. 134.   [36] Ibid. 133, 139.   [37] Ibid. 145 f.
[38] Ibid. 158.   [39] Ibid. 161, 152.
[40] *Ben Jonson*, ed. C. H. Herford and Percy and Evelyn Simpson (11 vols.; 1925–52), viii. 625.

for the horror of what Shakespeare is giving us comes through strongly despite his attitude of derision:

> But for our comfort, however felonious is the Heart, hear with what soft language, he does approach her, with a Candle in his Hand:
> OTH. *Put out the light and then put out the light;*
> *If I quench thee, thou flaming Minister,*
> *I can again thy former light restore—*
> Who would call him a Barbarian, Monster, Savage? Is this a Black-amoor?
> *Soles occidere et ridere possunt—*
> The very Soul and Quintessence of Sir *George Etheridge.*
> One might think the General should not glory much in this action, but make an hasty work on't, and have turn'd his Eyes away from so unsouldierly an Execution: yet is he all pause and deliberation; handles her as calmly: and is as careful of her Souls health, as it had been her *Father Confessor. Have you prayed to Night,* Desdemona? But the suspence is necessary, that he might have a convenient while so to *roul his Eyes,* and so to *gnaw* his *nether lip* to the spectators. Besides the greater cruelty—*sub tam lentis maxillis.*[41]

What is horrible in Othello's speech, as Rymer points out, is its combination of deliberation with tenderness, tenderness not rising in protest as nature would require but apparently at the service of Othello's desire for Desdemona's death. Othello finds in what he is about to do a terrible purity and beauty, and although it is not easy to feel him entirely sincere in this—to feel, that is, that his deepest motive is the sanctity of the claims of honour—it is also not easy to feel his deliberative and exquisitely sensitive preparation for the act as *merely* the self-deceiving rationalization of either the agonizing husband or the murderous egotist. We cannot readily conceive of a human self at Othello's centre; the bond of nature is ruptured; unlike, for example, Macbeth in his soliloquies before the murder of Duncan, there is a part of Othello which remains for us, as for himself, dreadfully, a spectacle. To the reader who looks to Shakespeare for representations of general nature, that

---

[41] *Critical Works of Thomas Rymer*, pp. 159 f. *Soles occidere et ridere possunt*: 'Suns that set may rise again; | But if once we lose this light, | 'Tis with us perpetual night' (Catullus, *Carmina* v, translated by Ben Jonson). In the poem, Catullus demands more and more kisses from his mistress—just like Othello, Rymer acidly suggests. *Sub tam lentis maxillis*: 'Poor Rome, doomed to be ground between those slow-moving jaws!' (Suetonius' *Tiberius*, xxi.) Among Tiberius' atrocities, Suetonius relates how 'tradition forbade the strangling of virgins; so, when little girls had been condemned to die in this way, the executioner began by violating them' (lxi).

spectacle presents a shocking and horrifying paradox: *the unnatural in man.*

Rymer responds to that situation as though he had heard the command of the Ghost in *Hamlet*: 'If thou hast nature in thee, bear it not.' Hamlet, like Shakespeare's other tragic protagonists, is to know and to bear that which the natural feelings of humanity cannot endure: and a critic who has nature in him and who perceives 'foul disproportion, thoughts unnatural' at the heart of the tragedies may feel and respond to pressures similar to those which Hamlet undergoes. Before considering Johnson's response to such pressures, this discussion of Rymer may be developed into the more general proposition that, for a number of eighteenth-century critics, to reject aspects of the tragedies as 'faults'—committing murder in the name of justice, so to speak—is a mark of sensitivity rather than the reverse. This proposition must not be pressed too hard. It does not apply to all the criticism that finds fault with the tragedies; one could not make a strong case of this kind, for example, with regard to Voltaire. Of those critics to whom it does apply, it generally applies only to one part of their minds. And unless the critic goes into some detail, it is impossible to say to what extent his preference for Tate's ending to *King Lear*, or his reprobation of Lady Macbeth as 'too monstruous for the Stage',[42] springs from a real sensitivity to what is shocking in those plays rather than from a mechanical application of criteria of poetic justice and decorum. But shock can, of course, itself generate mechanical postures of response; one may suppose that a genuine sense of shock, however small or little conscious, frequently played some part in such rejections of the tragic.

Some of the eighteenth-century criticism of *Hamlet* is strikingly perceptive in this way. The problem of what to make of the dark side of Hamlet's character was first explicitly aired in an essay published in 1736 and attributed to George Stubbes. The writer is troubled by Hamlet's bouts of strange exhilaration, of sardonic glee at the situation in which he finds himself:

HAMLET's whole Conduct, during the Play which is acted before the King, has, in my Opinion, too much Levity in it. His Madness is of too light a Kind, although I know he says, he must be idle; but among other Things, his Pun to *Polonius* is not tolerable. I might also justly find Fault with the

---

[42] *The Works of Mr William Shakespear. Volume the Seventh . . . With Critical Remarks on his Plays, &c.*, ed. Charles Gildon (1710), 394.

want of Decency in his Discourses to *Ophelia*, without being thought too severe. . . . HAMLET's Pleasantry upon his being certified that his Uncle is Guilty, is not a-propos in my Opinion. We are to take Notice that the Poet has mix'd a Vein of Humour in the Prince's Character, which is to be seen in many Places of this Play. What was his Reason for so doing, I cannot say, unless it was to follow his Favourite *Foible*, *viz.* that of raising a Laugh. . . . The whole Conduct of *Hamlet*'s Madness, is, in my Opinion, too ludicrous for his Character, and for the situation his Mind was then really in.[43]

Stubbes anticipates Johnson in his criticism of Hamlet's treatment of Ophelia, in his account of Shakespeare's 'favourite foible', and in his perception of much that is comic in Hamlet's 'madness'; he also resembles Johnson in touching on the unreasonableness of Hamlet's repeated delays:

To speak Truth, our Poet, by keeping too close to the Ground-work of his Plot, has fallen into an Absurdity; for there appears no Reason at all in Nature, why the young Prince did not put the Usurper to Death as soon as possible, especially as *Hamlet* is represented as a Youth so brave, and so careless of his own Life.[44]

'No Reason at all in Nature . . .': Stubbes is not prepared to open his mind to the possibility of an *unnatural* source for Hamlet's behaviour, but his comments nevertheless point towards the moral ambiguity of Hamlet's character. He is disturbed by the flippancy with which Hamlet can refer to his killing of Polonius, but finds it possible, with some difficulty, to vindicate Hamlet's behaviour here 'upon the Whole'.[45] But when it comes to Hamlet's sparing Claudius at prayer his tone rises from its prevailing note of mild academic reproof to a warmth that again anticipates Johnson:

HAMLET's Speech upon seeing the King at Prayers, has always given me great Offence. There is something so very Bloody in it, so inhuman, so unworthy of a Hero, that I wish our Poet had omitted it. To desire to destroy a Man's Soul, to make him eternally miserable, by cutting him off from all hopes of Repentance; this surely, in a Christian Prince, is such a Piece of Revenge, as no Tenderness for any Parent can justify.[46]

---

[43] *Some Remarks on the Tragedy of Hamlet* (1736), pp. 39 f., 35. For the attribution to Stubbes, see Brian Vickers (ed.), *Shakespeare: The Critical Heritage* (6 vols.; 1973–81), iii. 40. The essay was formerly attributed to Hanmer.
[44] *Some Remarks*, p. 33.   [45] Ibid. 43 f.   [46] Ibid. 41.

And his sensitivity to the moral problems at the heart of *Hamlet* also
extends to other areas:

The Scenes of *Ophelia*'s Madness are to me very shocking, in so noble a
Piece as this.[47]

LAERTES's Character is a very odd one; it is not easy to say, whether it is
good or bad . . .[48]

Stubbes's criticism of some aspects of Hamlet's behaviour as 'unworthy
of a Hero' was developed and extended by later critics. The chaotic
and haphazard manner of his ultimate revenge on Claudius was
found unsatisfactory by several critics besides Johnson, including
Charlotte Lennox, Arthur Murphy, and Francis Gentleman:

On returning, we do not find him taking any step towards punishing the
murderer; nay, most politely undertakes to win a wager for him; how
unworthy for him then does the catastrophe come about! when wounded
with a poisoned weapon himself, when he hears of his mother's being
poisoned, then and not before, urged by desperation, not just revenge, he
demolishes the king of shreds and patches.[49]

More noteworthy still is Smollett's inability to reconcile the sweet
young prince with the sentiments expressed in the 'To be or not to
be' soliloquy:

There is not any apparent circumstance in the fate or situation of Hamlet
that should prompt him to harbour one thought of self-murder; and therefore
these expressions of despair imply an impropriety in point of character. . . .
Nor is Hamlet more accurate in the following reflection.
      Thus conscience does make cowards of us all.
  A bad conscience will make us cowards; but a good conscience will make
us brave. It does not appear that anything lay heavy on his conscience.[50]

'Conscience' in that soliloquy may, of course, just mean the power
of reflection; but Hamlet speaks unequivocally of his bad conscience
often enough elsewhere for Smollett's general point to hold good.

---

[47] Ibid. 45.   [48] Ibid.
[49] Francis Gentleman, *The Dramatic Censor: Or Critical Companion* (2 vols.;
1770), i. 32. See also Charlotte Lennox, *Shakespear Illustrated* (3 vols.; 1753–4),
ii. 270–4, and Arthur Murphy in the *London Chronicle* for 17 Feb. 1757, repr. in
Vickers, *Shakespeare: The Critical Heritage*, iv. 278.
[50] From *The British Magazine: or Monthly Repository for Gentlemen and Ladies*,
May 1762: iii. 262 f. For the ascription to Smollett, see Vickers, *Shakespeare: The
Critical Heritage*, iv. 44 f.

It is indeed strange—unnatural—that Hamlet should exhibit such doubleness of character. This point was made most forcibly of all by Francis Gentleman, writing in 1770: 'We are to lament that the hero, who is intended as amiable, should be such an apparent heap of inconsistency.'[51] To the familiar list of Hamlet's faults, or inconsistencies, Gentleman adds the 'low chicanery' with which he sends Rosencrantz and Guildenstern to their deaths, as well as Hamlet's attitude to his killing of Polonius:

When the mistake is discovered, he has not common humanity enough to regret taking the life of an innocent inoffensive old man . . . and making himself the vindictive minister of heaven, is arraigning providence, for influencing punishment where no guilt has appeared; by the same mode of argument every rash, or bad man may palliate the most inordinate actions.[52]

Gentleman also cites Hamlet's blameable 'excess of spirit' at Ophelia's funeral, the 'mean prevarication' of his apology to Laertes, and his sparing of Claudius at prayer out of the desire for his damnation, which 'greatly derogates not only from an amiable but even a common moral character. . . . For a mortal vice or failing premeditately to plunge the perpetrator into a state of infinite misery, had we power, would be giving nature a diabolical bent.'[53] The case against Hamlet's amiable character has become a formidable one. Such observations as these bear directly on the tragic power of the play. Yet it should be remembered that these observations are offered not as perceptions about Hamlet but as strictures on Shakespeare's presentation of Hamlet. Nominally, they are intended to demonstrate Shakespeare's faultiness: Hamlet is not a horrifying case of the unnatural in man but rather 'an apparent heap of inconsistency.' The attitude is a judgemental one; for Hamlet to intend Claudius's damnation '*would* be giving nature a diabolical bent': the conditional tense announces that this is a moral absurdity which demonstrates Shakespeare's flagrant carelessness. Gentleman was happy to see the soliloquy cut in performance.[54] Yet the strength of his phrase and the way in which he gives his imagination to the possibility suggest how

[51] Gentleman, *The Dramatic Censor*, i. 33.

[52] Ibid. 30, 24 f.   [53] Ibid. 28, 29, 24.

[54] See *Bell's Edition of Shakespeare's Plays, as they are now performed at the Theatres Royal in London: Regulated from the Prompt Books of each House*, ed. Francis Gentleman (8 vols.; 1774), iii, *Hamlet*, p. 53 n.

the act of critical rejection could itself imply a form of acknowledgement of what is rejected. To give one further example, it is because
Gentleman feels himself critically free to reject whatever he regards
as unnatural that he can be so sensitive to the suggestions in the play
that the Ghost might be a figure of *evil*:

> The prince's address begins with becoming awe, yet I apprehend rises too
> suddenly into expressions ill applied to the venerable, well-known, beloved
> figure then before him; terror does indeed confound reason, but seldom gives
> birth to a passionate, presumptive effusion; wherefore I must be hardy
> enough to offer an objection against the following lines, as to their import;
>> Be thou a spirit of health, or *goblin damn'd*,
>> Be thy intents *wicked*, or charitable.[55]

Gentleman is sufficiently alive to this thought to repeat it twice more:

> On the prince's determination to watch, notwithstanding his violent agitation,
> he might have used a phrase less censurable than the following,
>> I'll speak to it, tho' *hell* itself should gape.[56]

> His remarks that the spirit he has seen may be a devil, and that the devil
> may have power to assume a pleasing shape, savour very strongly of a weak
> superstitious mind; and give us no exalted idea of the prince's head, however
> favourably we may judge of his heart.[57]

Beneath the moralizing surface of Gentleman's account can be
discerned the outlines of a far more disturbing play than he would
be prepared to recognize in *Hamlet*, but which his commentary serves
nevertheless to reveal.

By prefacing discussion of Johnson on the tragedies with this brief
consideration of Rymer, Stubbes, and Gentleman, I have wanted to
suggest how eighteenth-century criticism which recoils from certain
aspects of Shakespearean tragedy need not therefore be supposed
unintelligent about the plays, and so to amplify the significance of
Johnson's half-dozen notes expressing protest, dismay, or shock. At
the same time, I wish also to establish a distinction between such
accounts as these and the attitude of Johnson. For, Johnson is unique
among those eighteenth-century critics sensitive to what is shockingly
unnatural in the tragedies, in the degree to which he simply registers
his sense of shock without translating it into a pejorative judgement.
Rymer, Stubbes, and Gentleman reject as artistic faults those moments

---

[55] Gentleman, *The Dramatic Censor*, i. 17.
[56] Ibid. 16.   [57] Ibid. 22.

in the tragedies that are incompatible with their sense of general nature; Johnson, unexpectedly, is at these moments unwilling to claim any such critical authority.

This suspension of positive critical judgement can be illustrated, first, from his notes on *Othello*. In general, Johnson is able to find far more of nature in Othello than Rymer could do:

The fiery openness of Othello, magnanimous, artless, and credulous, boundless in his confidence, ardent in his affection, inflexible in his resolution, and obdurate in his revenge . . . are such proofs of Shakespeare's skill in human nature, as, I suppose, it is vain to seek in any modern writer. The gradual progress which Iago makes in the Moor's conviction, and the circumstances which he employs to inflame him, are so artfully natural, that, though it will perhaps not be said of him as he says of himself, that he is 'a man not easily jealous,' yet we cannot but pity him when at last we find him 'perplexed in the extreme.'[58]

This appears to be an absolute rebuttal of Rymer's reading. Other notes, however, suggest that this response to Othello was, at least at moments, achieved only under strain. On Iago's 'She did deceive her father, marrying you', Johnson has a long note explicable only on the assumption that he feels the force of Rymer's diatribe against the insane unreasonableness of Othello's jealousy, and is endeavouring to blunt the point of that attack by showing how Othello's mistrust of Desdemona can be seen as natural:

This and the following argument of Iago ought to be deeply impressed on every reader. Deceit and falsehood, whatever conveniences they may for a time promise or produce, are, in the sum of life, obstacles to happiness. Those who profit by the cheat, distrust the deceiver, and the act by which kindness was sought, puts an end to confidence.

The same objection may be made with a lower degree of strength against the imprudent generosity of disproportionate marriages. When the first heat of passion is over, it is easily succeeded by suspicion, that the same violence of inclination which caused one irregularity, may stimulate to another; and those who have shewn, that their passions are too powerful for their prudence, will, with very slight appearances against them, be censured, as not very likely to restrain them by their virtue.[59]

Such an obtrusive and dramatically discordant note, tugging so insistently at the reader's sleeve, suggests that Johnson is here making

<hr>

[58] *Yale*, viii. 1047.   [59] Ibid. 1032 f.

a point of supplying something which he feels Shakespeare does not, in fact, make sufficiently clear. Similarly, his exposition of the opening lines of Othello's soliloquy before the murder goes beyond what the text requires in order to emphasize that Othello *is* horrified, as nature would demand, by what he is about to do, however he may explain that horror to himself:

The abruptness of this soliloquy makes it obscure. The meaning I think is this. 'I am here,' says Othello in his mind, 'overwhelmed with horror. What is the reason of this perturbation? Is it want of resolution to do justice? Is it the dread of shedding blood? No; it is not the action that shocks me, but "it is the cause, it is the cause, my soul." '[60]

This steers the reader firmly away from that monstrous thought which Rymer had entertained, that Othello here is *not horrified enough*. Yet there was at least one moment in the soliloquy when Johnson, like Rymer, found the compassion of one human being for another impossible to extend:

> I must weep,
> But they are cruel tears. This Sorrow's heavenly;
> It strikes, where it doth love.

This tenderness, with which I lament the punishment which justice compels me to inflict, is a holy passion.

I wish these two lines could be honestly ejected. It is the fate of Shakespeare to counteract his own pathos.[61]

There is perhaps a half-hearted attempt at dismissiveness in the would-be magisterial tone of that remark about 'the fate of Shakespeare', as though this were merely another example of Shakespeare's exasperating fondness for inappropriate conceits; but his more authentic response is to be heard in the brief note at the end of this scene (in modern editions, at the point of Emilia's arrival): 'I am glad that I have finished my revisal of this dreadful scene. It is not to be endured.'[62] There is, as Rymer also felt, something at work in this scene which counteracts the pathos that might otherwise have allowed Johnson to endure Othello's action—something focused, for Johnson, in Othello's impassively self-savouring consciousness of his own pity and compassion, his 'cruel tears'. But where Johnson differs from Rymer is in his refusal to give any straightforwardly adverse judgement of the effect which this scene has on him. The terms he

---

[60] Ibid. 1044 f.   [61] Ibid. 1045.   [62] Ibid.

uses—'I wish', 'I am glad'—are those of naked personal sensation, without claim to the authority of evaluation; there is nothing to tell us whether his strong and unqualified praise of *Othello* in the general observation should be taken as including or excluding that one unendurable scene. In this there is a conscious reticence or restraint, as though in this one area of literary experience Johnson felt unable to move from response to judgement.

Just as Johnson does not say that the unendurable scene of Desdemona's murder is a fault, so he is careful not to say that Tate's ending to *King Lear* is an improvement:

A play in which the wicked prosper, and the virtuous miscarry, may doubtless be good, because it is a just representation of the common events of human life: but since all reasonable beings naturally love justice, I cannot easily be persuaded, that the observation of justice makes a play worse; or, that if other excellencies are equal, the audience will not always rise better pleased from the final triumph of persecuted virtue.

In the present case the publick has decided. Cordelia, from the time of Tate, has always retired with victory and felicity. And, if my sensations could add any thing to the general suffrage, I might relate, that I was many years ago so shocked by Cordelia's death, that I know not whether I ever endured to read again the last scenes of the play till I undertook to revise them as an editor.[63]

Johnson implies no judgement of the value of those sensations of shock. The double negative construction of the first sentence tends to suspend rather than to enforce any firm conclusion: 'I cannot easily be persuaded, that the observation of justice makes a play worse' is not the same as saying 'I am persuaded that the observation of justice makes a play better'. And when Johnson turns, characteristically enough, from theoretical considerations to the appeal to direct experience, the effect of that appeal is, quite uncharacteristically, not to settle the question in this instance but to suggest the impossibility, in this instance, of settling it at all: the public preference for Tate and Johnson's own sensations are put forward, not as decisive witnesses, but with a conscious critical helplessness as unsatisfactory substitutes for judgement, since neither the public nor Johnson, on Johnson's own admission, are capable of facing what is there in Shakespeare's ending. The formal hesitancy of the final sentence, with its conditional construction and negative verb, although positive

[63] Ibid. 704.

enough as to the shockingness of Cordelia's death, leaves the discussion of value in a state of uncertainty, of 'not knowing': on the one hand the end of *Lear* is painful in a way seemingly incompatible with the pleasure that Johnson expects from great literature; on the other hand the note pays ample tribute to the power of the scene in a way that would seem to be part of Johnson's strong general praise earlier in the same note:

There is perhaps no play which keeps the attention so strongly fixed: which so much agitates our passions and interests our curiosity. . . . So powerful is the current of the poet's imagination, that the mind, which once ventures within it, is hurried irresistibly along.[64]

A similar conscious inability to pass judgement also informs the other main notes of reservation on the tragedies. With regard to the blinding of Gloucester, which Joseph Warton had declared 'ought not to be exhibited on the stage',[65] Johnson invites us strenuously to hold back from outright condemnation:

My learned friend Mr Warton . . . remarks, that the instances of cruelty are too savage and shocking. . . . These objections may, I think, be answered, by repeating, that the cruelty of the daughters is an historical fact. . . . But I am not able to apologise with equal plausibility for the extrusion of Gloucester's eyes, which seems an act too horrid to be endured in dramatick exhibition, and such as must always compel the mind to relieve its distress by incredulity. Yet let it be remembered that our authour well knew what would please the audience for which he wrote.[66]

And with regard to *Hamlet*, although Johnson does have some unequivocally adverse criticisms to make, his response to Hamlet's reasons for sparing Claudius at prayer as 'too horrible to be read or to be uttered'[67] resembles his finding the scene of Desdemona's murder 'not to be endured' in deliberately stopping on the brink of condemnation; and, in his general observation on the play, remarks which begin in the manner of Stubbes or Gentleman by observing faults in the 'conduct' and 'poetical probability' of the action end as the open expressions of an attitude of emotional protest which pays conscious tribute to the power of that which it would gladly

---

[64] Ibid. 702 f.
[65] The *Adventurer* (2 vols.; 1753–4), facsimile repr., ed. D. D. Eddy (2 vols.; 1978), ii. 312 (no. 122).
[66] *Yale*, viii. 703.   [67] Ibid. 990.

reject: this is condemnation, but condemnation of a kind that might have come rather from an actor in the drama, embroiled, under pressure, and certain of nothing beyond his immediate passional response, than from a critic with access to some form of overview or possessed of sure criteria for judgement.

In all these notes, Johnson is torn between the impulse to reject and the obligation to acknowledge what is there, and he can do no more than offer the resulting tension as his fullest and furthest critical response. When it comes to what is tragic in Shakespeare, Johnson, that is to say, is out of his depth, and knows it. But it is a nice question how far this constitutes Johnson's limitation as a critic, and how far it is a mark of critical intelligence to find oneself out of one's depth in this way. At the end of this chapter I shall try to suggest what is lacking in Johnson's response to the tragic; first, though, it needs to be emphasized that there is nothing intrinsically inappropriate about being shocked by Shakespearean tragedy. Most modern criticism appears to experience little of Johnson's difficulty with the tragedies, but it would be a mistake to infer from this that 'our modern sensibilities are made of sterner stuff than those of our most cultured eighteenth-century ancestors'.[68] If we register less sense of shock at the presence of 'foul disproportion, thoughts unnatural', it is not that we are somehow tougher-minded than Johnson, but rather that our feeling for general nature is likely to be weaker than his, with the consequence that our capacity to be shocked and disturbed by the radically unnatural is likely to be weaker too. It is by no means obvious that this is an advantage. To *accept* the unnatural is to deny its force, or to alter its meaning; in order to feel it *as* unnatural with the urgency and alarm that Shakespearean tragedy proposes, it may be necessary to bring to the plays the most strongly confident sense of what is natural to humanity. It is true that Shakespeare's tragedies stagger and violate such confidence, but they also, for that very reason, depend upon it; a pre-condition of the tragic is Shakespeare's ability to hold in terrific equilibrium the strongest feeling for the natural with the strongest apprehension of forces dreadful to such feeling.

> Can such things be
> And overcome us like a summer's cloud
> Without our special wonder? You make me strange

---

[68] John Butt, *Pope's Taste in Shakespeare* (1936), 11.

> Even to the disposition that I owe
> When now I think you can behold such sights
> And keep the natural ruby of your cheeks,
> When mine is blanch'd with fear.

The tension of this situation—one which 'cannot be ill, cannot be good', and in which 'nothing is | But what is not'—is extreme. The thing cannot be: look, there it stands. It is to that shocking perception that Johnson's notes endeavour to be faithful, and in his capacity to be shocked he may well be closer to Shakespeare than the modern commentator who finds in the tragedies matter only for appreciation, exposition, and approval.

'Is there any cause in nature that makes these hard hearts?' Lear's question is, I take it, unanswerable, for it can be asked only at the very border between one's native land and an alien territory where 'nature' has no meaning. But among Johnson's critical contemporaries and immediate successors there was a growing movement to answer that question, and to answer it in the affirmative, by means of an appeal to psychology. This would seem to refute Johnson's sense of something in the tragedies that is 'not to be endured', but to look at these essays in the psychology of character is to see that they cannot, in fact, meet the point of Lear's question at all; the strength of Johnson's inability to do more than echo its terms is brought out by the comparison. Lord Kames, for example, explained Othello's 'unnatural' suggestibility to jealousy on the principle that 'fear, if once alarmed, has the same effect with hope, to magnify every circumstance that tends to conviction'. Hence, 'Othello is convinced of his wife's infidelity from circumstances too slight to move any person less interested', just as Shakespeare makes Posthumus in *Cymbeline* 'yield to evidence that did not convince any of his companions'.[69] Thomas Sheridan's exposition to Boswell of the consistency and naturalness of Hamlet's character was also based on the idea of fear:

Shakespeare drew him as the portrait of a young man of a good heart and fine feelings who had led a studious contemplative life and so become delicate and irresolute. . . . His timidity being once admitted, all the strange fluctuations which we perceive in him may be easily traced to that source. . . . When he has a fair opportunity of killing his uncle, he neglects it and says he will not take him off while at his devotions, but will wait

---

[69] Henry Home, Lord Kames, *Elements of Criticism* 11th edn. (1840), 67 f.

till he is in the midst of some atrocious crime, that he may put him to death
with his guilt upon his head. Now this, if really from the heart, would make
Hamlet the most black, revengeful man. But it coincides better with his
character to suppose him here endeavouring to make an excuse to himself
for his delay.[70]

William Richardson similarly argued that Hamlet's 'talk of damnation'
in this scene is merely his rationalization to himself of his unwillingness
to act,[71] a weakness in his character which stems from the fact that
his 'standard of moral excellence is exceedingly elevated' and he is
therefore 'exquisitely sensible of moral beauty and deformity'.[72]
His destructive, brooding feelings of disgust, together with the
'weakness' of character which prevents him from acting as he
would wish to, are the natural manifestations of this exquisiteness
of moral feeling, given the difficult situation in which he finds
himself, and he becomes 'an object not of blame, but of genuine
and tender regret'.[73] Richardson's essays on *Hamlet* were 'intended,
as the attentive reader will perceive, to remove some strong objections
urged by Dr. Johnson against both the play, and the character';[74]
Richardson's aim was to bring Hamlet back within the circle of the
natural, and all his essays on the tragedies interestingly suggest how
one of the main motives behind the new 'character criticism' was
the impulse to rebut the kind of difficulty raised by Johnson. Even
the inhumanity of a Macbeth could be seen in terms of the predictable
working out of the laws of normal human psychology:

. . . Thus, by considering the rise and progress of a ruling passion, and
the fatal consequences of its indulgence, we have shown, how a beneficent
mind may become inhuman: and how those who are naturally of an
amiable temper, if they suffer themselves to be corrupted, will become more
ferocious and more unhappy than men of a constitution originally hard and
unfeeling.[75]

Macbeth's fall is thus entirely intelligible: its cause lies in the principle
that limited gratification combined with strong imagination will
tend to increase the 'ruling passion', which, in Macbeth's case, is
ambition—a process expounded by Richardson with the aid of
Hutcheson's theories of association. Macbeth, it is true, speaks of

---

[70] *Boswell's London Journal 1762–1763*, ed. F. A. Pottle (1950), 234 f.
[71] William Richardson, *Essays on Some of Shakespeare's Dramatic Characters:
To which is added, An Essay on the Faults of Shakespeare*, 5th edn. (1797), 131–3.
[72] Ibid. 76, 78.   [73] Ibid. 141.   [74] Ibid. 138 n.   [75] Ibid. 68.

a *supernatural* soliciting, but for Richardson the soliciting to evil is only supernatural in so far as Shakespeare—somewhat unhelpfully—allowed himself to put forward such an idea for the sake of the undiscerning among his audience.[76]

Richardson's essays are open to criticism for the unsubtlety of much of their analysis, and for their invocation of a pseudo-scientific conception of psychology to make psychological description masquerade as explanation. But in the present context these criticisms are incidental; they could not, for example, be brought against the sensitive psychological interpretations of 'unnatural' characters and actions in Shakespeare that one finds in Coleridge's notes. The essential question here is whether such psychological interpretations, taken at their most illuminating and convincing, can be said to refute Johnson's sense of something shockingly unnatural in the tragedies—can be said, that is, successfully to treat Johnson's finding of something radically problematic in those plays as a *critical* problem, a problem of interpretation that admits of possible solution.

A strong case can be made, I believe, that however much such psychological readings add to our sympathetic understanding of the character in question, they do not touch the crucial point at issue for Johnson. In outline, the reason is this. Let us recall that Kames explains Othello's susceptibility to jealousy as the natural psychological effect of fear, and that Sheridan ascribes the 'strange fluctuations' in Hamlet's behaviour, such as his sparing Claudius and the reasons he gives for doing so, to his 'timidity'; Thomas Whately's essay comparing Macbeth and Richard III may also be mentioned here, in which Macbeth is humanized in so far as the quality chiefly distinguishing him from Richard is found to be his fearful self-regard.[77] Now, one may broadly agree that Hamlet, Othello, and Macbeth are all, at crucial points in their respective plays, men in the grip of fear, and that this fear palpably influences their actions in a manner profoundly and recognizably human: but this still does not meet the question of what it is that inspires such fear. Each of them is a man of unusual courage; there is nothing very timid about the way Hamlet challenges the Ghost. Yet each of them is terrified, arguably, by his intuition of what Rymer calls 'something horrible and prodigious, beyond any human imagination', and it is this which

[76] See ibid. 38–45.
[77] Thomas Whately, *Remarks on Some of the Characters of Shakespere* (1785).

is necessarily left out of a psychological reading which seeks to analyse action in terms of feeling and motive without sufficiently considering that a character's feelings and motives may be manifestations of or responses to realities not themselves psychological. By 'general nature' Johnson, as has been argued earlier, understands a true correspondence between our states of feeling and the course of the world, an ebb and flow of life *through* the flux of personal feeling and motive; a purely psychological account of Hamlet's or Othello's behaviour as 'natural' is not only something different from Johnson's understanding of 'nature', but ultimately cuts against it, since it implicitly denies any notion of a correspondence between our feelings and the nature of things by presuming the source and significance of states of feeling to lie within themselves. A purely psychological reading of the last scene of *Othello* may so far refute Rymer as to show that what is happening to Othello is happening to a human being like ourselves, but *what* it is that is happening remains a further question, one which cannot be answered by even the fullest and subtlest possible description of Othello's feelings. 'What are Othello's feelings?' is not the same question as '*What* does Othello feel?', where 'feel' is, emphatically, a transitive verb.

These propositions may be tested and illustrated by considering Coleridge's attempts to reconcile certain of the 'shocking' moments in the tragedies to nature by means of a psychological reading undoubtedly more sensitive than any that Johnson was able to provide. Coleridge was quite as capable of rejecting and condemning those aspects of tragedy shocking to his sense of the natural as any critic discussed in this chapter:

Take the admirable Tragedy of Orestes, or the husband of Jocasta, yet whatever might be the genius of Sophocles, they had a fault. There we see a man oppressed by fate for an action of which he was not morally guilty: the crime is taken from the moral act, and given to the action; we are obliged to say to ourselves that in those days they considered things without reference to the real guilt of the persons.[78]

But such horrifying moral ambiguity is just what Coleridge, unlike Johnson, claims *not* to find in Shakespeare's tragedies. Here is

[78] *Coleridge on Shakespeare: The Text of the Lectures of 1811–12*, ed. R. A. Foakes (1971), 87.

Johnson's note on Hamlet's sparing of Claudius at prayer, followed
by Coleridge's reply:

> This speech, in which Hamlet, represented as a virtuous character, is not
> content with taking blood for blood, but contrives damnation for the man
> that he would punish, is too horrible to be read or to be uttered.[79]

> Dr. Johnson's mistaking of the marks of reluctance and procrastination
> for impetuous, horror-striking fiendishness! Of such importance is it to
> understand the *germ* of a character.[80]

Johnson's phrasing is precise: it is not simply the desire for Claudius's
damnation which horrifies but the presence of such a desire in
one *represented as a virtuous character*: lilies that fester smell far
worse than weeds.[81] Coleridge's rejoinder follows the line taken by
Richardson: Hamlet does not really desire to damn Claudius, but
is merely seeking an excuse for delay, rationalizing his reluctance
to do the deed. This is certainly a possible reading, but by no means
as self-evident as Coleridge suggests; an actor would have to give
a very pointed performance of this speech to make it clear that
Hamlet's thoughts of damning Claudius are coming only from the
top of his mind, so to speak: the movement of the verse and the
intensity with which Hamlet dwells upon the thought tend, if
anything, to pull the other way. A neutral performance would,
perhaps, convey no more than that Hamlet's feelings at this point
are ambiguous and hard to discern. But even if one accepts Coleridge's
account, the question should still arise: why should Hamlet's rationalization of his reluctance take this monstrous form? And why should
he feel such reluctance to act—a reluctance which expresses itself
in such a horrific way—except out of an apprehension of something
shocking within himself to which the command of vengeance makes
a strong but terrible appeal? These questions have sufficient force
to suggest, at least, that Coleridge's reply to Johnson is not the clear
refutation that Coleridge takes it to be.

Another point of dispute between Johnson and Coleridge bears
on the same general issue. If there is within Hamlet something 'too
horrible to be uttered', Johnson feels its presence also in Hamlet's
treatment of Ophelia:

---

[79] *Yale*, viii. 990.
[80] Samuel Taylor Coleridge, *Shakespearean Criticism*, ed. T. M. Raysor, 2nd edn.
(2 vols.; 1960), i. 29 f.
[81] See Shakespeare's sonnet 94.

Of the feigned madness of Hamlet there appears no adequate cause, for he does nothing which he might not have done with the reputation of sanity. He plays the madman most, when he treats Ophelia with so much rudeness, which seems to be useless and wanton cruelty.[82]

Coleridge's most impressive attempt at answering this charge refers specifically to III. i:

Hamlet here discovers that he is watched, and Ophelia a decoy. Even this in a mood so anxious and irritable accounts for a certain harshness in him; and yet a wild upworking of love, sporting with opposites with a wilful self-tormenting irony, is perceptible throughout: *ex. gr.* 'I did love you' and his reference to the faults of the sex from which Ophelia is so characteristically free that the freedom therefrom constitutes her character.[83]

Here again, the text permits Coleridge's reading (that is, that Hamlet discovers that he is watched) without absolutely requiring it. But one may in any case grant the fidelity and insight of Coleridge's account of Hamlet's feelings. No critic can catch and transmit such impressions of feeling more finely than Coleridge, and it is by this means—as in the scene of Claudius at prayer—that he here defends Hamlet's human naturalness against Johnson. But is Hamlet to be identified simply with his feelings? Johnson, it is relevant to recall, vehemently opposed any suggestion that moral quality might inhere in a state of feeling as something more important than, and theoretically separable from, behaviour and action; he would have been deeply suspicious of Coleridge's reiterated insistence in his discussions of ethics on 'the primacy of "being" over "doing"',[84] as it appears for example in this 1803 notebook entry: 'Not what C. *has done?* or what has S. *done?* . . . but spite of it—what *is* C. or S. on the whole?'[85] For Coleridge the crucial thing is the intrinsic worth of the 'original self' prior to any consideration of conduct; hence his dissatisfaction with Greek tragedy, where what Oedipus and Orestes *are* is inextricably involved with what they have done and are to do. He could not have shared in the sentiment of sonnet 94: 'sweetest things turn sourest by their deeds'. By contrast, in all Johnson's

---

[82] *Yale*, viii. 1011.

[83] Samuel Taylor Coleridge, *Shakespearean Criticism*, i. 27.

[84] A. J. Harding, *Coleridge and the Idea of Love* (1974), 42.

[85] Coleridge, *Notebooks* (1957–), i. no. 1605. See also *Notebooks*, i. no. 1815; *The Friend*, ed. Barbara E. Rooke (2 vols.; 1969), ii. 314 f.; Harding, *Coleridge and the Idea of Love*, pp. 13, 37–42, 101–5.

moral writing the emphasis falls consistently on the choice of life, the use of talents, the relations of the self with others and with the world on which it acts.[86] Although Hamlet may indeed feel the scrupulous reluctance that Coleridge finds in him when he spares Claudius at prayer, it remains true that the issue of that feeling is the eventual consignment of Claudius to hell and the immediate release in Hamlet of the most barbarous and vengeful ideas; and although he may indeed feel a 'wild upworking of love' for Ophelia, he in practice treats her with what Johnson calls cruelty and even Coleridge concedes to be harshness. Is not part of the horror of these scenes the perception that there is something evil in Hamlet working itself out in his actions *despite* the humanity and naturalness of his feelings? His cruelty to Ophelia is all the more shocking, Johnson implies, for being 'useless and wanton', gratifying no imaginable feeling within Hamlet himself. It strikes Johnson as madness. What Hamlet feels and what he wills are strangely powerless to operate on the world, to issue in action; he appears impelled by forces which he cannot comprehend: 'Of the feigned madness of Hamlet there appears no adequate cause . . . Hamlet is, through the whole play, rather an instrument than an agent.'[87] Although Johnson does not develop that thought, it suggests a reading of *Hamlet* by comparison with which Coleridge's subordination of what Hamlet does to what he feels constitutes a softening of the play—a softening which can also be felt in a note contrasting the Ghost in *Hamlet* to the supernatural in *Macbeth*: 'In the first it is connected with the best and holiest feelings; in the second with the shadowy, turbulent, and unsanctified cravings of the individual will.'[88] For that note, printed in *Literary Remains* from an unknown source, we have only Hartley Coleridge's authority, and Raysor relegates it to a footnote. But something of the kind is implied by Coleridge's authenticated comment that the 'superstition' in *Macbeth* and *Hamlet* is 'not merely different but opposite', and accords well with his general account of the supernatural in Shakespeare as expressing a 'reverence for whatever arises out of our moral nature, even in the guise of superstition'.[89] Johnson, by contrast, speaks simply of 'the

---

[86] See Robert Voitle, *Samuel Johnson the Moralist* (Cambridge, Mass., 1961), 125–36, 149 f.; M. J. Quinlan, *Samuel Johnson: A Layman's Religion* (Madison, Wis., 1964), 101–25.   [87] *Yale*, viii. 1011.
[88] Coleridge, *Shakespearean Criticism*, i. 60 n.   [89] Ibid. 60, 138.

apparition that . . . chills the blood with horror' and foreshadows much modern speculation about the nature of the Ghost in the flash of anger that illuminates this unusually disturbing manifestation of Shakespeare's moral carelessness:

> The poet is accused of having shown little regard to poetical justice, and may be charged with equal neglect of poetical probability. The apparition left the regions of the dead to little purpose; the revenge which he demands is not obtained but by the death of him that was required to take it; and the gratification which would arise from the destruction of an usurper and a murderer, is abated by the untimely death of Ophelia, the young, the beautiful, the harmless, and the pious.[90]

Whatever the pieties of natural feeling associated with the Ghost, its practical influence is for evil.

Coleridge naturalizes other tragic protagonists similarly, giving primacy to their states of (conscious) feeling. 'Othello's *belief* not jealousy; forced upon him by Iago', he notes, contrasting the jealous vindictiveness of a Leontes to 'the feeling of high honor (as in Othello), a mistaken sense of duty'.[91] And Coleridge likewise responds to Lear as to the man Lear feels himself to be, a man more sinned against than sinning: 'All Lear's faults increase our pity. We refuse to know them otherwise than as means and aggravations of his sufferings and his daughters' ingratitude.'[92] Yet it is worth pausing for a moment over the delicacy of Coleridge's phrasing here: how is it possible to 'refuse to know' something? Such a refusal must itself involve a form of knowledge; it suggests what it denies, in a way which precisely reflects Lear's protestations of his innocence, or which may be more generally compared to Banquo's 'refusal to know' in *Macbeth*:

> Merciful Pow'rs!
> Restrain in me the cursed thoughts, that nature
> Gives way to in repose.

The man who had written *The Ancient Mariner* and *Christabel*—poems which appear to repeat the 'fault' of Sophocles in the ambiguity which surrounds 'the real guilt of the persons'—was not without sensitivity to the horror of nature violated, and in certain of the Shakespeare notes that sensitivity makes itself felt in the energy and

---

[90] *Yale*, viii. 1011.
[91] Coleridge, *Shakespearean Criticism*, i. 111 f.   [92] Ibid. 58.

anxiety with which it is denied, in the impression given of protesting too much. One clear example is his discussion of Edmund:

In the display of such a character it was of the utmost importance to prevent the guilt from passing into utter *monstrosity*—which again depends on the presence or absence of causes and temptations sufficient to *account* for the wickedness, without the necessity of recurring to a thorough fiendishness of nature for its origination. For . . . it becomes both morally and poetically unsafe to present what is admirable—what our nature compels us to admire—in the mind, and what is most detestable in the heart, as co-existing in the same individual without any apparent connection.[93]

Is there any cause in nature that makes these hard hearts? It is because Coleridge is so acutely alive to what is 'unsafe' in that question that he makes such haste to answer it in the affirmative. He goes on to explain at some length how Edmund can be 'accounted for' on the psychological principle that 'shame sharpens a predisposition in the heart to evil. For it is a profound moral, that shame will naturally generate guilt; the oppressed will be vindictive, like Shylock.' Edmund's wickedness, Coleridge argues, is the product of shame at his bastardy, at its public knowledge and the 'most degrading and licentious levity' with which Gloucester speaks of it; he has been denied 'all the kindly counteractions to the mischievous feelings of shame' that would have come had he been allowed to live at home; and he is motivated not by vindictiveness alone but by his desire for 'that power which in its blaze of radiance would hide the dark spots on his disk'.[94] As general psychology, this is highly persuasive, and as exposition of our dim and hardly conscious sense of Edmund's personal history it is plausible, although Coleridge overstates the case: he compares Edmund with Shylock, but we never feel in Edmund anything remotely like the bitter resentment of

> Fair Sir, you spit on me on wednesday last,
> You spurn'd me such a day; another time
> You call'd me dog . . .[95]

But, in any case, such psychological interpretation cannot account for *all* that Shakespeare suggests through Edmund; its inadequacy is most clearly to be felt in Coleridge's description of 'Thou, *Nature*,

---

[93] Ibid. 52. [94] Ibid. 55, 51 f.
[95] The quotation is taken from Johnson's 1773 edn., which offers an improved reading over 1765.

art my Goddess' as the attempt of a guilty conscience to justify itself:
'In this speech of Edmund you see, as soon as a man cannot reconcile
himself to reason, how his conscience flies off by way of appeal to
nature, who is sure upon such occasions never to find fault.'[96]
Whatever the feelings of shame and guilt may be from which
Edmund's mind is moving away, is there not in 'Nature' (as he terms
it) also something which he is positively and strongly attracted
towards? The power which he there invokes grows in the course
of the play into a power of evil that cannot be explained and
subsumed under the categories of moral psychology: Coleridge
himself came to the point of admitting this in respect of the blinding
of Gloucester. His response is given parenthetically in a note on the
play's opening:

With excellent judgement, and provident for the claims of the moral sense,
for that which relatively to the drama is called poetic justice; and as the
fittest means for reconciling the feelings of the spectators to the horrors of
Gloster's after sufferings,—at least, of rendering them somewhat less
unendurable (for I will not disguise my conviction that in this one point
the tragic has been urged beyond the outermost mark and *ne plus ultra* of
the dramatic)—Shakespeare has precluded all excuse and palliation of the
guilt incurred by both the parents of the base-born Edmund by Gloster's
confession that he was at the time a married man.[97]

There one can see Coleridge reaching out for the kind of 'accounting'
practised within the play by Edgar—

> The dark and vicious place, where thee he got,
> Cost him his eyes

—but there is a recoil as Coleridge finds the outrage to 'the claims
of the moral sense' too great to permit such a rationalization. On
the blinding scene itself, his marginal note reads: 'What can I say
of this scene? My reluctance to think Shakespeare wrong, and
yet—'.[98] This is not unlike Johnson's response to such moments; the
impulse to reject and deny is both provoked and held in check by
the power of what is represented.

The issues raised by Edmund's invocation of 'Nature' come up
again, more crucially, with regard to the lines in which Lady Macbeth
calls on the powers of darkness to stifle any impulse of compassion

[96] Coleridge, *Shakespearean Criticism*, i. 55.
[97] Ibid. 51.   [98] Ibid. 59.

within her. This soliloquy had been too much for the psycho-
logizing critics before Coleridge; Kames reluctantly concluded it 'not
natural', and even Richardson agreed with the common view that
Lady Macbeth was 'perhaps too savage to be a genuine representation
of nature'.[99] Coleridge, however, argued brilliantly against such
a view:

> The lecturer alluded to the prejudiced idea of Lady Macbeth as a monster,
> as a being out of nature and without conscience: on the contrary, her constant
> effort throughout the play was, if the expression may be forgiven, to *bully*
> conscience. She was a woman of a visionary and day-dreaming turn of mind
> . . . But her conscience, so far from being seared, was continually smarting
> within her; and she endeavours to stifle its voice, and keep down its struggles,
> by inflated and soaring fancies, and appeals to spiritual agency.[100]

To this report in the *Bristol Gazette* may be added Coleridge's own
notes on Lady Macbeth's soliloquy:

> Day-dreamer's valiance. . . . Feeding herself with day-dreams of ambition,
> she mistakes the courage of fantasy for the power of bearing the consequences
> of the realities of guilt. . . . All the false efforts of a mind accustomed only
> to the shadows of the imagination, vivid enough to throw the every-day
> realities into shadows, but not yet compared with their own correspondent
> realities.[101]

Although the notes and the lecture appear to differ on the question of how far Lady Macbeth's 'courage of fantasy' is itself the
expression of an uneasy conscience, the main point is entirely cogent.
Lady Macbeth's belief that she can absolutely set aside her 'human
kindness' is a delusion, and can be seen to be one even before 'the
realities of guilt' begin to bear her down: Coleridge, in his lecture,
not only remarks the significance of 'Had he not resembled | My
father as he slept, I had done it', but also finely observes that
the passage in which Lady Macbeth imagines herself dashing out the
brains of the baby at her breast, 'though usually thought to prove
a merciless and unwomanly nature, proves the direct opposite',
since she is here avowedly proposing the case of what would be
'most revolting to her own feelings': 'Her very allusion to it, and

---

[99] Kames, *Elements of Criticism*, 212; Richardson, *Essays on Shakespeare's Dramatic Characters*, 66.
[100] Coleridge, *Shakespearean Criticism*, ii. 221.
[101] Ibid. i. 64 f.; see also *Miscellaneous Criticism*, ed. T. M. Raysor (1936), 448.

her purpose in this allusion, shows that she considered no tie so tender as that which connected her with her babe.'[102] Coleridge successfully overturns any view of Lady Macbeth as a purely inhuman monster, 'a being out of nature'. But such psychological analysis, however convincing in itself, still cannot 'account for' all that is shocking in Lady Macbeth's dedication of herself to evil. From the fact that she is supported in this by 'the courage of fantasy', it does not follow that the evil to which she is so intimately attracted is itself fantastic, itself the product merely of 'day-dreamer's valiance'. She may not truly know the strength of her own natural feelings, but she is not *romancing* when she calls upon the powers of darkness in language which Johnson found to possess 'all the force of poetry, that force which *calls new powers into being*' (my italics).[103] The more we recognize in Lady Macbeth the psychology of a human being like ourselves, the more disturbing must be our awareness of a dimension beyond the natural:

> More needs she the Divine, than the Physician,
> God, God, forgive us all!

Her embracing of evil is not only a problem, which the actress, or the critic, may do something to illuminate: it also presents us with a mystery, a darkness in the play which cannot be made light.

In this respect, Johnson's ability to be shocked by the tragedies deserves to be seen as a strength rather than a weakness. It renders the experience of human nature at a limit and forced to endure the shock of intimate encounter with what lies forever beyond it; in its way, it is comparable to the unquestionable strength of Gloucester's ability to be radically shocked by Regan's and Goneril's treatment of Lear, or, more modestly, to the consternation of the Doctor in *Macbeth*: 'I think, but dare not speak'—which is not unlike Johnson's 'too horrible to be read or to be uttered'. At such moments, Johnson responds as though himself a character in the drama. But to make the point in that way is to indicate a failing as well as a strength in such immediacy of response, a failing located in the nakedness and painfulness of his engagement with what is 'unendurable' in the plays. The problem is not that Johnson finds moments in the tragedies intensely shocking, but that he finds those sensations of

---

[102] Coleridge, *Shakespearean Criticism*, ii. 221.
[103] *Yale*, v. 127 (*Rambler*, no. 168). For the context, see n. 110 below.

shock wholly painful. There is for him nothing which *mediates* the shockingness of the action to us in a form that we can not only endure but even, in however complex a sense of the word, take pleasure in.

At this point I want to recall Johnson's general proposition that 'Shakespeare has no heroes; his scenes are occupied only by men, who act and speak as the reader thinks that he should himself have spoken or acted on the same occasion'.[104] However appropriate to the great majority of Shakespeare's plays, it may be this tendency to think of 'heroes' and 'men' as mutually exclusive categories that cramps Johnson's full appreciation of the tragic. Shakespearean tragedy presents a situation unendurable to common human nature: but the protagonist, with all the feelings natural to common humanity, yet dares do more than may become a man: and by actively enduring the unendurable as we could not, he makes it possible for our minds to expand where they could only otherwise have been oppressed and overwhelmed. Johnson's response, however, might be described as being to tragedy without heroes, and is happiest with those situations which require something less than *heroic* endurance. Katharine's final scene in *Henry VIII* he pronounced to be

above any other part of Shakespeare's tragedies, and perhaps above any scene of any other poet, tender and pathetick, without gods, or furies, or poisons, or precipices, without the help of romantick circumstances, without improbable sallies of poetical lamentation, and without any throes of tumultuous misery.[105]

In that scene Katharine contemplates the injustice she has suffered, her fall, and her approaching end, with a noble patience; without being spiritless or unnaturally self-denying, her attitude is one of acceptance and calm magnanimity, and she is so far from being a heroic figure that the moral beauty of her response to affliction is presented as exemplary, as that which the reader would at least hope to feel on the same occasion. Johnson's derisive listing of those missing 'romantick circumstances' implies that anything more urgent or 'tumultuous' than Katharine here could only be a kind of Gothic frippery, a sinking into the false heroic. In this he is true to the scene. But such humane 'patience' is possible for Katharine, as it is not for Lear or Macbeth, only because there is nothing in her experience of affliction that is felt as radically disturbing or unnatural: a fall

---

[104] Ibid. vii. 64; discussed at the end of ch. 2, above.   [105] Ibid. viii. 653.

such as she suffers, like those of Buckingham and Wolsey in the same play, appears as part of the natural condition of earthly life, something that may and must be endured. Her submission to the common lot of humankind is thus, for Johnson, powerfully and unproblematically moving. But the sense of necessity to which Macbeth submits is of a very different kind, and Johnson's belief that Macbeth is essentially carried along by forces too great for him lends a note of positive disappointment to his general observation on the play:

This play is deservedly celebrated for the propriety of its fictions, and solemnity, grandeur, and variety of its action; but it has no nice discriminations of character, the events are too great to admit the influence of particular dispositions, and the course of the action necessarily determines the conduct of the agents.[106]

Johnson sees Macbeth, like Hamlet, as 'rather an instrument than an agent', and it is this, I think, which leads to his over-simplifying and flattening account of the kind of emotional engagement that the play provokes:

The passions are directed to their true end. Lady Macbeth is merely detested; and though the courage of Macbeth preserves some esteem, yet every reader rejoices at his fall.[107]

It is not necessary to find nobility or pathos in what Macbeth and Lady Macbeth come to at the end in order to feel that 'detestation' and 'rejoicing' are not felicitous terms for our feelings as we contemplate their ruin. The words would more properly describe Malcolm's response, who sees in Macbeth and his wife only 'this dead butcher, and his fiend-like Queen'; but we have known Macbeth as Malcolm cannot, and the effect of our knowledge is not indeed to soften Malcolm's moral judgement in any way but to leave us with a sense of something heroic in Macbeth that makes it impossible that we should give such a judgement in such a form. Johnson's 'though the courage of Macbeth preserves some esteem' goes some way towards acknowledging this, but in the movement of Johnson's sentence it leads inevitably to its own contradiction ('yet . . .'), existing only to create a provisional tension from which the release into rejoicing is all the more emphatic. Macbeth may be courageous, but this

[106] Ibid. 795.   [107] Ibid.

does not count for much: 'the events are too great to admit the influence of particular dispositions, and the course of the action necessarily determines the conduct of the agents'. A note on lines in Lady Macbeth's soliloquy further suggests how troubled Johnson was by this aspect of the play:

> All that impedes thee from the golden Round,
> Which fate, and metaphysical aid, doth seem
> To have thee crown'd withal.

For 'seem' the sense evidently directs us to read 'seek.' The crown to which fate destines thee, and which preternatural agents 'endeavour' to bestow upon thee.[108]

The point of this was not lost on Francis Gentleman—always ready to take a hint from Johnson—in whose acting edition of *Macbeth* the lines are annotated thus: 'We like not sentiments which inculcate principles that favour predestination.'[109] Johnson's proposed reading (for which there is no warrant in the Folio) does what it can to lighten that sense of predestination upon which he animadverts in his general observation on the play. There he implicitly recognizes some connection between what is 'too great' in the action of *Macbeth* and the play's 'solemnity' and 'grandeur'; but what he baulks at is the belittling of the responsibility and dignity of human agency that goes with Shakespeare's presentation of Macbeth as, essentially, dancing to the witches' tune.

Johnson's argument has its force. Macbeth is at no point the master of his fate; the presence of the 'weird sisters', together with that sense of an overarching dramatic irony which is so marked a feature of this play, create the strongest feeling of inevitability; from the first moment that the possibility is raised in our minds we know that Macbeth will kill Duncan, and from the moment that he does so his downward path is fixed beyond recall. Moreover, we are made aware of a perspective in which Macbeth appears as a positively derisory figure, the fool and dupe of the action—paltered with by the witches, unmanned by the appearance of Banquo's ghost and utterly dismayed by the vision of Banquo's issue, mocked outright

---

[108] Ibid. 763. This note was first printed in the 1745 *Observations on Macbeth*; see *Yale*, vii. 15.

[109] *Bell's Edition of Shakespeare's Plays, as they are now performed at the Theatres Royal in London: Regulated from the Prompt Books of each House*, ed. Francis Gentleman (8 vols.; 1774) iii, *Macbeth*, p. 15 n.

by his wife at the beginning and by Macduff at the end, in certain undeniable respects a dwarfish thief who wears a giant's robe.[110] Johnson's analysis is, in a way, perfectly accurate. His objection can only be met by embracing the paradox that although Macbeth is indeed the fool of his fate, he is at the same time a great and heroic figure who *actively* 'puts on the harness of necessity'. That expression comes from Aeschylus' *Agamemnon*; it describes the moment when Agamemnon resolves to sacrifice the life of his daughter Iphigenia for the sake of the expedition to Troy:

But when he had put on the harness of necessity, breathing a foul, unholy, sacrilegious change of soul, from that moment on he took to his heart a resolution that dared do all things.[111]

'Necessity' indeed sits heavily on Agamemnon here. His whole house lies under a curse; and Artemis will not let the Greeks sail until appeased by his daughter's blood. He was bound to do as he did. Yet Aeschylus does not present him as an instrument rather than an agent; it may be the harness of necessity, but it is Agamemnon who resolves to put it on; his action is allowed its full and terrible significance as action, and what might have been merely a submission to forces too powerful to resist, being inwardly embraced, becomes that awesome, essentially unholy quality of 'all-daring resolution' that distinguishes the tragic hero. Is not this something like *Macbeth*? But to think so depends on a readiness to find more of heroic stature in Macbeth than Johnson is willing to do.

To test these remarks, let us look at Johnson's note on Act I, Scene vii:

---

[110] It may be Johnson's over-enlarged responsiveness to this perspective that lies behind his notorious remark in *Rambler* no. 168, where, referring to Lady Macbeth's 'Come, thick night . . .' (which he attributes to Macbeth, strangely enough), he states that he can 'scarce check' his 'risibility' at the expression used, 'for who, without some relaxation of his gravity, can hear of the avengers of guilt *peeping through a blanket?*' (*Yale*, v. 128). In context, this is not as crass as it seems: Johnson is avowedly impersonating the eighteenth-century reader for whom Shakespeare's words have acquired misleading associations; his explicit point is that to find the expression risible is a *mis*reading of the passage, and there is ample evidence in the same essay of how powerfully his own imagination is gripped by the scene. But that alone does not entirely account for the curious vigour and clumsiness of such a remark.

[111] *Agamemnon*, ll. 218–21. Some modern translators miss what I have taken to be the point of the lines by changing the Greek active verb ἔδυ—'he put on'—into a passive idea; thus Raphael and McLeish: 'So binds the king necessity', and Lattimore: 'But when necessity's yoke was put upon him'.

The arguments by which Lady Macbeth persuades her husband to commit the murder, afford a proof of Shakespeare's knowledge of human nature. She urges the excellence and dignity of courage, a glittering idea which has dazzled mankind from age to age, and animated sometimes the housebreaker, and sometimes the conqueror; but this sophism Macbeth has for ever destroyed by distinguishing true from false fortitude, in a line and a half; of which it may almost be said, that they ought to bestow immortality on the author, though all his other productions had been lost.

> I dare do all that may become a man,
> Who dares do more, is none.

. . . She then urges the oaths by which he had bound himself to murder Duncan, another art of sophistry by which men have sometimes deluded their consciences, and persuaded themselves that what would be criminal in others is virtuous in them; this argument Shakespeare, whose plan obliged him to make Macbeth yield, has not confuted, though he might easily have shown that a former obligation could not be vacated by a latter: that obligations laid on us by a higher power, could not be overruled by obligations which we lay upon ourselves.[112]

This must have been amongst the most important of those scenes in which Johnson found that 'the course of the action necessarily determines the conduct of the agents': it is Shakespeare's 'plan' that 'obliged him to make Macbeth yield', Johnson says, pointedly outlining the grounds on which Macbeth might have resisted Lady Macbeth's 'sophistry', and hinting a disappointment that a man capable of resisting the imputation of cowardice as magnificently as Macbeth does should be brought down by the emotional blackmail and weakly sophistical arguments of his wife. The decision to go on with the murder is seen as an option which Macbeth might 'easily' have declined; his final yielding appears, therefore, a weakness, forced upon him somewhat belittlingly by Shakespeare's predestination of the action, a mere lapse into that 'false fortitude' which he has himself authoritatively identified and condemned:

> I dare do all that may become a man,
> Who dares do more, is none.

In those lines, embodying as they do the formula 'not heroic but human' with the utmost trenchancy and force, Johnson plainly feels

---

[112] *Yale*, viii. 767 f. Except for the final clause, this note was first printed in the 1745 *Observations on Macbeth*; see *Yale* vii. 17 f. Its early date is, however, probably not significant, as the view expressed is thoroughly compatible with the general observation written for the edn. of 1765.

that Macbeth is given what is essentially the last word, that he speaks with unquestionable authority; there is crystallized here a truth central to Johnson's sense of what makes Shakespeare a classic.[113] Yet it is significant that in praising those lines, Johnson should choose to imagine them as a fragment isolated from its context, for in context they by no means possess the finality which he ascribes to them. Lady Macbeth has what is, dramatically, a very strong reply:

> What beast was't then,
> That made you break this enterprize to me?
> When you durst do it, then you were a man.

Johnson writes as though the sophistry were all on Lady Macbeth's side, the truth all with Macbeth's resistance, but it is at least equally true that, in the dramatic working of the exchange, Lady Macbeth is pressing home a truth from which Macbeth is on the run—the truth, that is, of his 'black and deep desires'. Despite Johnson, we cannot envisage how this exchange could turn out otherwise than it does; it is more than just the plan of the play that obliges Shakespeare to 'make Macbeth yield', for with part of himself Macbeth *does* dare do more than may become a man, even though all the sources of natural feeling within him recoil in horror at such resolution. Johnson's phrasing ('Shakespeare . . . might easily have shown . . .') suggests that he did not find it likely that a man of such strong and intelligent natural feeling would, in reality, have yielded at all, and it is presumably a dissatisfaction of this kind that makes itself felt in his general observation on the play. But what Macbeth comes to at the end of the scene—

> I am settled, and bend up
> Each corporal agent to this terrible Feat

—is not well described as a 'yielding', but is rather an assent to the necessity of the thing, a putting on of the yoke of necessity that may fairly be described as *heroic*: Macbeth here transgresses the bounds of action which can be referred to the general feeling of mankind, he goes beyond what the reader 'thinks that he should himself have spoken or acted on the same occasion': his resolve, as he himself best knows and feels, is an awful, fearful thing, a thing to be

---

[113] Cf. Nekayah in *Rasselas*, ch. xxix: 'He does nothing, who endeavours to do more than is allowed to humanity' (Johnson, *Works* (1825), i. 263).

wondered at. Such resolution puts nature on the rack, and cannot be sustained without the extinction of Macbeth's humanity, but it is not therefore a piece of 'false fortitude': Johnson's entirely characteristic equation of the conqueror with the housebreaker is here out of place. Shakespeare's presentation of the heroic in *Macbeth* is not what it was in *Henry IV*.

It is, paradoxically, because of our simultaneous sense of Macbeth as a man in the grip of forces which he is powerless to resist that his resolve actively to embrace what is his can strike the true heroic note. To realize this is not only to see a way past Johnson's objection that the course of the action necessarily determines the conduct of the agents; it also makes it possible to escape his harrowing experience of certain moments in the plays as 'not to be endured' while retaining his full sense of the shockingness of what is there represented. For the hero is a man like ourselves who is yet also not a man like ourselves: daring to endure more than may become a man, and sacrificing not only his life but also his common humanity in the process, he grapples with the unendurable where we could only have covered our eyes, and so mediates it to us in a form which we can begin to accept. Macbeth is more clearly and unequivocally such a hero than any of Shakespeare's other tragic protagonists, and it is therefore with regard to *Macbeth* that Johnson's response is most plainly in need of revision; with the other tragedies the case is more debatable. Hamlet is least convincingly the hero, and a reader who finds that Hamlet never quite puts on the yoke of necessity may well feel Johnson's criticisms of the play to be well made. In *Othello* one sees Shakespeare making a more determined attempt to lift his protagonist above the common run of humanity, albeit partly by an exotic and glamorous nobility that may be thought to invite its own nemesis: the painfulness which Johnson records is in part, perhaps, the painfulness of Othello's failure to sustain the sense of greatness that he so potently suggests. But the grandeur of Lear's final speeches is of a quite different kind. The most unexalted and fundamental human emotions are given with an awesome, hardly human energy of spirit: if Lear is now at last an irrevocably broken man, he is also here a figure whom we dare not presume to pity. This is not how *we* should suffer in such a situation, we may feel, remembering that Lear's first words on entering are spoken in passionate reproach of Albany and the rest for their shocked passivity in grief. In one sense he is not 'suffering' at all, as Gloucester, for example, suffers, but with an immense, lucid agony giving himself wholly to the sense of intolerable pain and injustice and love. We shall not find the ending of *King Lear* as merely painful as Johnson does in proportion as we can feel that Lear, like Macbeth, comes with his own hands to put on the harness of necessity.

INDEX

Abrams, M. H. 78, 79 n.
Addison, Joseph:
  on Boileau and Bouhours 29
  on Caliban 113
  Johnson on 16, 27, 75, 107
Adler, J. H. 99 n.
Aeschylus' *Agamemnon* 194
All's Well that Ends Well:
  Johnson on Bertram 17
  Johnson on Parolles 50, 87
Antony and Cleopatra:
  Hazlitt on Cleopatra 103-4,
    109
  Johnson on Enobarbus' miserable
    conceit 134
  quibble as 'the fatal Cleopatra'
    54, 144-5
Arbuthnot, John 109 n.
As You Like It:
  Johnson on Frederick's conversion
    17
d'Aubignac, Abbé 159, 160 n.
d'Aucour, Barbier 27
Audra, E. 31-2

Badawi, M. M. 11, 69
Bate, W. J. 25 n., 52 n.
Beaumont and Fletcher, Rymer
  on 161, 165
Boileau Despréaux, Nicolas 19,
  25, 28-36, 84
Borgerhoff, E. B. O. 29
Bouhours, Dominique 28-37
Bradley, A. C., on Emilia 164
Brody, Jules 29 n., 31
Bunyan, John 61-2
Burney, Fanny, on Caliban 119

Carlyle, Thomas, on Coleridge
  88
Chaucer, Geoffrey:
  Dryden on 45-7
  Hazlitt on 93

Churchill, Charles 114
Coleridge, Samuel Taylor:
  character analysis in the tragedies
    182-90
  on dramatic illusion 125-6
  on Falstaff 86-8
  on *Hamlet* 88-91, 183-5
  on Johnson 11-12, 66, 183
  on *King Lear* 186-8
  on Lady Macbeth 188-90
  on mind as originating experience
    63-82
  on organic unity 126-7,
    129-31
  on Othello 186
  and Polixenes 77
  and primacy of being over doing
    184
  on *Romeo and Juliet* 141,
    150-2
  and sexuality 81-2
  on Shakespeare's characters as
    species 69
  on Sophocles 182, 184, 186
  on *Venus and Adonis* 81-2,
    90
  on word-play and conceit
    148-53
  on Wordsworth 70-7
Colman, George 4, 114, 116,
  117
Comedy of Errors:
  Johnson's lack of interest in 120
Coriolanus:
  Hazlitt on the imagination's
    love of power 105
  Johnson on Coriolanus and
    Achilles 58-61
  Schlegel and Coriolanus 83
Cowley, Abraham, Johnson
  on 27-8, 38, 55
Crabbe, George, Hazlitt on 93
Cruttwell, Patrick 159

Cymbeline:
Johnson on Belarius 17
Johnson on Posthumus' miserable conceit 134
Kames on Posthumus' jealousy 179

Damrosch, Leopold 22, 42 n., 111
Dennis, John, on Pope 33
dramatic illusion 5, 97–9, 125–6
Dryden, John 27, 32, 45–7, 57–8, 108–9, 143–4, 158
Dutton, G. B. 159

Eliot, George 43, 50
Eliot, T. S. 1, 60, 159
Euripides' *Hippolytus*, Rymer on 165–6
Ewton, R. W. 79 n.

Falstaff *see Henry IV*
Flint, Bet 50–1
Folkenflik, Robert 52 n.
France, Peter 36 n.
Fruman, Norman 81 n.
Fussell, Paul 4 n., 39 n.

Garrick, David 6, 99
Gentleman, Francis 171–3, 193
Gibbon, Edward 32
Gildon, Charles 117–18, 169
Goethe, Johann Wolfgang 13, 128
Guthrie, William 5–6, 115–17

Hagstrum, Jean 21–2
Hamlet:
Coleridge on 88–91, 183–6
Hazlitt on 100–1, 109
and the heroic 197
Johnson on 118, 158, 177–8, 183–6
Johnson on Polonius 21
morally problematic 100–1, 169–73, 177–8, 183–6
psychological interpretation 179–80, 183–6

word-play in 148, 150
Hawkins, John 5–6, 40
Hazlitt, William:
on Burke 105
on Caliban 119
on Chaucer 93
on Cleopatra 103, 109
on Coriolanus 105
on Crabbe 93
on Falstaff 96
on Hamlet 100–1, 109
on Hogarth 93
on Iago 109
on the imagination 92–106
on individuality of Shakespeare's characters 106–9
on Johnson 11, 23, 40, 106–7
on Lake poets 105
and Lamb 95, 100–1
on Lear 92, 94–5, 102–6, 110–11
on the politics of poetry 105
on Richard II 103
on the 'ruling passion' 109
on Schlegel 10, 91–2
on Scott 92–3
on Shelley 94, 107
on Spenser 92
on Titian 94
on *Troilus and Cressida* 91 n.; quoted 104
Henry IV:
Hal and Falstaff 47–50, 52–4, 61, 85–8, 96, 115, 132
Johnson on Lancaster's 'violation of faith' 18
Henry V:
'the king is but a man' 52
Henry VI:
Johnson on Iden's 'damnation' of Cade 18
Henry VIII:
Johnson on Katharine 191–2
Heywood, Thomas 95 n.
Hirsch, E. D. 79 n.
Hogarth, William, Hazlitt on 93
Homer 19, 27 n., 33, 58–60
Hurd, Richard 113

identification with characters in
    drama 95-6, 99-101, 108
illusion *see* dramatic illusion
irony 80-4, 147, 150

James, Henry 43
Jenyns, Soame 33, 38
Johnson, Samuel:
    on Addison 16, 18, 27, 75, 107
    his assertiveness 6-9, 39-43
    on Berkeley 7
    on Bet Flint 50-1
    and Boileau 19, 25, 28
    on Bouhours 35
    on Cowley 27-8, 38, 55
    on definition 37
    Dick Minim 4, 38
    on dramatic illusion 5, 97-9
    on Dryden 27, 32, 45-7,
        57-8, 108-9, 143-4
    evolution of his critical stance
        8, 19, 34
    and 'general nature' 21-8,
        44-7, 49-50, and *passim*
    on good humour 47-51,
        53-4, 57-8
    on the heroic 52-60, 191-7
    and Homer 27 n., 58-60
    on Hume 7
    on individuality 45-8, 109-11,
        116-17
    on Jenyns 33, 38
    on love 47-51, 142-4
    on metaphysical poetry 27-8, 81
    on Milton 23, 54-5, 58
    his moralism 16-21
    on the novel 19-21
    and 'particular manners' 20-1
    on Pope 33, 54-60, 109
    on Prior's *Solomon* 27
    his reviewers 4-6
    and romance comedy 17-18
    on Rymer 158, 160
    his scepticism 24-5, 37-43
    on the shockingness of tragedy
        173-9, 183-6, 190-1
    on Smith's *Phaedra and
        Hippolitus* 97
    on stoicism 38
    his style 38-9
    on Swift 56
    and Wordsworth 74-5
    see also Shakespeare; titles of
        Shakespeare's works
Jonson, Ben 128, 167
Julius Caesar:
    Johnson on 20

Kames, Lord 98, 179, 189
Kant, Immanuel 63, 78
    on the organic 129-30
    on the poetic imagination
        65-6
    on the sublime 82-3
Kean, Edmund 100
Kenrick, William 4-5
King John:
    Johnson on Constance 110-11
    Johnson on the Bastard 53
King Lear:
    Coleridge on 186-8
    Hazlitt on 92, 94-5, 102-6,
        110-11
    Johnson on 95-7, 176-7
    Johnson on Oswald's loyalty
        18
    Kent and Rymer 164
    Lear as hero 197-8
    Schlegel on the ending 83
Kinnaird, John 102 n.
Korff, H. A. 79

Lamb, Charles 94-5, 100-1
La Mesnardière 159
Lascelles, M. M. 42 n.
Leavis, F. R. 16, 22-3
Le Bossu 159, 162
Lennox, Charlotte 171
Lloyd, Robert 98
Locke, John 37, 109 n.
Lockridge, L. S. 68 n., 81 n.
Longinus 32
love 47-51, 142-5, 153
Lovejoy, A. O. 68 n.
Love's Labour's Lost:
    Johnson on 132 n.

Macbeth:
 Coleridge on 188–90
 Johnson on 118, 190, 192–7
 Johnson and the Doctor 190
 Lady Macbeth 169, 188–90,
  194 n.
 Macbeth and Agamemnon
  194
 Macduff 101–3
 Richardson on 180–1, 189
 and shockingness of tragedy
  178–9
Mahood, M. M. 146–8
Mason, H. A. 29 n.
Measure for Measure:
 Johnson on Angelo 17
 Johnson on 'Be absolute for
  death . . .' 122–4
Merry Wives of Windsor:
 Johnson's lack of interest in
  120
 Johnson's objection to profanity
  in 18
metaphysical poets 27–8, 81
Midsummer Night's Dream:
 Johnson on 118
 quoted by Colman 114
 Warburton on 113–14
Milton, John 23, 54–5, 58,
  104, 157
Molière 29–30, 84
Montagu, Elizabeth 113, 117
Montaigne, Michel de 31, 41
Morris, Corbyn 49
Much Ado About Nothing:
 Johnson's lack of interest in
  120
 Johnson on Leonato 110
Muirhead, J. H. 79
Murphy, Arthur 171

'nature' 18–34, 44–6, and
  passim
neoclassicism 23 n., 29, 159,
  160 n., 162
Nuttall, A. D. 131 n.

Orsini, G. N. G. 77 n.

Othello:
 Bradley on Emilia 164
 Coleridge on 186
 Guthrie on 115
 Hazlitt on Iago 109
 Johnson on 174–6
 Kames on 179
 Othello as hero 197
 Rymer on 158, 160–9

Park, Roy 95 n.
Pierce, C. F. 9 n., 42 n.
Pope, Alexander 3
 Essay on Criticism 31–3, 36
 and Johnson 33, 54–60, 106,
  109
 on Rymer 158–9
Popper, Karl 10

Rapin, René 159
Richard II:
 Hazlitt on Richard 103
 Richard's miserable conceits
  133, 148–50
Richard III:
 Richard's singularity 116–17
Richardson, William 180–1, 189
Robinson, Henry Crabb 11–12, 76
'romantic' defined 10
Romeo and Juliet 134–52
Rowe, Nicholas 112–13
Rymer, Thomas 158–69

Sachs, Arieh 21, 42 n.
Salingar, Leo 49
Schelling, F. W. J. 77–9
Schlegel, August Wilhelm:
 on Boileau 84
 on Caliban 125
 on comedy 83–6
 on dramatic illusion 99, 125
 and Hazlitt 10
 his influence 11
 on Johnson's Shakespeare 12,
  135, 141
 on *mimesis* 15
 on poetic language 74 n.,
  145–6

and Prospero 84, 124
on romantic and classical art 67
on *Romeo and Juliet* 134–5,
  138–41, 145
on Shakespeare's characterization
  111–12
on Shakespeare's irony 80,
  82–4, 147
on the supernatural in
  Shakespeare 111–12
on tragedy 82–3
and transcendental idealism
  78–9
on unity in art 126–31, 134,
  138–40
on word-play and conceit 145–7
Schlegel, Caroline 138 n.
Schlegel, Friedrich 13, 90, 127
Scott, Walter, Hazlitt on 92–3
Seneca's *Phaedra*, Rymer on
  165–6
Shakespeare, William:
  his bombast 157
  his characters—species or
    individuals 5, 45, 106–11,
    114, 116–17
  compared to Hal and to Falstaff
    52–4
  dramatic illusion 5, 97–9, 125–6
  his faults 2, 16–18, 53–4,
    126–53, 156–7
  and the heroic 51–4, 60–2,
    191–8
  our identification with his
    characters 95–6, 99, 101,
    108–11
  his irony 80–5, 145–7
  his language 74–5, 157
  his 'mingled drama' 44–5, 84
  in performance 99–101
  his power of invention 27 n.,
    112–15, 118–21
  psychology and tragedy
    179–90
  his relation to his audience
    53, 57
  the scene as unit of his
    achievement 129

supernatural in 13, 111–26
and tragedy 60–1, 101–6,
  156–98
unity in 126–31, 134–40
his word-play and conceits
  131–6, 144–53
see also titles of individual works
Shaw, George Bernard 61–2
Shelley, Percy Bysshe, Hazlitt on
  94, 107
Sherbo, Arthur 3, 44 n.
Sheridan, Thomas 179–80
Smallwood, P. J. 23 n.
Smollett, Tobias 171
Sophocles, Coleridge on 182,
  184, 186
South, Robert 25
Staël, Madame de 83
Stock, R. D. 3, 21–2, 44 n.
Stubbes, George 169–71
Swift, Jonathan 56

Tempest 112–26
  Prospero and Schlegel 84, 124
  theatrical performance 99–101
Theobald, Lewis 113
Thrale, Hester 28, 63
Tieck, Ludwig 125
Titian, Hazlitt on 94
Troilus and Cressida:
  Hazlitt on 91 n.
  Johnson on 20
  quoted by Hazlitt 104
Twelfth Night:
  Johnson on the ending 18
  Orsino on fancy 153

unity, organic *see* Shakespeare

Venus and Adonis:
  Coleridge on 81–2, 90
Voitle, Robert 40 n.
Voltaire 117, 118, 169

Warburton, William 109 n.
  113–14, 117–18
Warton, Joseph 113, 118,
  121–2, 124, 177

Watson, George   159
Weinbrot, Howard   24 n.
Wellek, René   23-4, 79
Whately, Thomas   181
White, Ian   42 n.
Wimsatt, W. K.   21-2

Winter's Tale:
   Polixenes on art and
      nature   77, 115, 124
Wordsworth, William   8 n., 70-6

Zimansky, C. A.   159-60